TEAM TRAINING

FROM STARTUP TO HIGH PERFORMANCE

TEAM TRAINING
FROM STARTUP TO HIGH PERFORMANCE

Carl Harshman

Steve Phillips

McGraw-Hill, Inc.
New York San Francisco Washington, D.C. Auckland Bogotá
Caracas Lisbon London Madrid Mexico City Milan
Montreal New Delhi San Juan Singapore
Sydney Tokyo Toronto

Library of Congress Cataloging-in-Publication Data

Harshman, Carl L.
Team training : from startup to high performance / Carl Harshman and Steve Phillips.
p. cm.
ISBN 0-07-026925-4 (pbk.). — ISBN 0-07-912220-5 (looseleaf)
1. Employees—Training of—Handbooks, manuals, etc. 2. Works groups—Handbooks, manuals, etc. I. Phillips, Steve L. II. Title
HF5549.5.T7H324 1995
658.3'124—dc20 95-4747
CIP

1 2 3 4 5 6 7 8 9 0 EDW/EDW 9 0 0 9 8 7 6 5

ISBN 0-07-026925-4 (pbk.)
ISBN 0-07-912220-5 (looseleaf)

The sponsoring editor for this book was Richard Narramore, the editing supervisor was Fred Dahl, and the production supervisor was Donald F. Schmidt. It was set in Palatino by Inkwell Publishing Services.

Printed and bound by Edwards Brothers, Inc.

We dedicate this work to
Jesse, Parker, Cody, Ryan, and Todd
for the spirit of excellence and teams in their lives

CONTENTS

ACKNOWLEDGMENTS

With a field and topic that are changing faster than we can write about them, our only salvation is the assistance (physical and spiritual) of lots of friends, colleagues, and clients. As the content of this book evolved over the past few years, we received a lot of input and guidance from consumers. Notably, what is now known as the King County (Seattle) Department of Metropolitan Services was the application site for the initial model. Kathy Coronetz, the Internal Coordinator, the respective site coordinators, including Sydney Munger and Kate Leone, as well as the cadre of internal trainers all helped refine and improve the modules. The LTV Steel-Direct Hot Charge Complex, and the internal consultants, Dave Craven and Bill Pecek, were also helpful in field-testing some of the modules.

The State of Washington Employment Security Department and the LTV Steel-Direct Hot Charge Complex were pilot sites for the team certification process and moved certification from concept to reality with the quality of their efforts.

Colleagues, including JoAnn Schindler, Tom Kramer, Pattie Grimm, and Marianne Garr, provided input and content to various modules. Without their help, the final product would not have been as good as it is. Along the way, we were supported and helped by Ann Marie Toney, Tony DiCostanzo, and Kelly Koeberlein, who did a lot of the typing, editing, and hand-holding.

Richard Narramore of McGraw-Hill was the source of inspiration and encouragement. Without Richard, the project would not have come to fruition as quickly or as well as it did.

Finally, we owe a debt of gratitude to our partners, Ellen Harshman and Sally Phillips, for their moral support, editing prowess, and general willingness to be abandoned for our computers and teams.

Carl Harshman
Steve Phillips

ACKNOWLEDGMENTS

For More Information on Implementing Teams

Carl Harshman and Steve Phillips are leading team consultants and are available to discuss your team implementation effort:

Carl Harshman & Associates, Inc.
6361 Clayton Road
St. Louis, MO 63117
Tel.: 314-721-5416
Fax: 314-721-0524

Phillips Associates
23440 Civic Center Way, Suite 100
Malibu, CA 90265
Tel.: 310-456-3532
Fax: 310-456-8744

INTRODUCTION

THE TEAM MOVEMENT

Some say it's a fad that is bigger than hula hoops, convertibles, and the Beatles. Around the world, business, industry, and government are zealous participants in the new "team" movement. Fueled in the late 1970s by the Japanese approach to employee involvement in business, public and private American organizations have tested a variety of team structures and activities over the last decade. These range from temporary teams, such as a task force, to permanent structures like self-directed work groups.

In *Teaching the Elephant to Dance* (1990), Jack Welch, CEO of General Electric, said:

> We have found what we believe to be the distilled essence of competitiveness. It is the reservoir of talent and creativity and energy that can be found in each of our people. That essence is liberated when we make people believe that what they think and do is important—and then get out of their way while they do it. [p. 5]*

Teams are a powerful tool for getting at that talent, creativity, and energy.

THE TEAM APPROACH

The team approach—how teams are structured and what they do—depends on:

1. How long the team will be in place.
2. The nature and extent of the team's involvement in the business.

The time frame for a team structure can be short- or long-term. For example, a task force on purchasing, parking, or food service represents short-term involvement. *Problem-solving work groups* in a work area are generally in place for a longer period (a year or two). More permanent structures, such as *self-managing work teams,* represent a long-term involvement strategy.

The extent of involvement in the business is a function of the issue or need as well as the organization's willingness to open or alter old boundaries between "thinking" and "doing." In classic work systems, *thinking* is the domain of management; *doing* is the domain of workers. New work systems blur those distinctions. With the shift toward involvement and empowerment, employees at every level have a different and, in many cases larger, role in thinking related to their work and the business. This manual is an attempt to expand and extend the considerations about and approaches to implementing and developing teams.

*J. A. Belasco, *Teaching the Elephant to Dance* (Crown Publishers). Copyright © 1990 by James A. Belasco. Reprinted by permission of Crown Publishers, Inc.

Our approach to teams is firmly rooted in the assumption that teams are the means to, not the ends of an organizational transformation effort. This perspective is important because the organizations of the 1980s would often institute a team process and then sit back and wait for the benefits to roll in. As the quality circle movement aptly demonstrated, this often was not the case. Here are three important principles related to the installation of teams in the organization:

1. *Teams are not the answer: They are the question.* Actually, teams are part of the question. The larger issues are: How do you want to run the organization in the future, and what do teams have to do with that philosophy and strategy? What will you need to change to make teams a real asset: power structures? decision-making patterns? communication and information processes? reward systems? All these questions surface when teams are implemented. Unless you are ready to begin answering some of them, the team process should wait.
2. *Teams will create more problems than they solve.* This is not good news, but somebody has to say it. Teams are a wonderful addition to the workplace and, if successful, will become a major asset to the business. But in the early going—generally a year or more—teams create a great deal of havoc in organizations striving for stability and predictability. For a while teams begin to work on issues related to the quality of work life, product quality, and productivity. They simultaneously, however, put enormous stress on the power structures, management paradigms, union representatives, information systems, and the like. Don't look for a way to avoid this problem; it cannot be found. The organization can, however, prepare itself for the tensions created by a team process and put in place structures and processes from which to learn and change. (See Harshman & Phillips, 1994.)
3. *You may be training teams, but teams are the key to learning.* This is perhaps the most difficult principle to understand. We tend to think of learning in the team process as the activities and outcomes related to the development of the team. This is one form of learning. The assumption is that the teams' learning will translate into problem solving and decision making that improve the organization's functioning. To the extent the organization listens and implements the ideas put forth, one kind of learning takes place. This learning is what Chris Argyris and Donald Schon (1978) called "single loop learning" or what Peter Senge (1990) refers to as "adaptive" learning. It is change related to adjustments in the present paradigm. We believe the ultimate value of teams is their role in the deeper learning processes of the organization. As they begin to function, teams provide the means and the data for the organization to understand what works and what does not. They are like the electronic scopes we hook up to modern automobile engines to determine how it is functioning and what might be wrong. The team provides insights to the organization that are presently not available. The data are there, but the historical blinders and filters prevent us from seeing what is obvious to others. By implementing a team process, the organization opens itself to all kinds of new learning and commits, at least implicitly, to hear and respect the data.

Quality circles were often an example of using teams for adaptive or single loop learning. The primary intent of their formation was the improvement of quality or productivity. The teams were trained in quality techniques (and perhaps some basic team processes) and pointed toward quality problems, which the effective teams solved with considerable success. Any team process can do that. One that is also dedicated to higher-order learning in the organization will be viewed through a different set of lenses. Our experience indicates that unsuccessful teams are not effective because of a lack of training or motivation. They fail to succeed at the expected level because of systemic characteristics and barriers. Using teams to understand and overcome these barriers yields the ultimate value. There are two keys to having teams help change the larger context.

1. Helping them understand their role in this function
2. Setting up mechanisms and structures to monitor and learn from the team activity

For example, if you tell teams throughout the training that their role is not only to solve problems or to make improvements, but also to help improve the overall organization, they will begin to view their role beyond the bounds of traditional work. We have, for example, observed a pattern of problems with teams that are a result of a middle management grid blocking and deflecting team input. On the surface, it all looked legitimate, but over time and with constant dialogue with the teams, the real problem became clear.

That brings us to the second recommendation—the creation of a structure or mechanism by which to monitor the pattern of team functioning. The organization will derive the least value from teams if you train them and turn them loose to perform without support or oversight. We are not talking about support just from the existing management system (which is a given), but from an independent organization or group. For example, in one large organization, the internal trainers who were organized to deliver the training for teams also became the support structure to work with teams over a two-year period. They would sit in on team meetings, conduct progress reviews, collect unobtrusive data, and work as a team analyzing the patterns of team data searching for the sources of success and failure.

Beyond the group of trainers was a steering committee whose task was to listen to and understand what was working and not in the organization based on the teams' experience. The steering committee consisted of 12 managers and labor leaders who were trained and oriented in the role of overall change of the organization. As a steering committee they had the ultimate responsibility to understand the patterns and do something about them. Two examples demonstrate the larger learning role. In one, the steering committee observed that company policy constantly got in the way of quick, effective responses to problems. There was so much red tape that individuals and teams literally gave up when it came to creating permanent fixes. In another case, a pattern indicated that a powerful middle manager was a major blocker of data and progress.

In both cases, the steering committee's role was to find ways to change the context so that these characteristics did not impede the organization's ability to get better.

Note that neither of these problems is unusual for an organization. Yet they were not obvious to the leadership even though they had been there for years. It was the team process that surfaced the data and provided a mechanism for understanding the true nature of things.

The approach to developing teams influences the quality of the work the team does and its longevity. If team development is seen as a one-shot training event, the effort is not likely to contribute much to a long-term involvement strategy. If, on the other hand, the team strategy is viewed as an ongoing, complex, learning process, the result can increase the chances of long-term success.

The key to using these modules for long-term development is to focus on the ultimate goals, not just on the objective of completing the training. One client, for example, chose to focus on the completion of training rather than on the growth of the teams. We advised spreading the modules out over a two-year period in order to give the teams time to absorb the learning and the organization a chance to adjust to it (see the discussion in the prior section). In this case, the steering committee wanted to demonstrate commitment and to get results; so they pushed to complete the entire set of modules within a year. The result was a group of overtrained teams in the middle of an organization that was not ready to empower them. The effect was to lose the value of the investment both in terms of training (the teams) and change (the organization).

We believe that it is critical to be clear about the long-terms goals of the effort and to understand that the ultimate success of teams is a product of both the teams and their work (to which training is primarily related) and the organizational context within which the teams must function.

Our advice is to go slow rather than fast in delivering modules to the teams so that the organization has an opportunity to understand both the rate of development of the teams (how much they can absorb) and the ability of the organization to support this new source of energy, input, and power.

Developing a team can be compared to learning to play golf. Anyone who has attempted the game knows that golf cannot be learned in a week, nor can one get beyond the fundamentals by reading a book or watching one of Jack Nicholas's videos. Rather, one learns golf by acquiring knowledge about it (stance, grip, swing, which club does what) and going to the driving range or course to practice. Actually hitting the ball (and the resulting score) tells golfers whether they are learning. And, since the game of golf requires complex eye-hand-body coordination (to say nothing of what is required of the mind), it is not likely that one will become proficient at golf right away. Instead, one learns, practices, gets feedback (*#@*% slice!), and returns to learn. With enough teaching/coaching, time, practice, and, most of all, patience, someday the game may all come together. Breaking a 100 (with honest scorekeeping) is typically a milestone for the golfer. Then the target is 90, and so forth. Golfers keep moving the goal and doing what they can to move toward that goal.

If we extend the analogy to the development of a team, the approach to teaching and learning is different than if team development is viewed like teaching someone to add numbers (2+2=4) or install spark plugs in a car. Teaching addition might be done in one or two sessions, after which participants have the skill to add the numbers every time they encounter them. The task of installing spark plugs requires a certain basic set of knowledge and skills; beyond that only the context changes. This is not the case with team development. Learning and development make for a continuous process characterized by increasing complexity.

These business team development materials are based on the assumption that:

- ✓ The development of effective, permanent work teams is an ongoing, complex learning process.
- ✓ The process requires a basic set of skills and relationships as a foundation from which continuous improvement of team functioning and performance evolves with teaching, coaching, and experience.

IMPLICATIONS FOR USING THE MODULES

The real question is: How does the preceding information affect the delivery of training to the teams? The first and most important implication is that you are concerned with the development of groups of complex individuals in the middle of a complex organization. That means you need to *plan* the development of the teams, not just *schedule* the training. Here are some thoughts regarding planning and delivery:

1. What is the long-term vision for the organization? That is, do you have a statement of what you are trying to become? The vision should be a product of the top-level, strategic leadership of the organization. If you have an organizational vision, have the leadership help you understand how the team process fits into achieving the vision. You can use this information to determine *how much of what kind* of training is likely to be needed. For example, if the vision focuses primarily on improving the present organization, you may want to limit the training to basic team skills and problem solving. If, on the other hand, the vision is for an empowered, team-based organization, you will probably want to expose the teams to the entire range of modules.
2. Think about the development of the teams, not just the delivery of the training. The implication of this recommendation is that you may "package" modules to allow for development. One organization, for example, organized the modules into four groups, each of which was delivered in a series. There was a period of "absorption" time between the groups of modules to allow the teams to understand the application of the learning to their work and to integrate the knowledge and skills with what they presently knew and did.
3. Trainers are more than just conveyors of the content of the modules. They are the eyes, ears, and brains of the development process. As such, those who deliver the modules must "listen." By *listen* we mean pay attention to the teams as you deliver succeeding modules. Their formal and informal discussion provide significant clues to both the impact of the prior training and to the organizational dynamics that impact their functioning. You may hear discussions, for example, that lead you to conclude that you should slow down or repeat portions of a module that did not "take." The difference between delivering learning by book, video, or computer is the human touch and sensitivity afforded by those who are with the teams throughout the development process.

THREE KINDS OF DEVELOPMENT: THE BUSINESS AND THE TEAM

The team development process focuses on three areas:

1. Team members' relationships to each other and the team

2. Team members' relationships to the business
3. Team members' skill in quality, process, and productivity improvement

No one kind of development is sufficient in itself. Putting problem-solving or quality-improvement skills into a dysfunctional group lessens the chance that the skills will be used well or perhaps at all. Doing relationship training (e.g., conflict resolution, listening) without business skills adds little, if anything, to the team's contribution to the business. And teaching the team process improvement techniques when team members do not get along or have no sense of their business goals or operation tends to be futile.

Our approach to team development is based on the assumption that task (business) functions go hand in hand with team interpersonal development. Each is a necessary, but not a sufficient condition for success of the team. As a result, the manual includes modules designed to improve relationship development, business development, and quality/process/productivity.

Teams at Various Levels

Most of the discussion of team processes and the vast majority of team implementations are aimed at work groups at the first (touch labor) level of the organization. There is good reason for this in the mind of implementers. Primarily, the goal is to tap the knowledge and skills of employees who historically have been omitted from the decision-making and managing processes. Teams are the primary vehicle for achieving that goal.

A major limitation of most team processes is that the organization *implements a team development process only at the first level of the organization.* This approach omits the critical managing levels above the first-level teams. Why does this happen? First, many management groups with which we have worked report that they already function as a team. Therefore, there is no need to do any work with them. Secondly, and more prevalently, most management organizations assume that teams are for the workers, not management. So, whether by design or by omission, the focus of team attention on the first level of the organization and not on the entire organization leaves management off the hook in terms of living the process themselves.

Here is our fundamental stance on the approach to teams: *In the long term, unless the entire organization operates in a team process, nobody will operate in a team process.* That is, the organization cannot sustain a deep, powerful team process at the first level of the organization with a traditional, hierarchical, manager-based system. Everyone from top management to first-line supervision, line and staff, needs to understand and be a part of teams. Only through this "saturation" approach can the organization hope to achieve a shift in culture required to obtain maximum gain from teams and to provide the teams a chance to "teach" the organization.

People at all levels and in all functions in the organization need to explore and implement the team process. Not everyone should, or will, proceed in the same direction or at the same pace. And the content of some modules will differ according to level. For example, top management teams are more likely to do strategic rather than operational planning.

Adjustments in the content of the materials can and should be made for the particular level and function being trained. The adjustments can range from a shift in emphasis in the module to a major revision of the content.

There are several implications for delivering the modules to different levels of the organization:

1. See what's already been done. Upper-level management teams, for example, have often been exposed to various kinds of training. Be sure to know what they have done so that you do not repeat it in the modules (or that you make modifications to account for the prior learning).
2. Be sure the module is at the right level. We tried to construct modules for broad application. In some areas, however, we approached the topic with the notion of teams at the first or second level of the organization. Probably the modules on business planning are the best examples. It is likely that the top-level management teams in most organizations have a planning process in place. If so, the modules are not likely to be useful to them. Instead, if the top-level teams want to improve planning, you may have to go outside the modules to find something like an advanced strategic planning workshop to meet their needs.
3. You may have to vary the "homework." In the modules we have tried to make the exercises practical so that teams have usable products from their efforts. These products will vary, however, depending on the level of the organization involved. In Module 9, Team Vision, work with the top-level teams may focus on developing the organization's vision; work with front-line teams may focus on how they see themselves fitting into the organization's vision.

Mostly, we are trying to emphasize that the team modules do not represent a cookbook approach to training and team development. They are a *resource.* To be applicable and valuable, they need the careful thought and input of those who have to deliver the content and those who have to lead the organization into which these enlightened, empowered teams will be placed.

A CUSTOM APPROACH

The actual team development modules included in this manual should be a product of the organization's analysis of the team strategy best suited to its mission, vision, and organizational change strategy. In general, the materials are divided into three levels:

1. Problem-solving groups and task forces (problem-solving focus)
2. First-generation business teams (business meeting focus)
3. Second-generation business teams (business management focus)

Although there are no clear divisions between levels, by working with the organization, you may include the topics that meet the team development needs for this particular time and your specific strategy.

CREDENTIALING TEAMS

Perhaps the major contribution of this manual is the explanation of the concept of credentialing or certifying teams. The concept gives management teams and steering committees a tool with which to plan, manage, and evaluate the team implementation process. The certification process is outlined in Chap. 3.

No matter how you cut it, a team process has to do with redefining power in the organization. Teams force organizations to rethink *who* has *what kind* of power and *how much.* This is no easy or painless task. In implementing teams, you tamper with a fundamental mechanism of the culture. The implications are potentially overwhelming. On one hand, those of us who have worked with organization transformation for a period of years know and understand how difficult it is to redistribute power from upper and middle levels of the organization to the lower levels. At the same time, those involved in team processes understand how difficult it is to create mature, effective teams who are able to make good use of the power they acquire.

The questions of how to transfer power (and authority) and to encourage the mature use of that newly acquired authority are central questions addressed in Chap. 3 on team certification. The notion of team certification is one of the most viable ways we have seen to define an orderly transition of power and to do it in such a way that those acquiring the power provide some assurance that it will be put to good use.

The next chapter is dedicated to the subject of using this manual. Remember, you can do anything from a single module to a full-blown, self-directed work team certification process with the resources in this book.

2 HOW TO USE THIS MANUAL

ORGANIZATION OF THE MANUAL

The team development exercises and lessons in this work manual are designed to help any team as it moves toward more skills, more empowerment, and more ability to manage itself. The modules consist of three content areas:

1. Team and interpersonal development
2. Process, quality, and productivity improvement
3. Business planning and management.

Although we have put the modules in a specific order, your organization may want to combine, rearrange, skip, or delete modules as required. Also, we have designed most modules to fit in a two- to four-hour time block. The modules can be altered, combined, or otherwise adjusted to meet your specific delivery needs.

PACE OF THE TRAINING

By *pace* we mean the speed with which you deliver the modules to teams. What comes to mind is one author's work with the design of a curriculum for an alternative college. The task involved packaging courses for an intense weekend format with a class meeting Friday night, Saturday, and Sunday. A professor of business in the planning group said we could not put introductory accounting in the weekend program because the material required time to practice and absorb, and the weekend format did not permit that kind of time. This is also the case with some aspects of team development. It will take time for some teams to practice the skills taught and, in other cases, to integrate the material with existing knowledge and skills. The key is to "listen" in the broadest sense to the teams and to adjust your pace to their learning, not your schedule.

SCHEDULE OF THE TRAINING

Packaging the training is another decision point. We recommend a two- to four-hour time commitment to a module (depending on the module) every two weeks. This gives the team a chance to use the new knowledge and tools before they move on. If training cannot be scheduled every two weeks, we suggest combining two modules and running a full day every month. Our experience is that more than eight hours of team training a month does not give team members adequate time to practice and fully comprehend the new material. Less than eight hours of team training a month may serve to diffuse the learning, weaken its impact, and stall momentum toward new team behavior.

FACILITATION

We recommend that a qualified facilitator work with the team as it goes through the materials. As team members become more mature at teaching, presentation, and process skills, they may be able to facilitate the training without an outside facilitator. In the beginning, however, an experienced facilitator can be a powerful asset to the team by modeling effective presentation skills and training competencies.

TRAINERS

The manual is designed so that the organization can use internal trainers to deliver the materials. There are a variety of ways to do this. The most common is to assign the training department responsibility for delivering the modules to the teams.

An alternative—and one we recommend—is to use the training department (if you have one) to train and support a pool of trainers who come from the ranks of the teams. We have used this approach and find that it has several advantages:

- ✓ It allows the organization's talent to emerge and grow with the effort.
- ✓ It provides a broader base of trainers than would normally be available, and the process can move faster as a result.
- ✓ It creates a pool of on-site trainers who are typically also members of teams who can coach and support the teams as they learn and implement the skills.

INSTRUCTOR'S GUIDE

We wrote the modules in instructor guide format. These come complete with already designed, easy-to-copy flipcharts and handouts. The instructor's guide at the beginning of each module provides the organization with a comprehensive resource to manage its own team development process.

At the same time, it should be treated as a guide. If you find other materials that are more appropriate or that work better, replace what is there. If you find a different approach yields better results, use it. The goal is to create a set of materials and a method of delivering them that yield the best possible outcome.

3 CERTIFICATION: A RADICAL NEW WAY TO EMPOWER TEAMS*

WHY CERTIFY TEAMS? THE RATIONALE FOR THE CREDENTIALING PROCESS

Credentialing or certifying teams is a powerful tool to manage the implementation of the team process and to motivate teams to learn and grow. The application of this concept may be the most useful tool to appear this decade. The concept of team certification is just emerging and there have been very few field tests. This chapter outlines the:

- ✓ Rationale for the certification process.
- ✓ Assumption underlying it.
- ✓ Certification structure.
- ✓ Model and levels of certification.
- ✓ Strategy for implementing certification.
- ✓ Roles of various groups in the process.

There are two major challenges in the implementation of a team process. One is a transformation issue, the other a logistical (implementation) issue. The transformation problem, in our experience, is by far the more difficult to understand and solve. *It is fundamentally an issue of transferring power and authority to first-level teams.* If, as we believe, the installation of a team process is a means to an end of changing the organization, then a core issue in that change is how to move power and authority from traditional levels and structures to the teams. Often, the organization will talk of "empowering" teams, but the reality is little more than a variation on the old individual environment.

At the same time, we have witnessed organizations in which the implementation of a team process and the empowering of teams moved beyond what either the organizations or the teams were able to handle. That is, the process resulted in "too much, too soon," and both the teams and organization suffered as result.

In any case, the orderly and rational transfer of power in the organization is the single most important issue underlying a team process. You must provide teams enough power to legitimize their new role, and you must find a way to help management transfer their power to teams. Moreover, you need a structure and process that will guide and facilitate that transformation. The organization will find itself in the middle of a situation in which the teams tend to believe that they never have as much power and authority as they need, and managers (deep down) believe that the organization is "giving away the farm" with the empow-

*Much of the translation of theory into practice is credited to work in the State of Washington—Employment Security Department and the LTV Steel-Direct Hot Charge Complex (Cleveland, Ohio). The hands-on efforts of these clients made the development of the certification process possible to this stage.

ering of teams. Neither, of course, is correct. But unless the organization has some visible and structured way of dealing with the issue, it goes underground to be fought out in the traditional tunnels of the paradigm of managing. The team certification process provides a structured and orderly way for the organization to define power and authority, a way to develop structures and individuals to assume new levels of power and authority, and, most important, a vehicle for managing the redistribution of that power and authority.

When asked why he used primarily a running game rather than a passing offense, Woody Hayes, the infamous coach of the Ohio State Buckeyes football team was reported to have said something like, "... because in a passing offense, three things can happen and two of them are bad." The same may be true with the transfer of power to teams. The larger organization can give teams too little, too much, or just the right amount. Examples of giving teams too little power abound throughout the country. The evidence? The teams and the team process disappear after a time. Teams given too little power and authority will simply cease to function or to be effective after a period of time. Too much power is less frequent, but happens nonetheless. One organization, when moving to a team-based structure, created a new business unit with totally self-managing work teams. The members of the teams came out of a traditional workplace and were given minimal training. The result was a long struggle that ranged from anarchy by team members and teams to attempts to regain control by management. It seems to be a case of making too big a shift too quickly. Giving teams too little or too much power tends to end up with the same result—management tends to regress to the prior state and recapture the power from the teams.

The logistical challenge is in organizing the team development process and in managing the implementation of that process with teams that have widely differing abilities and interests in growing as teams. Typically, we see a team process put on a schedule and implemented across the board in an organization. Such an approach usually results in a relatively normal distribution of team effectiveness. About 20 percent of the teams do very well, about 20 percent do very poorly, and the remaining 60 percent are somewhere between the other two groups.

The key to success is the middle group. You will always have some high-performing teams, and there will always be some mediocre to poor teams. If, however, you can move a large portion of the "average" teams toward the high-performing end of the continuum, the investment in teams will pay off. How do you do this? Here are some suggestions:

1. Pay attention to the pace of team development. Being certain that teams understand and acquire the information and skills and integrate those skills with their work is more important than completing the training on schedule. If you appear to be going too fast, slow down. If the teams appear to be getting bored, speed up.
2. Treat the teams as your customers. Pay attention to their needs and requirements, and be sure they have the support they need to be effective.
3. Use strategies such as team certification to encourage teams to keep growing and improving their performance.

The certification process provides several useful tools for the organization. First and foremost, define the training, development, and performance standards for implementing teams. Interestingly, this process takes the definition of teams and their development out of the hands of external trainers and consultants and puts it back in the hands of the organization where it belongs. Second, the certification process provides a vehicle for setting targets of accomplishment for teams, but provides within those targets the freedom for teams to move at their own pace. Finally, perhaps the most useful tool is the definition of power and authority transferable to the teams once they achieve a certain level of development.

That is, the organization defines exactly what teams will be able to do as a result of achieving levels of certification. For example, new (or new levels of) authority might include:

- ✓ Having the authority to expend a certain level of budget without approval of a superior.
- ✓ Setting work or vacation schedules.
- ✓ Developing or changing work processes.
- ✓ Providing a variety of customer service functions (e.g., telephoning cus tomers, making customer site visits).
- ✓ Managing overtime.

Notice that these are not minor authorities, but represent areas traditionally in the domain of management.

In summary, the team certification process provides a mechanism to facilitate transformation from an individual, hierarchical organization and culture to an empowered, team-based culture and one to help the organization structure and manage a team process.

PRINCIPLES OF THE TEAM CERTIFICATION PROCESS

1. The certification process should move teams toward what the organization is trying to become. The assignment of authority is not a random process, but should be directed to what the teams will be doing in the future organization. As organizations are flattened and shrunk, more and more authority and responsibility will be assumed by groups and teams of people who do the work. The certification process will support role redefinition by focusing training and skill development on the critical areas of team functioning.
2. The certification process and training programs should be compatible and reinforce each other. Once the organization has a clear picture of where it is headed in the future, if teams are part of that picture, the organization will undoubtedly pursue a team development process that includes training. We contend that the training program should be linked conceptually and operationally to the certification effort. This allows teams to see that the training is related to the skills and behaviors required of them and, when they demonstrate the acquisition of pertinent knowledge and skills, the certification process reinforces the growth with the allotment of new authority.
3. Certification should be designed and carried out so that teams can move through "stages of growth." Each stage should consist of an increasingly complex set of skills and knowledge. The first stage (called "Basic" in one client firm) should be difficult enough to represent a "stretch" for the team. That is, they should have to work to achieve success. Certification requirements might include demonstrating an understanding of the organization's and the team's business, development of a team purpose statement, demonstrating the ability to conduct effective team meetings, and so forth. At the same time, the requirements at the first level should not be so stringent as to dis-

courage the team. For example, having to present a business plan is probably too much to ask at this stage.

4. Recognition plans should reinforce teams' efforts in certification. The organization can use media (newsletter stories), create events (recognition dinners or meetings), or provide a discretionary budget for the team to use in improving the work area or business.
5. The certification process should help teams answer the question: What's in it for us to become a certified team? In general, certification is a tool to help transfer power and authority from the management hierarchy to the teams. Presumably, the acquisition of power and authority will give the team the ability to increase the performance of their business and to make their efforts more successful. As a result, team jobs may be easier, money might be better (if, for example, the organization has a profit- or gain-sharing program), or the general quality of life on the job might be improved.

DESIGNING THE CERTIFICATION PROGRAM

How is the certification program effort organized? What should the program consist of? How does it operate?

The Certification Organization

The first step in the process is the creation of a certification organization. The organization consists of a committee or set of committees that develop(s) certification requirements, procedures for reviewing requirements, and a system for certifying teams. Depending on the size of the organization, one committee can perform the range of functions. In larger organizations, there may be several levels of committees. Figure 3-1 is a sample organization for a certification process in a large business. This structure shows three levels of certification organization:

Policy Committee. This committee is responsible for the overall design of the certification process, for the development of policies to guide the process, and for specifying the administrative procedures to implement it. In addition, the policy committee, in conjunction with the business units at the next level, designs the overall structure of the process. The policy committee should consist of representation from top leadership of the management team, union officials (if a union is present), and any internal resource people who could be helpful (e.g., training).

Certification Committee. In an attempt to keep decision making at the proper level, we recommend the actual certification be administered at the business unit level. Administration of the process includes:

1. Being certain that teams are receiving the necessary training and support.
2. Evaluating team products (e.g., purpose statement) and activities (e.g., quality of team meetings).
3. Recommending or awarding certification.

Leaders at this level are most familiar with the requirements of the business unit, know the kinds of teams within it, and are in the best position to support the certification process. The certification committee should consist of business unit leaders, union leaders at the business unit level (if they exist), resource people, and two or three representatives from the various levels and functions in the unit.

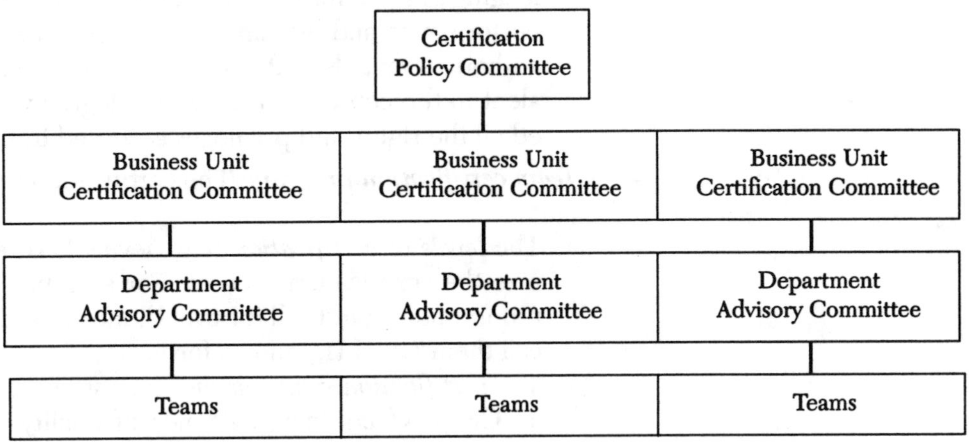

Figure 3-1. Certification organization.

Who Designs the Certification Program? The program should be designed by a committee of the leadership of the key stakeholders in the organization. If, for example, there is a steering committee in place that is responsible for a joint labor-management process or for organizational transformation, this committee could take responsibility for the design process. The committee could do the design themselves or create and oversee a task force to create it for them.

The design of the certification process can take from one to twelve months depending on the number of people involved in the design, the complexity of the organization and the program, and the intensity of the design effort. There is no right way to do the design. One organization's design committee met approximately once a month for ten or eleven months to create the design. Another organization did the design in about six months (in a larger and more complex organization) by meeting at least once a week.

How Do the Committees Interact? Either top management or an organizationwide steering committee should have the ultimate responsibility for success of the certification process. Within the process, the policy committee should have primary authority for the structure and content of team certification. The certification committee is the "manager of operations." This committee administers the certification effort and recommends and/or confers certification of the teams.

What Is in the Design? The certification program plan should consist of the following:

✓ *Certification organization:* This is the organization responsible for over seeing the certification process. This organization is responsible for essen tially three functions:

1. *Being certain that teams are trained and supported:* Providing training and support for teams involves developing and/or overseeing a training plan for teams (for the training needed to fulfill certification requirements) and the in-house support staff to coach and counsel the teams as they begin to implement learning.
2. *Auditing and assessing teams' performance and achievements:* The audit and assessment function involves measuring teams' products (e.g., purpose statement) and activity (e.g., team meetings or problem-solving products) against the standards defined in the program.
3. *Doing the actual certification of teams* (see Fig. 3.1.): Certification involves the actual conferral of the certification. This involves acknow-

ledging in some formal way that the team has achieved a certain level of performance and learning and that they are now eligible to utilize the authority available in that level of certification. (This is somewhat equivalent to the conferral of a college degree with its phrase "and is granted all the rights and privileges accorded to this degree.")

✓ *Team certification program:* The certification program consists of three parts:

1. The *levels of certification* (e.g., levels I, II, etc.) define how you organize the certification process. For example, you may begin with basic requirements (and call it Level I), move to advanced requirements (and call them Level II), and so forth.
2. The *certification requirements* consist of three things:
   a. The *products* (e.g., evidence of quality problem solving) and *outcomes* (e.g., successful team meetings) required to demonstrate competency are the first.
   b. The *standards for completion* define how the products and outcomes will be measured (e.g., the team will have demonstrated the ability to use a structured problem-solving process to solve at least one problem which is within their realm of authority).
   c. The *training and development* defines the training modules or other developmental experiences that the team is expected to complete to acquire the knowledge and skills necessary to produce the products and outcomes at the level of the standards (e.g., Module 10, Team Business Meetings, would be listed in the level related to holding successful team meetings).
3. The *levels of authority* define what the team will be able to do as a result of achieving certification at a given level. For example, upon achieving Level I certification, the team acquires the right to schedule and run its own team meetings and/or is henceforth given input to the operating budget for the department/team.

Figure 3-2 shows the relationship between the components of the certification program and some examples of those components.

Levels of certification	Certification requirements			Levels of authority
	Products and outcomes	Standards for completion	Training and development	
I	Regular and effective team meetings	a. Team generates regular minutes, which include the dates and times of meetings as well as the significant content and outcomes. (An independent observer provides satisfactory feedback to the team about the quality of its meetings at least twice during a three-month period.)	Team completes Module 10, Team Business Meetings.	Team provides input to team scheduling and assignments.
II				For Level II
III				For Level III

Figure 3-2. Certification program.

One organization entitles Level I the "Basic" team development; another calls it the "Problem-Solving Team" level. The categories in Fig. 3-2 can and usually do have multiple listings, as shown in the sample certification program later.

✓ *Implementation strategy and action plans:* This is the general approach to certification. It includes the general model to be employed, the certification processes, and the assignment of responsibility.

Levels of Certification

An organization can create as many levels of certification as it wishes. In general, however, we recommend three levels of certification.* Two levels seem to pack a lot into each category and extend the amount of time a team must work to achieve certification. That reduces the potential to recognize and reinforce a team's movement in the desired direction. More than three levels puts too much detail and bureaucracy into the process. Thus our recommendation of three.

Level I certification indicates that the team has basic information about the business and about the team's functioning, as well as an orientation to the operation of a team. Team operation includes team meetings and some problem solving.

Level II certification is aimed at improving the team meetings, getting a quality improvement process in place, upgrading the level and focus of problem solving, and defining internal supplier/customer relationships. This level of certification typically requires more team leader/facilitator training.

Level III certification leads to full status as a business team. At this level, the team is demonstrating its ability to implement solutions to complex business problems, is creating and implementing successful business plans, is working to satisfy the requirements of internal and external customers, is developing budgets and financial plans to support their business, and is planning their future team development.

One organization identified the three levels of certification with the following titles:

✓ *Level I—Problem-solving work team:* In general, problem-solving work teams give input and recommendations to management for decisions. At Level I, teams have responsibility for some team functions, but final decisions on business issues reside with management.

✓ *Level II—Business work team:* Business work teams (1) may provide input to business decisions, (2) make some decisions jointly with leadership, or (3) have decisions that affect their immediate business delegated to them. In general, BWTs have the authority to make many decisions that affect their immediate work life and give input on larger issues in the business.

✓ *Level III—Self-directed work team:* A number of traditional management functions are in the hands of the team. Leadership roles shift to coaching and support of the team, such that it is successful in carrying out its broader responsibilities. In general, SDWTs run the daily business of their unit. They manage daily decision making and problem solving.

*This is not a fixed number. One company, for example, uses two levels of certification for its teams. Your organization should choose the number of levels appropriate to your vision, goals, and strategy.

Each organization can vary the boundaries between levels and the content of each level to fit its vision and needs. The beauty of the approach is its flexibility.

Certification Requirements

There are two kinds of requirements for certification:

1. Successful completion of training and developmental activities
2. Products or deliverables

Products and deliverables constitute the evidence that the team has completed the requirements for the given level of certification. The team demonstrates accomplishment in two ways:

1. They provide the review committee with physical documents such as a mission statement, vision, or signed team commitment.

2. A person outside the team reviews team activity for successful conduct or completion of requirements (e.g., successful team meetings) based on the certification requirements. For example, the documentation might include the following:

   ✓Meetings are held regularly.

   ✓Meetings are run according to the team meeting model.

   ✓Minutes/records are kept of the meeting and distributed to key groups.

   ✓Meeting leadership is satisfactory.

   ✓Team members judge the meetings to be valuable.

The reviewer would observe meetings to see that the pertinent activities were occurring and that the overall quality of the meeting was acceptable. Figure 3-3 contains a sample certification program for the basic level.

Review or certification committees and individual reviewers should be chosen carefully and oriented to the task they will perform. The selection and orientation processes are typically the responsibility of the change-related steering committees. The concern is that the review and certification processes neither be so loose that team members view them as a joke nor so tight that the organization never shifts any authority to the teams.

If the selection and orientation are done carefully and with planning, the third key element is a monitoring and evaluation process that provides continuous and accurate feedback about how the process is working. In general, the feedback should include some good data (teams enjoyed the challenge of the certification) and some complaining (they thought it was too tough). The balance would indicate that the certification is a "stretch" for the teams, but that it was worth it.

Basic team level

Products and outcomes	*Standards to demonstrate successful completion*	*Training support materials and aids*
A. Team business profile, including team business goals and objectives for the next 6 months/1 year	1. Team business profile sheet completed (Team Manual). 2. Flipcharts, worksheets documenting group input into determining products, services. 3. Flipcharts, worksheets documenting group input into the top 4–5 priority goals and objectives to be achieved.	1. Team manual, sections 1 and 2
B. Team mission statement	1. A mission statement that includes the ultimate purpose of the team, the reasons for its existence, and the boundaries within which it operates. This should be 25–50 words in length. 2. Documentation of the date this was completed, those present and participating in developing and approving the team mission statement.	1. Team manual, section 2
C. Team vision statement	1. A team vision statement that includes the team's desired future state in terms of outcomes, characteristics, and function. This should describe what the team aspires to be if it could "be all that it can be." 2. Documentation of the date this was completed, those present and participating in developing and approving the team vision statement.	1. Team manual, section 3
D. Team role assignments	1. All roles have been assigned to one of the team members, and the minutes indicate that team members have filled these roles for a minimum of three meetings.	1. Basic work team meeting minutes form. 2. Form that lists and defines all the roles being developed.
E. Signed Team Commitment Form	1. A signed Team Commitment Form all team members that they can support the team mission statement, the team vision statement, the team goals and objectives, and the team role assignments.	1. An appropriate form will be developed.
F. Regular team meetings	1. The team has conducted a minimum of three team meetings. 2. The minutes of the meetings indicate that the team is following the team meeting model contained in the work team training. 3. The agenda of the meetings and the minutes indicate that the meetings have included information sharing, discussion and input of important issues, and problem-solving and/or decision-making activities.	1. Team manual, sections 5, 8, 9 2. Basic work 3. Team meeting minutes form.

Figure 3-3

Basic team level *(continued)*

Products and outcomes	*Standards to demonstrate successful completion*	*Training support materials and aids*
G. Tour: Prefab to final processing	1. All members of the team have completed this tour developed by a team composed of representatives from each area and facilitated by the internal consultants. 2. Team prepares a summary of major points of impact they learned from this tour: (1) what they learned about how what they do affects other units/components, and (2) how what other units/components do affects them.	1. Tour procedures and scheduling needs to be developed
H. Conduct internal customer visits	1. Engage in specific conversations between the team, or a subcommittee of the team, with at least one internal customer to (1) clarify issues/problems, (2) establish standards, (3) develop agreement on standards, (4) develop a written agreement and obtain approval of process procedures, and (5) coordinate activities and working relationships. 2. Prepare a summary of the visit with action steps that implement some change, either in customer, the team, or both.	1. Customer and supplier analysis from the work team training 2. Team manual, section 3 3. Step 2 of the quality training manual.
I. Successfully solve a type I problem	1. Identify a list of problems under the control of the team. 2. Select one problem from the list and apply systematic problem-solving techniques to develop a solution and action plan for solving the problem. Use minutes or other supporting documents (flipchart) that this was done. 3. Provide evidence that the action plan was implemented and the outcome evaluated.	1. Team manual, section 8 2. Work group proposal form, proposal tracking chart 3. Basic work team meeting minutes form
J. Demonstrate use and understanding of the quality problem-solving model	1. Demonstrate an understanding of quality-related problem solving through its application to a new problem or to the problem in section I above.	1. Step 2 of the quality training manual

Advanced team level

Products and outcomes	*Standards to demonstrate successful completion*	*Training support materials and aids*
A. Successful team meetings	1. Over a reasonable period of time (6 months) the team meetings reliably result in completing the meeting agenda. Objectives for the meeting are achieved. 2. Complex issues are carried to completion across several meetings. 3. The agenda of the meetings and the minutes continue to indicate that the meetings have included information sharing, discussion and input of important issues, and problem-solving and/or decision-making activities.	1. Team manual, sections 5, 8, 9

Figure 3-3 *(Continued)*

Advanced team level *(continued)*

Products and outcomes	*Standards to demonstrate successful completion*	*Training support materials and aids*
B. Three type II issue proposals developed to resolve team business problems	1. Identify a list of problems involving issues that go beyond the team itself, such as with customers, suppliers, other teams. 2. Select three problems from the list and apply systematic problem-solving techniques to develop a solution and action plan for solving the problem. Use minutes or other supporting documents (flipchart) to show that this was done. 3. Provide evidence that an action plan has been developed and accepted by those whose cooperation is required for successful implementation.	1. Team manual, section 8 2. Work group proposal form, proposal tracking chart 3. Basic work team meeting minutes form
C. Internal supplier contract	1. All major suppliers have been identified, along with the input each provides. 2. The standard(s) for each have been identified using delivery times, cost, quality, accuracy of information as appropriate. 3. A contract has been executed for at least three suppliers.	1. Business team training, module 16 2. A contract form will need to be developed.
D. Internal customer assessment and follow-up plan	1. All the customers, both internal and external, have been identified along with the product or service provided. 2. The customer requirements have been determined for each customer using the customer standards form. 3. Customer ratings have been obtained from the top two customers, a feedback meeting has been held with each, and a corrective action plan has been developed for both customers if needed.	1. Business team training, module 15 2. Customer standards form, page 13 3. Customer rating and feedback form, page 15
E. Quality plan and documentation	1. Statistically monitor the process. 2. Approve standards. 3. Diagnostics/advanced statistics/design of experimental trials with expert assistance. 4. Demonstrate understanding of the quality model programming and use of statistical packages.	1. Steps 3 and 4 of the quality training manual
F. Team leader/facilitator certified	1. The team facilitator has completed the basic work team development program. 2. The team and the team facilitator have received structured feedback from the internal consultants using the team meeting evaluation form, have taken corrective action where needed, and perform at least at a satisfactory level on all dimensions. 3. The team facilitator has assisted the group through the problem-solving cycle for at least one type I and one type II problem.	1. Business team leader training, module 8 2. Team meeting evaluation form, page 16

Figure 3-3 *(Continued)*

Master team level

Products and outcomes	Standards to demonstrate successful completion	Training support materials and aids
A. External customer visit	1. Depending on the size of the team, at least one customer visit has occurred for each five team members (teams with less than five members = one visit; teams with 6–10 members = two visits, etc.). 2. Where possible, at least two team members visit the same customer at the same time. 3. Team members summarize in writing for the team how the team's product/service is used by the customer, the degree to which customer standards are being met, additional customer needs, possible corrective action.	1. Business team training, module 15 2. Customer visit report form to be developed
B. Successful implementation of three type II business team problem proposals	1. Provide evidence that the action plans were implemented. 2. Evaluate the effectiveness of implementation; develop steps for follow-up and refinement where indicated.	
C. Team development plan	1. The team conducts an assessment of the individual and team strengths and areas for potential improvement. 2. Team members determine both individual and team objectives for improvement. 3. The team constructs an action plan for developmental activities to achieve the objectives for improvement and obtains approval and funding where needed. 4. The team implements the plan and assesses the degree to which the objectives were achieved.	1. Business team training, module 22 2. Contracting: Assessment of the experience, pages 4–5 of Module 22 3. Team contract, page 6 of Module 22
D. Successful achievement of three annual business team goals and objectives	1. The team has constructed a complete business plan that has annual business goals of the team that are clearly linked to the goals of the business unit. 2. Action plans to achieve at least three business team goals and objectives have been developed and implemented. 3. The team has documented the achievement of at least three annual business team goals and objectives.	1. Business team training, Module 21 2. Business plan, page 11 of Module 21
E. Quality plan and documentation	1. Statistically identify process and product performance. 2. Approve standards and product specifications. 3. Diagnostics/advanced statistics; set up trials without requiring expert assistance 4. Capable of training others in the quality process and quality model programming (input programming, nonstandard programming).	1. Step 5 of the quality training manual

Figure 3-3 *(Continued)*

Levels of Authority

The levels of authority are the exchange medium in the certification process. As teams achieve levels of knowledge and skill in participating in the business and begin to demonstrate new abilities, the transfer of authority represents the reward for their effort and commitment.

The key is to set the levels of authority high enough to (1) motivate the teams to achieve and grow and (2) effect a real transfer of power to other levels of the organization. If you do not do both, the chances of the certification program making a real difference are lessened considerably. A sample Levels of Authority chart is included as Fig. 3-4. This figure is a compilation of all the authority available to teams divided into the categories that equate to the three levels of certification. You can relate this figure to the one on certification in Fig. 3-2 by taking the information in the Level I column and attaching it to the certification table. That is, if the team demonstrates that it has fulfilled all the requirements for Level I, these are the kinds of authority they earn. The same holds for levels II and III. If we had more space, we would include the information in the table that describes the products and outcomes, standards, and training for the respective levels.

Training to Support Certification

Various resources are required to support teams' creation of the products and deliverables for certification. Typically, training courses or modules are organized by topic or skill. Our goal is to provide most of the essential training modules in this manual.

Some blocks of training may currently be available within the organization. Others (not included in the manual) may need to be created or acquired outside the organization. Still others may need to be modified to fit your situation. For example, the module called Roles in the Team can be adjusted to the roles you define for your teams (e.g., communicator, safety, quality).

Regardless of the source, it is important to have a comprehensive training plan to support the implementation of the certification process. If the training plan is going to support certification, you need to do the following:

1. Design the certification program and training to support the teams' development.
2. Develop a tentative schedule for making the training available (over a period of probably 18 to 24 months).
3. Identify the trainers who will deliver the modules. Potential trainers include:
   a. Outside vendors or consultants.
   b. The personnel in your human resources or training department.
   c. A team of in-house trainers and coaches who both deliver the modules and support the teams during their learning periods. We have used a variety of salaried and hourly personnel in this fashion (some full-time, some part-time) and find them to be extremely valuable. In addition, the new "work" provides a challenge and an opportunity to grow that often does not exist in today's downsized organization.
4. Orient the trainers, launch the teams, and begin the training process. We normally have teams request training as they need and want it. That means the organization operates an on-call system. But the ability to respond to

Level I	*Level II*	*Level III*
Teams plan, problem-solve, and recommend for management approval, changes in work environment: type I problems.	Teams plan, problem-solve, and implement solutions for changes in work environment. Management informed/ management approval on specified type 2 problems. (Requires changes in philosophy, structure, systems, policies, and skills.)	Run daily business of the unit. Manage decision making and problem solving.
Determine training needs.	Schedule training with budgeatry approval.	Determine schedules and approve training.
Train new employees.	Develop and/or select training programs	Evaluate new employee job knowledge and recommend training needs.
Monitor and report team vacations.	Schedule vacations.	Schedule days off.
Determine work needs.	Determine work assignments.	Schedule team work assignments and using supervisor as resource.
Selection of team leaders.	Selection of supervisor.	Supervisor becomes team resource.
Plan/lead work team meetings.	Determine work procedures.	Manage work procedures.
Provide input; assist in budget preparation.	Prepare cost budget. Monitor/control costs.	Manage cost budget (spend money within limits).
Contact and resolve internal customer concerns.	Contract with external customers and suppliers for resolution for issues.	Visit and resolve external customer problems.
Generate ideas for meeting customer needs.	Generate and implement ideas for meeting customer needs.	Use customer needs in building team business plan.
Set team objectives.	Provide input to team goals.	Set team goals.
Monitor team goals.	Monitor team goal performance.	Track team goal performance over time.
Provide input to hiring process.	Interview candidates; make recommendations.	Do team hiring.
Handle individual team performance problems, excluding discipline (problem-solve).	Handle individual team performance problems excluding discipline; send cases to peer review board.	Handle individual team performance problems, including discipline.
Input to team work life conditions in plan.	Take responsiblity for overall work life conditions. Monitor/oversee repair work orders.	Manage overall work life condition. Manage maintenance function.
Request maintenance help. Maintain safety and housekeeping.	Plan safety and housekeeping.	Manage safety and housekeeping.
Implement quality improvement processes.	Plan quality improvement processess.	Manage quality improvement processes.
Generate ideas to improve productivity/cost/quality.	Generate and implement within limits) ideas to improve productivity/cost/quality.	Plan and manage productivity/cost/quality processes in the team's business.

Figure 3-4. Levels of authority.

teams' needs and schedules emphasizes the new role they play in the organization. It may be possible to schedule multiple teams in the same session, but remember that they have to work in their respective exercises. So you need to be able to facilitate and coach the number of teams involved.

All this occurs in the context of the larger training mission and program of the organization. There is likely to be training related to skill development, new social programs (e.g., diversity), and new products going on at the same time. Coordination is the key to make the effort high-quality and to have all the pieces fit together.

Failure to plan and deliver quality training will negatively affect the success of the effort.

IMPLEMENTING A CERTIFICATION PROCESS

Implementing a certification process is an extensive and varied process. It will require resources on the part of the organization. Figure 3-5 shows the steps to implementing a certification process. Essentially the steps to implementation begin with the design committee, move through the design process, and end with the implementation and evaluation of the effort.

With something as new as certification, however, the design and development process will be ongoing. There is not enough experience or a sufficient foundation on which to design and implement a program that is as good as it will be after you have had some experience with the effort.

1. Form a certification design committee.

   Launch the committee.
   Outline the planning process and set a schedule.

2. Design a certification organization.
3. Create the certification program.

   Identify certification levels.
   Identify content areas.
   Identify products and outcomes.
   Determine related training and support.

4. Specify the certification process.
5. Create a recognition process.
6. Design a plan to monitor and evaluate the certification program
7. Review the plan with key stakeholders.
8. Create the final plan.
9. Communicate the program to the employees.

   Use the organization's publications.
   Hold orientation meetings.

10. Implement the certification program.
11. Monitor and evaluate the certification program; implement improvements based on the evaluation.

Figure 3-5. Steps to implementing a team certification process.

Barriers to the Certification Process

There are at least three key barriers to the implementation of a successful certification process:

1. *Commitment:* The certification of teams requires an extensive commitment on the part of the organization. The commitment takes the form of people, money, and time. You need people to design, oversee, and support the effort. You need money to fund the development of training, trainers, materials, and the like. You need time to do the training, coaching, and learning.
2. *Patience:* In today's world of "make it happen yesterday," when the executive suite is filled with people looking at the next quarter's stockholder meeting, there is often not the patience to look out three to five years and see what kind of investment it will take to create a high-performance workplace. As a result, there is sometimes less patience than the organization needs to get the program in place and keep it going until the payoff begins.
3. *Willingness to change:* Certification is based on a presumption of a shift in power in the organization. Unless the people and structures with the power are willing and able to somehow redistribute it, there will be little or no chance of success in the long term. This, of course, is one of the issues at the heart of the efforts to change the culture of organizations.

What to Do?

Invest the time and effort at the outset to assess the probability of success. It will not be an easy or clear decision. If you have the kind of organization that is not hampered by the three barriers, you may well have an organization that does not need certification, either to develop teams or to transfer power. Most of the remaining organizations have the opportunity to use the certification effort as a learning tool. In this vein, the certification process is just one element of a larger effort to bring about a substantive change in the organization—a change that includes a great deal more than just developing teams.

In any case, be aware of the potential stumbling blocks and deal with them as best you can before the fact rather than after the fact.

CONCLUSION

This chapter has provided an overview of a team certification process. Certification is a tool with which to integrate organizational change, training, and empowerment into a single process. It is neither simple nor easy. The experience of organizations over the next decade will yield a concept and process that add to the strength and viability of the organization of the future.

4 TEAM CERTIFICATION QUESTIONS AND ANSWERS

This chapter addresses questions that arose in the development of the certification program for the client whose case is outlined in Chap. 5. We share them to give you an idea of the issues that emerge when you are designing a certification effort.

Is there ever a reason to decertify teams? If so, what is it?

We would not decertify teams. The organization should be committed to keeping teams competent and functioning. Any time a team reaches the point where you might want to decertify it, there is probably some combination of failure in the team and failure in the organization. Work on solving the issue rather than punishing the team.

You might want to think about renewal of certification (as they do in the professional licenses). The certification design could stipulate a certain amount of team training each year as part of renewal (topics chosen by the team) and/or evidence of orientation/ development of new members, etc.

Would certain conditions, such as high turnover in a team, merit having them go through certification again?

Think about several things:

1. As long as at least some percentage (e.g., 33 percent) of the team members have been through formal certification, the team itself does not need to recertify.
2. Each team (or the overall effort) should have a way to integrate and develop new team members. The new member process should differentiate between members coming from other teams (who might have had training) and those who are new to the organization. (*Note:* You might ask teams to experiment with solutions to this problem and submit suggestions based on their experiences.)
3. The organization could set up quarterly or semiannual training sessions for people new to the organization. This would give you a way to cover more people at one time.

What about teams that claim they have the knowledge and skills in certain areas? Should they have to go through the training and generate the evidence?

Having been involved in higher education programs that provide means for adult learners with a lot of life and professional experience to earn credit toward a college degree, we are familiar with alternative ways of demonstrating knowledge and skills. Teams could also demonstrate knowledge and skills in an alternative manner. For example you might create a portfolio review process to which teams would submit material for review (maybe something as simple as a memorandum with endorsement by a supervisor or manager).

What incentive is there for teams that already have a fair amount of authority to pursue certification?

There may be no direct incentive. You should consider the present levels of authority when you design the program. Remember, the certification has to be a "stretch" beyond what the teams currently do (in terms of work) and what they currently have (in terms of authority). The problem is finding a way to make similar gates onto the certification road.

The teams that presently have more authority may actually have a lot more than they can use. Training might expand their repertoire of skills, and certification might expand the role of the team in its business. (*Note:* The option in the preceding case enabled teams to request authority beyond what is in the model and get a review of a revision for their situation.) And, if you have the portfolio process to certify existing knowledge and skill, the teams do not "lose" anything that adds value.

Some people or teams will not pursue certification because "there is nothing in it for them." They believe that certification represents more work and that they should be paid more or be given incentive to engage in this effort. Is it a good idea to honor their request?

For some, that may be true. We would not recommend that you create monetary or other kinds of special "incentives" to motivate teams to pursue certification. We recommend that you send the following messages to the organization:

1. If you want to participate in a team and the certification process, and if you want to have more influence in discussions about the organization and its business, you are free to do so under the auspices of the agreement.
2. Some individuals or teams may refuse to proceed on the basis that the process lacks incentives or rewards. This process is not about money or other "carrots." It is about transforming a whole culture of work, at the core of which is redistributing power. If you begin to mix in old culture techniques (e.g., goodies for learning), it will confuse and confound people. The principle is: Do the right thing and be ready to take the heat from up to 20 percent of the people who want you to buy their commitment.
3. The issue of more work for more pay may be a problem. By and large, you are designing different (rather than more) work. Actually, a lot of outcomes of empowering people result in less work. You surely do not reduce pay in such cases.

One aim of this process is to shift the work effort from exclusively doing toward thinking. It is impossible to put a monetary value on that shift.

At the same time, the leadership of the organization will need to pay attention to whether some cases result in significantly different jobs that merit pay increases. To ignore a case or cases of adding a lot of work would result in questions about justice and equity.

In general, we recommend that the organization adopt overall compensation systems that allow all employees to participate in the financial success (or stewardship) of the organization. This is a broad-based form of incentive that ties the efforts of the teams to the overall performance of the organization.

Are we not just creating another whole bureaucracy with the certification structures and committees? Doesn't that contradict what we say we are trying to do with the organization?

Yes, there is a vulnerability of being looked at as additional "overhead" since the certification process does not add immediate value. At the same time, organizations putting in serious efforts to change need some structures and processes to facilitate that change. This is one of those processes.

The best we can recommend is:

1. Don't create unnecessary bureaucracy and paperwork.
2. Get rid of bureaucracy where and when you find it as part of getting better.
3. Work at creating "substance," not form, in the certification effort and manage it at the local level.

The key, we believe, is to understand the underlying strategy. [This also relates to the issue of a local certification committee (LCC) leadership control, discussed in Chap. 5.]

Finally, there is the issue of the extra work involved. In spite of what Phil Crosby said, quality is not free and neither is substantive change. The organization will have to invest time, money, and effort in changing from a hierarchy-centered to a team-centered culture and organization. And people will have to make the investment while continuing to run the organization in the traditional fashion. This creates stress and fatigue. You don't want to overload the system, but neither do you want to short-circuit the effort required to make a real difference.

Don't we need to be consistent across the organization in the requirements for certification and how we administer the effort?

Consistency is an issue. On one hand it would be difficult, if not impossible, to create an exact replica of the system across the various divisions, businesses, and cultures of the organization. At the same time, to create a system with such great variability may suggest inequities that will result in questions of justice. These inevitably lead to discussions about dissolving the process (especially if it is voluntary).

Remember: Team certification is more like an art than a science. Everyone wants a formula, the chemicals, and tools to make it happen. Instead, we provide a blank canvas, some brushes and paint, as well as suggestions about what and how to draw. From that point it is up to the organization to make it work.

How do responsibility and accountability relate to certification and the transfer of power?

Authority, responsibility, and accountability are inseparable (although they are often separated in the classic organization). As such, the plan should designate how the three are related in the operation of the teams. The simplest way to do that is to think of the team as a leader and ask the question: If this were an individual to whom we were granting the authority to do *x*, what responsibility and accountability does she or he have? Who has the responsibility and accountability when he or she does not? If you ask and answer these questions for teams, the division of authority and related responsibility and accountability will be clear.

Can teams begin to do things in the certification program after they have completed a given module or sequence, or do they have to wait until they have finished the certification for the entire level?

Our original (and somewhat linear) thinking was that authority would transfer at the point of certification (a kind of "baptism"). Such thinking limits our options. For example, once teams have completed team meeting training, they could have the authority to set up and run their own meetings even if they are not fully certified. These meetings will also probably turn out to be one of the more valuable learning experiences in their curriculum.

5 TEAM CERTIFICATION: A CASE OVERVIEW

INTRODUCTION

This section is devoted to sample information from an emerging certification program. The content and process are in the formative stages and will evolve over the first two years of the effort. Because of the developmental nature of the effort and sensitive issues in the client firm, we have not identified the location of this process. Perhaps by the time the book is printed, the organization will be far enough along to permit public review of and learning from the effort.

Most of the information is condensed from the working documents used in the planning of the certification effort. Much of the discussion in developing strategies is not captured here. The intent is to provide an overview of an actual case, not a complete how-to-do-it manual.

BACKGROUND

The decision by the organization to implement team-based management raised numerous issues, one of the most complex being how real authority is transferred from current management to teams. Management questioned how to know when teams are ready to accept increased authority. On the other hand, many staff have doubts that management will ever relinquish significant authority to teams.

To clarify the issue of transferring authority, the organization is adopting a team certification process. In the process, the organization will divide teams into three different levels, each with increasing degrees of authority. A team certification process provides more and better guidelines for this transfer of authority than any of the alternatives explored.

The following overview provides the rationale for certification, the major players (their roles and responsibility), the timelines, the criteria, and the process.

Rationale for a Certification Process

Team certification is a powerful tool to manage the implementation of the team process and to motivate teams to learn and grow. This tool has three major components:

1. Defining the training, development, and performance standards for implementing teams

2. Providing a vehicle for setting targets of accomplishment for teams and the freedom for teams to move at their own pace
3. Providing a definition of power and authority transferred to the teams once they achieve a certain level of development

The certification process provides a structured and orderly way for the organization to define power and authority, and, most important, provides a vehicle for managing the redistribution of it. The creation of structure to guide and facilitate the orderly and rationale transfer of power in an organization is the single most important issue underlying a team process.

CERTIFICATION ORGANIZATION

The following sections describe the people and groups involved in the certification process as well as their roles and responsibilities.

Major Players, Their Roles, and Responsibilities

The major players in the certification process include the certification design team, the local certification committee (LCC), the area steering committee, the team and the cost center manager.

Certification Design Team. This team is appointed by, and reports to, the design and oversight committee. The certification design team is charged with designing the certification program. The design responsibility includes developing the certification requirements (criteria), the procedures for reviewing the requirements, and a system for certifying teams.

Local Certification Committee (LCC). To keep decision making at the proper level, the actual certification of teams will be administered at the local level. Leadership at this level is most familiar with the requirements of the business and the teams. Therefore, a "local" certification committee is in the best position to implement the actual certification of teams.

The local certification committee is created by the area steering committee (ASC). The LCC should reflect the following membership mix:

- ✓ Standing members:
  - Cost center manager for the team
  - An ASC member from outside the team's cost center
- ✓ Potential members:
  - Union leadership at the local level (if available)
  - Two or three representatives from other levels/functions
  - A team trainer

The specific functions of the local certification committee include:

1. Being certain that teams have been trained.
2. Assessing teams' performance and achievements.
3. Doing the actual certification of teams.
4. Providing feedback to teams and ASCs regarding the certification results.

It is important that members of the LCC have the following knowledge and understanding:

1. The day-to-day business of the team and cost center
2. The vision/goals of the ASC for creating a team-based environment
3. The philosophy and procedures of team certification

The membership of the LCC may change for each team certification. To build consistency, an ASC may choose to have some members from the potential membership of the LCC as standing members of the LCC for a period of time (e.g., six months). The cost center manager and ASC member always adjust according to the particular team seeking certification.

Area Steering Committee. In general, the ASC is responsible for supporting the certification process in their area. This includes:

✓ Creating local certification committees (LCCs).
✓ Teaching local teams and leadership about the certification process.
✓ Communicating about the certification program.
✓ Assuring that teams are scheduled for training.
✓ Coaching teams that are having difficulties.
✓ Monitoring the certification process and assisting in resolving disputes.
✓ Providing feedback to coordinators and/or DOC.
✓ Celebrating the success of teams by providing recognition.

Cost Center Manager. For true authority to be transferred to teams, the cost center manager must be a key player in the certification process. Unless the manager believes that the team is capable of exercising the authority to be transferred, the implementation of team-based management will never get beyond the discussion stage. It is essential that the manager be a part of the certification task team because real authority will not be transferred without the manager's active participation.

The Team. The team has the responsibility to initiate the certification process when they feel the requirements for the desired level have been met. In general, certification requirements for a level involve the following:

✓ Completion of the training requirements
✓ Demonstration of specific outcomes, products, and/or assignments (as de scribed in the certification model)

Team Trainer. The role of the team trainer includes:

✓ Training teams.
✓ Supporting the teams on an "as-needed" basis.
✓ Assisting the local certification committee.
✓ Keeping the ASC informed on progress, issues, successes, etc.

TIMELINES (SAMPLE FOR LEVEL I)

January	Certification design process completed.
	Team trainer selection process completed.
	Training of team trainers begins.
February	Training of team trainers completed.
	Level I training begins.
	Teams complete other certification requirements.

May	Level I training ends.
	First teams complete other certification requirements.
June	Most teams complete other certification requirements.
	Teams are ready for Level I Certification.

Certification Process

The certification process (at this point still in the refinement stage) is as follows:

1. A team notifies the area steering committee upon completion of the requirements for a given level of certification.
2. The area steering committee, in partnership with local business leadership, selects a local certification committee (LCC) to oversee the certification process.
3. The LCC reviews the team's products and procedures according to the criteria outlined in the certification program.
4. When the LCC determines that a team has met all certification requirements, the team, the area steering committee, and local leadership plan the recognition activity to celebrate the team's success.
5. If, for some reason, the LCC determines that the team has not met the requirements for certification at the next level, a member of the LCC meets with the team to explain the rationale for the decision and to discuss what the team needs to do to achieve the desired level of certification.
6. After this level of certification is complete, the team can request training for the next level of certification.
7. Business leadership related to the team receives notification of the certification along with a description of the authority and responsibility the team now has as a result of the certification.

SAMPLE TEAM CERTIFICATION PROGRAM: LEVEL I

This is the certification for what the organization calls problem-solving work teams. These are first-level teams that give input and recommendations to management for decisions. At Level I, teams have responsibility for some team functions, but final decisions on business issues reside with management.

Outcomes	*Demonstrations of successful completion*	*Training*
1. Understand the current change strategy for moving toward a team-based organization.	a. Team members read and discuss the memoranda on the change process and on new directions. Indicate completion in team meeting minutes. b. Team discusses similarities and differences between the current strategy for change and efforts of the past. Indicate completion in team meeting minutes.	Module 1: Orientation to Change and Team Development Plan

Outcomes	*Demonstrations of successful completion*	*Training*
2. Team understands its current strengths and weaknesses, sets team objectives and undertakes activities for improvement.	a. Survey of team strengths and weaknesses completed. b. Work sheet documenting team's plan for reinforcing strengths and addressing weaknesses. c. List of activities implemented as a result of (c), the outcome(s) of those activities and the team's next steps.	Module 2: Changing Organizational Paradigms
3. Team holds regular and effective team meetings.	a. The team has conducted a minimum of four team meetings. b. Team has created ground rules for operation (using guide in training materials). c. Meeting minutes indicate the team is using effective meeting guidelines and the consensus process to make decisions. d. Team ends meetings with a simple verbal assessment of "What went well and what did not." Summary of this assessment is included in minutes. e. Team has administrered the team meeting evaluation form. f. Documentation that a neutral "outsider" (trainer, co-worker, coordinator, etc.) has observed one of the meetings and has given the team feedback on task and process observations. g. Summarized results of (c) and (d); outline of action steps for improvement.	Module 6: Communication Listening, and Feedback Module 10: Team Business Meetings
4. Team demonstrates-understanding and use of problem-solving model on *two* type I work-related issues.	a. Worksheets or flipcharts documenting team brainstorm list of work issues and the two type I issues selected for resolution. (*Note:* Work on one issue at a time.) b. Worksheets documenting steps I (identifying the problem) through VIII (submitting the proposal) of the problem-solving process. c1. If proposal is accepted, provide evidence that the action plan was implemented and the outcome was evaluated or c2. If proposal is conditionally accepted (e.g., decision maker will support proposal with a few modifications acceptable to team), rewrite proposal to include modifications, provide evidence the action plan was implemented and the outcome evaluated. or c3. If proposal is rejected and/or team and decision maker cannot reach agreement, attach to part (B) a written summary of the decision maker's rationale for rejection and whether the team has any inclination to pursue the issue further.	Module 12: Problem Solving (*Note:* Type I issues are those that are primarily under the control of the team.)

Outcomes	Demonstrations of successful completion	Training
5. Demonstrate understanding of approaches to conflict resolution. Demonstrate use of effective conflict resolution skills.	a. Complete individual self-assessment exercise in training module b. Provide worksheet(s) documenting: The primary types and causes of conflict in the team. Strategies for helping team members become more effective in dealing with conflict. c. Create a conflict resolution "case study," describing an actual conflict and how it was resolved. Where appropriate, the example should reflect aspects of the integrative negotiating process outlined in the training.	Module 7: Conflict Strategies and Integrative Resolution
6. Creation of team standards.	a. Team identifies areas of basic common responsibilities. For example: Maintaining safety and housekeeping in work area Providing OJT to new employees Answering the phone Other (to be determined by team) b. Written action plan (who does what and when) for managing these	None

SAMPLE TEAM CERTIFICATION PROGRAM: LEVEL II

This is the certification program for Level II teams. The organization calls them business work teams (BWTs). They will have completed the Level I certification as well as the requirements in the following table. The business work teams (1) may provide input to business decisions, (2) make some decisions jointly with leadership, or (3) have decisions that affect their immediate business delegated to them. In general, BWTs have the authority to make many decisions that affect their immediate work life and give input on larger issues in the business.

Outcomes	Standards to demonstrate successful completion	Training
1. Team understands the organization's basic business.	a. All team members view organization's business orientation video. (*Note:* Local leadership will participate in this effort to help teams understand how they fit in the big picture and to answer business questions that may arise.) b. Team designs and completes a tour of the organization's primary business units. c. Team prepares a summary of the major learning from the tour including: How the team's affects other units/areas. How the work of other units/areas affects the team.	Module 5: Orientation to the Business Business Orientation (video to be developed) (*Note:* Need to coach local leadership as to their role.)

Outcomes	Standards to demonstrate successful completion	Training
2. Team creates a mission statement.	a. Team creates a mission statement that includes the ultimate purpose of the team, the reasons for its existence, and the boundaries within which it operates. b. Documentation of the date this was completed and a list of those whose input was considered in creating the mission statement. c. Mission statement signed by all team members.	Module 8: Organizational Mission and Purpose of the Team
3. Team creates a vision statement.	a. A team vision statement that includes the team's desired future state in terms of outcomes, characteristics, and function. This should describe what the team aspires to become if it could "be all that it can be." b. Documentation of the date completed and a list of those whose input was considered in creating the vision statement. c. Vision statement signed by all team members.	Module 9: Team Vision Organization, Region, and Division Vision Statements
4. Develop an empowerment plan between teams and leadership.	a. Team reviews minimum authority levels described in Level II certification and decides if any revisions are necessary to meet the needs of their team. If not, team documents that this review occurred and that no changes are needed.	Basic business training: budget, personnel, procurement, and sexual harassment.
	b. If team decides modifications are needed in the Level II description of authority (e.g., a team may need to exercise some authority in areas not covered by the certification model), they should propose revisions using the decision-making exercise as a guide.	Module 11: Decision Making
5. Team business information needs are identified and and fulfilled.	a. Completed business information needs form b. Agenda of team meetings indicates that business information and team performance feedback data are discussed in meetings. performance feedback data are discussed in meetings.	Module 21: Business Information Management
6. Customer and supplier awareness is enhanced.	a. Worksheet illustrating results of customer customer exercise, including: Identification of team's customers Identification products and/or services for those customers.	Module 17: Customer Analysis
	b. Worksheet illustrating results of supplier exercise, including: Identification of team's suppliers. Identification of products/services used by the team from their suppliers.	Module 18: Supplier Analysis
7. Team success indicators are identified.	a. Completed success indicator exercise worksheet b. Evidence that team receives performance feedback data concerning these indicators (should be a part of team's business information needs assessment).	Module 16: High-Performance Business Teams: Quality and Process Improvement Overview

Outcomes	Standards to demonstrate successful completion	Training
8. Team demonstrates understanding and use of the problem-solving model to to address two type 1 work-related issues.	a. Brainstorm a list of problems that involve issues that go beyond the team itself, such as problems with customers, suppliers, other teams etc. b. Select two problems from the list and document working through the issue, following the steps in the problem-solving model. Provide minutes, flipcharts, or other supporting documents. c. Provide evidence that an action plan has been developed and accepted by those whose cooperation is required for successful implementation.	Review Module 12 (Problem Solving)
9. Team holds regular and effective business team meetings	a. Minutes indicate that team meets regularly. b. Agendas, following the team meeting model, include: Sharing business information and team performance feedback data. Discussing issues. Problem-solving and/or decision-making activities. c. Meeting minutes indicate the team is following effective meeting guidelines. d. Team members give each other feedback on behaviors that contribute to effective or ineffective meetings. e. Team administers the business team evaluation form every six months. f. Documentation that a neutral "outsider" (e.g., trainer, co-worker, coordinator, etc.) observed the team meetings once every six months and has given the team feedback on task and process observations. g. Summarized results of (e) and (f); outline of action steps for improvement. Evidence that action steps have been implemented.	Module 15: Personal Styles Team Effectiveness Review Module 10 (Team Business Meetings)
10. Team demonstrates understanding of of organization budget basics.	a. Present current budget for the team. b. Indicate relationship between team's budget and the business unit's financial plan and projections and make some suggestions about how changes in the team's budget could improve its business performance.	Basic training on budget (to be designed)
11. Team demonstrates understanding of organization's personnel basics.	a. Fill out sample form.	Training in person nel (to be designed)
12. Team understands organization's purchasing and procurement basics.	a. Team reviews three months' purchase orders for the group.	Training in purchasing and procurement (to be designed)

Level III is the highest Level of certification. These teams are called self-directed work teams (SDWTs). In the self-directed work team, a number of traditional management functions are in the hands to the team. Leadership roles shifts to coaching and support of the team, such that it is successful in carrying out its broader responsibilities. In general, SDWTs run the daily business of their unit. They manage daily decision making and problem solving.

Outcomes	*Standards to demonstrate successful completion*	*Training*
1. Empowerment plan between team and organizational leadership is refined.	a. Team reviews minimum authority levels and decides if any revisions are necessary to meet the needs of their team. If not, team documents that this review occurred and that no changes are needed. b. If team decides modifications are needed in the Level III description of authority (e.g., a team may need to exercise some authority in areas not covered by the certification program), they should propose revisions using the decision-making exercise as a guide. c. Written verification of modifications agreed upon between team and leadership. This agreement includes what, if any, additional business training the team needs to carry out successfully these additional responsibilities. d. Documentation of any additional business training received.	Advanced business training (provided by the organization) Review Module 11: Decision Making
2. Team business plan is developed and three annual team goals are achieved.	a. The team has constructed a complete business plan that has annual business goals of the team that are clearly linked to the goals of the company, division, and region. b. Action plans to achieve at least three team goals and objectives have been developed and implemented. c. The team has documented the achievement of at least three annual team goals and objective	Module 22: Business Planning I, Module 23: Business Planning II, Review of division and regional goals.
3. Team improves in areas of customer analysis and contracting.	a. Team completes the customer exercises contained in the customer analysis module. b. Team visits at least three customers (internal and/or external) to discuss the customer feedback form. Where possible, at least two members visit the same customer at the same time. Discussion should include: Issues and problems. Customer expectations and standards. Team performance to those expectations. Strategies for improvement. c. Prepare a summary of the visits with action steps that implement some of the changes agreed upon between customer and team.	Module 17: Customer Analysis
4. Two proposals addressing type II problems are implemented.	a. Provide evidence that action plans were implemented for the type II problems. (These are the same problems the team worked on for Level II certification.) b. Evaluate the effectiveness of implementation. Develop steps for follow-up and refinement where indicated.	Review Module 12: Problem Solving

Outcomes	Standards to demonstrate successful completion	Training
5. Team improves in areas of supplier analysis and contracting.	a. Team completes the supplier exercises contained in supplier analysis module. b. Team visits at least three suppliers (internal and/or external) to discuss/understand: Issues and problems. Team expectations/standards. How supplier is performing with regards to the expectations. Strategies for improvement. c. Create a contract with the suppliers that contains agreed-upon expectations and standards.	Module 18: Supplier Analysis Review Module 7: Conflict Strategies and Interest Negotiation

TEAM CERTIFICATION PROGRAM SUMMARY OF AUTHORITY LEVELS FOR TEAMS

The table on the facing page summarizes the kinds of authority and responsibility the teams acquire with each level of certification. Note that at the inception of the certification program, some teams already had authority in some of the named areas. There was not, however, consistency across the organization, and there was no clear path to acquiring the authority. By and large, the system was paternal at best and tended toward being autocratic for the most part. In addition, as noted in the preceding certification process, teams have the right to request authority or responsibility not presently listed in the table. This provides moderate flexibility for the organization and the teams to adapt themselves to the business and the certification process as needs arise and experience is gained.

MOVING AHEAD

This section has offered an overview of one organization's work with the team certification process. There is, of course, a great deal more to be said and written on the subject of certification. The early pilot projects in the United States will provide the learning and evidence we need to make this into one of the most important tools available to help transform the human system in organizations.

Level I: Problem-solving work team	*Level II: Business work team*	*Level III: Self-directed work team*
Identify training needs.	Schedule training with budgetary approval.	Schedules training when needed.
Provide on-the-job training for new employees.	Develop and/or select training programs.	Evaluate new employee job knowledge and employees recommend training needs.
Recommend work team scheduling.	Schedule vacations.	Determine alternative work schedules.
Understand new role of supervision.	Provide input to selection of supervisor.	Provide input to selection of supervisor.
Plan/lead work team meetings.	Determine work procedures.	Manage work procedures.
Provide input to resource needs (human and capital).	Prepare cost budget with supervisor; monitor/control costs.	Manage cost budget (spend money within limits).
Recommend solutions to work issues.	Develop and implement solutions to work issues (within Level II authority).	Develop and implement solutions to work issues (within Level III authority).
—	Contact, understand, and problem-solve customer and supplier concerns.	Visit with customers and suppliers; contract for standards and resolution of issues.
Set and monitor team objectives.	Provide input to team goals.	Set team goals.
—	Monitor team goal performance.	Monitor team goal performance.
—	Provide input to hiring process; participate in candidate interviews.	Do team hiring.
Problem-solve team meeting performance problems.	Provide feedback to team members regarding performance issues.	Recommend to supervision how to handle individual team performance problems (including discipline).
Input to team work life conditions; request maintenance help.	Input to team work life conditions; request maintenance help.	Input to team work life conditions; request maintenance help.
Maintain safety and housekeeping in work area.	Plan safety and housekeeping.	Manage safety and housekeeping.
Recommend ideas for improving productivity, cost, quality, and customer service.	Generate and implement ideas to improve productivity, cost, quality, and customer service (within Level II authority).	Plan and manage productivity, cost, quality, and customer satisfaction processes in the team's business.

TRAINING MODULES

Module 1

Orientation to Change and the Team Development Plan

(3 hours)

Objectives

✓ To orient the team to organizational change, the organization's overall plan, and the role of teams in that plan.

✓ To clarify the team's expectations about what is to come.

Materials Needed

✓ *Flipchart:* Objectives, Key Learning Points, and Topics (copy from this page)

✓ *Handouts:* Teams and the Change Process in Complex Organizations (page 48)
The Role of Teams and the Team Development Process (page 52)
Our Organization's Attempts to Change (page 53)
Current Organizational Change Strategy (page 54)
Hopes and Concerns Survey (page 55)
Evaluation (Appendix)

Key Learning Points

✓ Understanding the history, goals, and strategy for the organization's change strategy.

✓ Understanding the role of teams in the change strategy.

Topics

✓ Teams and the Change Process

✓ The Role of Teams and the Team Development Process

✓ History of Change

✓ The Organization's Change Strategy

✓ Hopes and Concerns

✓ Evaluation

Procedural Outline

Time	Activity
50 minutes	*Overview:* This is the kickoff module. Consequently, you can expect several questions from the team as to the nature of the training such as what is it, how long will it take, what is expected of the team members, whether the training is mandatory, what the members get for completion, etc. In this module, the idea is to answer all these questions and any other concerns the team may have. Additionally, help the team understand the history, goals, and strategy of the change process.
	Preparation: Be prepared to answer all questions regarding the team training and change process. Reading through the materials in the handouts Teams and the Change Process in Complex Organizations and The Role of Teams and the

Team Development Process should help. If you don't know the answer to a question, do not guess or make something up. Simply acknowledge that you do not know the answer and tell the team you will try to find out.

15 minutes *Open the Session:* Open the session by introducing yourself and giving as much background as you can about the nature of the training and the change process. Also, post and explain the objectives, key learning points, and the topics to be discussed. Ask the participants if they have any questions or concerns. If the team wants additional information or if you feel the team would benefit from a solid background on organizational change, hand out Teams and the Change Process in Complex Organizations and The Role of Teams and the Team Development Process. Answer all their questions and concerns about the training and/or the change process.

5 minutes *History of Change:* Introduce this section by explaining that most organizations have a long history of attempts to change. The employees often refer to these efforts as the Program of the Month. It is important to understand what attempts have been made and the perception of the success of those efforts. *Note:* The next exercise will help bring some of the potential cynicism to the surface and allow teams the freedom to share their current perceptions of the potential of this effort to succeed.

45 minutes *Your Organization's Attempts to Change:* Introduce this exercise and explain that most organizations have made several attempts to change various aspects of their operation. Those changes may range from restructuring the entire organization to cultural change or total quality management training programs. Your task is to identify as many formal efforts to change the organization as you can recall and to assess the success or lack of success of those efforts. Hand out Our Organization's Attempts to Change and instruct the participants to individually:

1. List all the formal attempts to change the organization they can recall.
2. Rate each attempt in terms of their perception of the level of success achieved with the effort.
3. Give their opinion about what made the effort successful or unsuccessful.

Once all participants have completed their individual lists, you should compile a group list. Once you agree on the major events or attempts, give them respective ratings. Then spend as much time as you need to discuss what made each attempt successful or unsuccessful.

Current Organizational Change Exercise: The discussion about past change efforts should be a fairly lively one. When it draws toward a close, distribute the Current Organization Change Strategy Sheet and work with the participants to answer as many of the questions as possible. These are the major questions that should be answered in preparation for the team being part of an overall change effort. After the team has discussed these questions and their answers, pose the following question: Why will this effort be successful? Work with the team and brainstorm this question. Record as many answers as you can on a flipchart in front of the group.

20 minutes *Hopes and Concerns Survey:* After the team members have thought about this change effort and why it might be successful, have them complete the Hopes and Concerns Survey handout.

30 minutes After everyone has completed the survey, have each member share a hope and a concern in a round robin fashion until all the items on each person's survey have been mentioned. Hold a brief discussion about any themes or trends.

15 minutes *Summary/Close:* Summarize this session by stating this was the first in a series of training sessions designed to help the team reach high performance. This introductory session was designed to orient the team to the organizational change, the overall change plan and the role of teams in that plan. It was also designed to answer any and all of the team member's questions and to create a level playing field for everyone by facilitating a discussion centering around team expectations and concerns. Remind participants that change takes time and to remember to "catch people doing things right." Change is hard and although we may all try to do things differently, many times people revert to old behaviors. This should be expected. Remind team members to be helpful when folks slip back. Thank them for their time. Ask them to take a moment to complete the evaluation (Appendix).

TEAMS AND THE CHANGE PROCESS IN COMPLEX ORGANIZATIONS

Today, the leadership of companies and unions often make a commitment to substantial changes in their workplaces. A central assumption in making such a commitment is that the change occurs when the entire organization acquires the commitment and skills to learn and to change rather than when the change is imported by external agents or as a formal, structured program. The individual, team, and organizational learning underlying such change is experiential and occurs over time through careful and thoughtful structures and activities.

A strategy that combines a broad, team-oriented approach with the general aim of deeper involvement of employees in the organization seems to be the most effective in creating significant, permanent change. Through various committee and team structures, an organization can put into place the vehicles for *both the change and the learning* that must proceed it. Teams of employees, properly trained and guided, will become internal sources of energy and talent. They will not only improve the operation of the business, but will also foster different styles of decision making, more open and honest communication, and better listening throughout the organization. In organizations with bargaining units, when this approach is used, a more cooperative, positive relationship develops between labor and management.

A broad, effective approach to organizational change should include both a structure to guide the process and a series of activities to prepare the organization and to support and encourage the change along the way. Our experience with organizational change efforts typically includes:

1. Development of a steering committee (learning) structure to design, implement, and oversee the team process.
2. An initial assessment of the existing workplace to define strengths, weaknesses, and needs.
3. Orientation and training of management, supervision, and union leadership so that each understands the process and their respective roles.
4. Development of an internal communication strategy that gets essential business information to teams and generally informs the members of the organization on critical issues.
5. Installation and development of business units, work teams, task forces, and other involvement approaches appropriate to the specific organization and vision.
6. Ongoing learning and coaching in order to help focus the change process and to be certain that the effort has permanent effects.

The following sections outline what is involved with each phase of the process.

The Steering Committee. The change and team processes should be developed and guided by a top-level steering committee. This committee should consist of the leadership of key stakeholders (top management, functional areas, unions, and others) and should be empowered to create a vision and design the team strategy.

Besides creating the vision and the strategy, the steering committee sets the boundaries of the process, the general goals that all stakeholders can support, and the "tone" that should be reflected in the overall change effort.

Diagnosis. This is part of the preparation that is necessary to understand the present organization—its strengths and weaknesses. The diagnostic process can include a survey and interviews with representatives from all levels and functions of the organization. The process should allow employees to talk openly about their workplace, its strengths, and its weaknesses. The goal is to get the various functions and levels to begin to explore and to agree on the diverse perceptions of the organization. The diagnostic process allows stakeholders and the outside consultant time to discuss the differences within and between specific work areas and levels.

The diagnostic process should provide the foundation for:

1. Later discussion on the best strategy for, and issues in, the change process;
2. A long-term plan.
3. An ongoing evaluation of the effort and an assessment of progress at some point in the future.

Our experience is that if a team strategy is launched in a facility that has not done adequate preparation (i.e., development of structure, diagnosis, planning), there is a great danger of releasing team energy into a process the organization is not ready to manage and support.

Orientation and Training of Leadership. The leadership orientation process provides the critical transition from commitment to installation of the team strategy. It is an attempt to develop a common level of awareness throughout the organization as well as to begin to build the change skills and behaviors that are necessary to make teams successful. We suggest a leadership orientation approach that includes the following:

1. A two-day awareness session for managers, supervisors, and union leaders who are going to be affected by the process. This is an intense orientation to present ways of managing people and making decisions and about the assumptions that drive those practices. This experience also prepares the middle management, first-line supervision and union officials for their roles in the months to follow and gives them an opportunity to talk openly about current practices.
2. Another step is team building at various levels to begin creating a hierarchy that understands and can support the team process at the first level.
3. The third phase involves going into specific areas and installing business teams, structured team meetings, task teams, problem-solving groups, and/or cross-functional teams depending on the change strategy adopted.

The orientation, training, and team development processes can be seen as stages of learning. It begins with an introduction to the change effort, moves to preparation of the hierarchy for a new team culture, then builds specific skills into first-level teams and their leadership.

The Communication Strategy. A comprehensive communication strategy is essential to the overall change effort. It provides the vehicles and content for better decision making as well as for building the credibility essential to long-term organizational change. The communication process will typically focus on three areas:

1. Essential business information
2. Performance feedback
3. Human interest/motivation.

The change process should study existing vehicles and content in light of the organization's vision and the communication's mission.

The aim is to develop a more open system of information sharing and better listening than is ordinarily in place. The success of teams is based, in part, on the success of the communication and information system that supports them. Change is difficult, if not impossible, without good, credible information systems and processes.

Consulting and Learning. All the elements of change to this stage are designed to generate a structure and strategy that provide the data, energy, and experience for the change. It is now a question of how well various levels of the organization can learn from this process. Individuals and teams should be ready and able to learn, not only from the ideas that come from the teams, but also about the existing attitudes, behaviors, systems, and policies that discourage the openness, teamwork, sharing, participation, and involvement that cultural change ultimately requires.

This learning process is ongoing and in the early stages is very difficult to understand. Further, it often does not yield the immediate results to which top management is accustomed. This causes frustration for managers and puts stress on the teams and the change process.

Be assured that complex organizational change is not a "black box" solution to a passing interest in symbolic participation efforts. Substantive change requires an open, complex process that moves an organization toward its vision *if* the organization is prepared to take risks, to listen, and to learn. The impact of teams on change toward high-performance organizations depends on all three elements.

How Will We Know If Teams Are Successful? There is a strong bias toward quantitative measurement of everything in work settings in this country. Further, the key measure for most organizations is improvement in the bottom line.

Quantitative measurement provides a good set of controls, but it also brings with it a history of some things that are antithetical to cultural change. If people were punished for lack of numbers, for instance, they would tend to do only what was necessary to get the numbers or to fabricate them if all else failed. A legitimate team process needs an atmosphere of openness, trust, and cooperation in which people can plan and problem-solve, not blame or operate from fear.

For these reasons, our recommendation is to use forms of measurement that already exist—indicators of quality and efficiency—and not to create new ones for this process. Further, we advocate an evaluation process that looks at means *and* ends as we search for the deeper reasons for variations from the targets. Finally, even in systems that achieved the numbers, the approaches to that achievement often resulted in a failure to break through the "ceiling" and determine what was possible. This process should support significant improvements as long as teams do not suffer for early failures and mistakes and are not punished for performing very well (e.g., with layoffs).

Conclusion. The kind and extent of change envisioned with teams requires an extended period of time to achieve. We do not believe that it can occur as a result of isolated training or in establishing a team participation process. Instead, we believe that it involves an organic, systemic change in people's attitudes and behaviors. At the same time, it requires an organization to look at its structures, procedures, and policies.

In addition, the team process must be structured and coached in such a way as to help the organization and its members understand the strategy and process of change as the first step in moving toward an ongoing, adaptive organization for the future. Such a process is not simple. It challenges a large number of people with a substantive history and old expectations, as well as structures, policies, and procedures that are not prone to be flexible and open. For all these reasons, we take a complex view of, and approach to, the change. In so doing, we set up a formal, structured strategy, combined with training and ongoing coaching and learning that support the major thrust of the long-term culture change effort.

THE ROLE OF TEAMS AND THE TEAM DEVELOPMENT PROCESS

Teams are the *means,* not the *ends,* of an organizational change effort. As such, we need to review what functions high-performance teams serve in changing an organization and the implications of this role for how the team operates.

TEAMS AND ORGANIZATIONAL CHANGE

Teams serve the following purposes in changing organizations:

- ✓ They bring first-hand knowledge to the resolution of problems and issues resulting in better decisions, more effective resolution to problems, and more commitment to the successful implementation of decisions and solutions.
- ✓ More involvement serves as an intrinsic motivation to employees, who tend to enjoy their work more and to experience jobs as more challenging.
- ✓ Teams force the organization to provide more and better information to the front line units so that they can make better decisions about the business and get more immediate feedback about their performance and what is working.
- ✓ A team process tends to increase cooperation between functional areas, departments, and shifts, thereby decreasing the amount of resources lost to needless competition, blaming, and buck passing.
- ✓ The number and severity of problems between labor and management tend to decrease as problem solving addresses issues at the point of occurrence.
- ✓ Trust levels grow among all the players.
- ✓ Teams create an environment in which authority and responsibility have to be redefined and redistributed in order for the process to work over the long term.

The roles of team members change, and, for that to happen, the roles of management, supervision, and staff also change.

OUR ORGANIZATION'S ATTEMPTS TO CHANGE

Change Strategy	Rating of Success					Reasons for Success or Lack of It
	None	Some	Moderate	Great Deal	Extremely	
Example: First-Line Supervisor Training Program	1	2	3	4	5	Couldn't use on the job what they learned.
1	2	3	4	5		
1	2	3	4	5		
1	2	3	4	5		
1	2	3	4	5		
1	2	3	4	5		
1	2	3	4	5		
1	2	3	4	5		
1	2	3	4	5		
1	2	3	4	5		

CURRENT ORGANIZATIONAL CHANGE STRATEGY

What is your organization's current strategy to change?

A. What are the goals of the change effort?

B. What is the overall guiding structure for the effort (e.g., a steering committee)?

C. Has there been an assessment of the current state of the organization? If so, has everyone seen the results?

D. Has there been an orientation to the process for everyone?

E. Has there been any preparation/training of leadership for the change?

F. Is there a communication strategy for the change effort?

G. Is upper and middle management going to be involved in a team development process?

H. If you have a collective bargaining unit, has the leadership been involved in the design and implementation of the process?

I. Are there any forms of reward or recognition planned for successes in the effort?

J. How will success be measured?

K. What is the plan (curriculum) for developing teams?

HOPES AND CONCERNS SURVEY

HANDOUT 1-5

Take a few minutes to answer the following questions:

1. What are your **hopes** about *this work group becoming more of a team and more involved in the business?*

To the right of each hope is a blank labeled "Rating." After you list all your hopes, put a number beside each hope to indicate how *important* a hope it is. Use the following scale:

1	2	3	4	5
Very little importance	Some importance	Moderate importance	Serious importance	Very serious importance

Hopes	Rating
a. ______________	______
b. ______________	______
c. ______________	______
d. ______________	______
e. ______________	______

2. What are your **concerns** about *this work group becoming more of a team and more involved in the business?*

Again, to the right of each concern is a blank labeled "Rating." After you list all your concerns, put a number beside each concern to indicate how *serious* a concern it is. Use the following scale:

1	2	3	4	5
Very little concern	Some concern	Moderate concern	Serious concern	Very serious concern

Concerns	Rating
a. ______________	______
b. ______________	______
c. ______________	______
d. ______________	______
e. ______________	______

Module 2

Changing Organizational Paradigms

(2 hours)

Objectives

✓ To help teams understand the concept of "paradigm" and how it plays a role in the day-to-day operations of the organization.

✓ To obtain the team's assessment of the organization's existing paradigms and to outline how those need to change.

Materials Needed

✓ *Flipchart:* Objectives, Key Learning Points, and Topics (copy from this page)

✓ *Handouts:* Paradigms: The Traditional vs. the High-Performance Organization (page 58)
Paradigms: Present and Future (page 59)
How Does the Paradigm Shift Affect Your Team? (page 60)
Evaluation (Appendix)

Key Learning Points

✓ Understanding organizational paradigms.

✓ Determining the critical paradigms in the existing organization as well as those that need to emerge if the organization will move toward the vision.

Topics

✓ Traditional vs. High-Performance Paradigms

✓ Paradigms: Present and Future

✓ Evaluation

Procedural Outline

Time **Activity**

30 minutes *Introduction:* Open this session by posting and explaining the objectives, key learning points, and session topics. Next ask the participants if anyone knows what a "paradigm" is. If the participants have been exposed to this term, have a discussion and clarify its definition. If they have not, simply define "paradigm" as a rule or principle of operation. Further explain that organizations often have a series of these rules or principles that add up to "the way we do things around here." Hand out Paradigms: The Traditional vs. the High-Performance Organization sheet. Explain that the characteristics of the left (the traditional) are representative of the classic hierarchical, top-down organization. The principles on the right are characteristic of contemporary, high-performance organizations. Review both lists with the participants and have a discussion about which principles and/or characteristics are more typical of their organization. Also, discuss which principles should be in effect if starting a business.

Now that the team has looked at traditional vs. high-performance principles, have the members look specifically at their organizations.

45 minutes *Paradigms: Present and Future:* Distribute the Paradigms: Present and Future handout. Explain that Thomas Kuhn in *The Structure of Scientific Revolutions* says, **paradigms** *are the cumulative values, methods, procedures, and the like that we use to view and manage the world around us.*

Explain the instructions to this exercise. Tell the team members to think about their workplace for a moment. It is structured and run on the basis of several paradigms. These are the rules, assumptions, principles, procedures, and "laws" that govern how work is managed and how it is done. There are paradigms for leadership, decision making, communication, motivation, and so forth.

The team's task is to identify the major paradigms for the organization. List them in the chart distributed. Included are some characteristics they might want to use to describe the existing paradigms. Or they can include some of their own in the blank lines. (The first line is an example of a paradigm statement about quality.)

After they make the list, tell them to go to the column labeled "Continue or Change?" and indicate whether the existing paradigm should be continued (that is, keep doing what they are doing) or changed.

After everyone has completed their statements, hold a discussion about the perceptions of the existing paradigms and whether they are the right ones for the future of the organization.

Next, have the team members think about their organization in the future. Have them assume they want to be a thriving, successful, dynamic operation. What are the characteristics of the paradigm that are not parts of their business paradigm at present? List them in the characteristics of the paradigm of the future table. Be sure to discuss each team member's response.

30 minutes *How Do Paradigms Affect the Team?* After they list and discuss the paradigms of the future, have the team members complete the handout How Does This Paradigm Shift Affect Your Team?

Have the team members indicate how the adoption of the principles and practices of the new paradigm outlined on the previous table will affect the structure, membership, skills, and/or operation of their team.

(*Note:* Be sure to remind participants not to worry about whether they have control over the possible changes; just think about what they will be under the new paradigm.)

15 minutes *Summary/Close:* Wrap up this session by recapping what a paradigm is, which paradigms the team members feel are currently in operation, which ones members desire, and how the team members feel the current paradigm characteristics are affecting their team.

The key exercise in this module is the team's examination of existing and future paradigms of business. By discussing paradigms, the team begins to understand the forces that got the organization where it is and that keep it there in spite of evidence to the contrary. They also know, based on experience and intuition, what changes in the paradigm are required if the organization is to move toward excellence through the establishment of teams.

Distribute the evaluation and ask participants to take a moment to complete the form and hand it back. Thank them for their time.

PARADIGMS: THE TRADITIONAL VS. THE HIGH-PERFORMANCE ORGANIZATION

Traditional Organization Paradigms	High-Performance Organization Paradigms
Command-demand/paramilitary orientation	Community/commitment orientation
Top are thinkers; bottom are "doers."	Everyone is a thinker and doer.
Quantity is all that's important.	Quality is the primary value.
Information flows primarily downward; only good news flows up.	Information moves in all directions; listening and learning are everywhere.
Extrinsic motivators dominate: pay, benefits, status symbols ...	Intrinsic motivators are important: involvement, information, respect ...
Short-term planning and payoff	Long-term vision and payoff
Internal independence and competition	Horizontal teamwork and cooperation
Isolated layers and structures	Integrated vertical teams
Midlevel grid specialists control, enforce, compete ...	Midlevel shares expertise and vision, with strong internal customer orientation.
Employee evaluation based on punitive assumptions and tools.	Positive orientation with emphasis on quality and development.
Machine analogy (impersonal)	Living organism/system analogy
Rigid rules, policies, and programs	"Loose anchors": outcome criteria, benchmarks, and guidelines
Customer/client seen as a passive recipient, a bother, or the enemy.	Customer/client seen as an ally, partner, and active participant.
Labor-management relations are highly adversarial.	Labor-management relations are based on collaborative problem solving.

PARADIGMS: PRESENT AND FUTURE

Characteristic	Characteristics of the Existing Paradigm	Continue or Change?
Example: Quality	Quality is only important if we are making quota (quantity).	Change
Leadership		
Communication		
Motivation		
Supervision		
Labor relations		
Decision making		
Customers		

Characteristic	Characteristics of the Paradigm of the Future	How Does This Affect Our Team?
Example: Quality	Quality comes first; it is the most important thing we do.	
Leadership		
Communication		
Motivation		
Supervision		
Labor relations		
Decision making		
Customers		

HOW DOES THE PARADIGM SHIFT AFFECT YOUR TEAM?

Characteristic	How Does This Affect Our Team?
Example: Quality	We will no longer be dependent on other departments to determine our quality. We will have to be trained in quality techniques.
Leadership	
Communication	
Motivation	
Supervision	
Labor relations	
Decision making	
Customers	

Module 3

Consensus in the Team

(2.5 hours)

Objectives To introduce the team to consensus decision making and instruct the team in its use during the training and development process.

Materials Needed

✓ *Flipchart:* Objectives, Key Learning Points, and Topics (copy from this page)

✓ *Handouts:* Consensus is Achieved When Every Member Can Say ... (page 66)
Consensus Includes/Does Not Include (page 67)
How Consensus Works (page 68)
Helpful Hints (page 69)
Remaining Training Modules (page 70)
Evaluation (Appendix)

Key Learning Points

✓ Understanding the concept of consensus and how to reach it.

✓ Understanding and agreeing on how consensus decisions will be made in the team.

Topics

✓ Consensus: What Is It?

✓ Consensus: What's the Alternative?

✓ Consensus: When to Use It

✓ Consensus: How It Works

✓ Helpful Hints

✓ Handling an Impasse

✓ Consensus Exercise: Planning the Team's Development

✓ Evaluation

Procedural Outline

Time	Activity
10 minutes	*Consensus: What Is It?* Post and explain the objectives, key learning points, and topics to be covered. Also tell the team that consensus is not always what people think it is. Explain that consensus decision making and problem solving is a method in which all the participants actively discuss the various dimensions of the issue and come to agreement about the resolution or decision. The strength of the process is in the fact that the group pools the knowledge and experience of all its members to reach a solution or decision. Write the following on a blank flipchart:

Consensus is achieved when every member can say:

> I have had an opportunity to express my views fully and they have been thoughtfully considered by the group. Even though this solution may not be the one I believe is optimal, I think it will work and I support it.

Be sure to emphasize that the goal is to (1) achieve the best possible decision or solution and (2) get maximum support from those who have to implement and/or live with the decision.

20 minutes To further define consensus, we should look at what it includes and what it does not include. Write the following on a blank flipchart and have a team discussion about each one of these variables.

Consensus includes:

✓ Pooling opinions.

✓ Effective listening.

✓ Discussing ideas and differences.

✓ Not getting all you want.

✓ Agreement to the point that everyone "can live with it."

Consensus does not include:

✓ Voting.

✓ Majority rule.

✓ Minority rule.

✓ One-person rule.

✓ Bargaining.

Summarize the discussion by suggesting that consensus is one *process* by which a group or team makes a decision (product). Teams should note that consensus is not appropriate or necessary for all decisions. Using consensus does not preclude a one-person decision (e.g., the team leader deciding something), voting, or bargaining, depending on the situation or the goal. Several other methods of decision making include having the leader make the decision, voting, and a numeric method. The following describes the strengths and weaknesses of each.

(*Note:* You may or may not want to teach the team about all these options. It depends on how much time you have and how in depth you want to go.)

10 minutes *Alternatives to Consensus:* There are a number of ways to make decisions. The process chosen depends on several factors:

✓ *Time:* How much do you have before a decision has to be made (urgency factor)?

✓ *Information:* Who has all the *essential* information to make the *right* decision (the data factor)?

✓ *Involvement:* Who has to understand and support the decision in order for it to be implemented successfully (the commitment factor)?

How an organization or team makes a decision or solves a problem depends on the answers to all three questions. Consensus is most useful and appropriate when (1) you have enough time, (2) multiple people possess essential information to understand the decision or problem context and to develop a good solution, and (3) the understanding and commitment of a group or team are essential to a successful outcome.

If the criteria for a good decision or solution are the correctness of the decision (did we get it right?) and the commitment to make it work (does the team understand and agree with it?), then we can look at some alternative ways of making decisions and evaluate their strengths and weaknesses on the basis of the two criteria.

Approach	*Description*	*Strength(s)*	*Weakness(es)*
Leader	A single person, usually the team leader, makes the decision.	Quick; best when leader has most or all the knowledge required.	Decision maker may lack essential knowledge or information in complex situations.
Voting	The majority makes the decision.	Quick; assures that at least 51% of the people buy the decision.	Majority are not always right (think about politics); 49% of people may be opposed (that's a lot!).
Numeric	A quantitative criterion is established as the threshold for a decision.	"Hard date" criterion; does not require much thought after threshold is set.	Criterion may not be right; may not apply; lots of people may not agree with it.

Each method of decision making has an appropriate application. In a team, not all decisions should be made by the leader, nor should all decisions be made by consensus. Choosing the right decision method is the first important step. Beyond that, consensus is the most complex and difficult of the various methods because of the steps and the involvement of multiple team members.

When to Use Consensus: Be sure to tell the team that consensus is vital for any decision that must be supported by all members of the group, even those who dissent originally. It may be used to select an issue, agree on causes of a problem, choose a solution, develop a plan, and/or build a strategy for evaluation.

30 minutes *How Consensus Works:* Post the How Consensus Works flipchart and explain that in the decision-by-consensus process the first and very important step is to identify the decision to be made or the problem to be solved. Once that is done and agreed upon by those who have to reach consensus, you can begin the process. In the consensus process, each group member should:

1. *Prepare his or her own position* as well as possible prior to meeting with the group (but realize that the task is incomplete and that the missing pieces are to be supplied by other group members).
2. Feel obligated to *express his or her opinion* and explain it fully, so that the rest of the group has the benefit of all members' thinking.
3. Feel obligated to *listen to the opinions and feelings of all other group members* and be ready to modify one's own position on the basis of information, logic, and understanding.
4. *Avoid using "win-lose" techniques* such as voting, compromising, or giving in to keep the peace. Differences of opinion are helpful. In exploring the differences, the best course of action will make itself apparent.
5. *Alter the solution* so that all can support it; don't try to alter people's minds.

6. *Decision by consensus is difficult to attain* (so take all the time you need), and not every decision will meet with everyone's unqualified approval. There should be a general feeling of support from all members before a group decision is made. Take all the time you need to listen, consider all members' views, make your own view known, and be reasonable in reaching a group decision.

When everyone in the group reaches a decision with which they can live and which they are willing to support, the group has consensus. *Note:* Consensus does *not* mean that every team member must be 100 percent in favor. The Saturn Corporation consensus process, for example, asks that the person feel at least 70 percent in favor in order to be supportive. And a team should not be held up by one person who is opposed if that person is unable to offer the group some alternative that will help and be accepted.

20 minutes *Helpful Hints to Building Consensus:* Be sure to emphasize that consensus is not easy, but that there are some other helpful hints. Hand out the Helpful Hints sheet and briefly have a group discussion on how to overcome some common barriers. Also explain to the team that at times things may come to an impasse. If an impasse occurs, help the team understand the following strategies:

10 minutes *Handling an Impasse:* In the event the team gets stuck during a discussion on an issue, try the following:

✓ *Take a short break.* Walk away from the issue for a time. Continuing to pound away at something or someone often "freezes" the person or causes everyone to lose sight of the real issues.

✓ *Review your criteria or standards to see if the subject or idea fits.* The discussion should not be a free-for-all. There should be goals and standards that guide you toward the right decision (for example, how much time you have, how much money is available, how many staff are available). Check the discussion against the standards to be sure you are in the ballpark.

✓ *Determine whether standards should be changed.* If your discussion or idea is outside the guidelines or standards, you may want to consider altering the standards if enforcing them would cause you to reject a great proposal.

✓ *Adjourn and "sleep on it."* Sometimes you just have to walk away from a discussion for a while. In the meantime, however, everyone should be trying to gather more data (not just "lobbying" outside the room).

✓ *Inject humor to break tension.* Lighten up! Although what you are doing is serious business, a little humor can sometimes unstick a deadlock.

✓ *Ask a person to present the opposite view from his/hers.* This is an uncomfortable, but powerful tool. If two or three team members are locked in on positions, ask them to present and defend the other's position or proposal. This serves two purposes: (1) It helps everyone understand whether the person is interpreting the proposal the same way as the person who made it. (2) It often provides some insight to the speaker that will help her or him make adjustments or improve the proposal she or he has made.

Now that the team members have a good understanding of consensus tell them they will be conducting an exercise.

45 minutes *Consensus Exercise—Planning the Team's Development:* There are a lot of textbook exercises on which the team could practice its newfound knowledge of consensus. However, the most powerful teacher is "live" experience. That's what this exercise uses.

Team Goals for Training and Development

The Task: To establish five training and development goals for the team development process. Have each team member individually list the five most important goals this team should reach in the next three years. After all participants have written their individual goals, help the team organize to reach consensus on the goals for the entire team.

After the group has agreed on the training and development goals, the team members need to give some indication of what they think they need to pursue in terms of training and development.

Developmental Needs of the Team

The Task: To reach consensus on the top five (priority) topics for training and development of the team.

Distribute the Remaining Training Modules handout.

Remaining Training Modules

- ✓ Overview of the Organization's Business
- ✓ Communication, Listening, and Feedback
- ✓ Mission and Purpose of the Team
- ✓ Creating a Team Vision
- ✓ Resolving Conflict in the Team
- ✓ Team Business Meetings
- ✓ Decision Making
- ✓ Problem Solving
- ✓ Learning Styles
- ✓ Roles in the Team
- ✓ Roles in the Organization
- ✓ High-Performance Business Teams: Quality and Process Improvement Overview
- ✓ Customer Analysis
- ✓ Supplier Analysis
- ✓ Quality and Continuous Improvement
- ✓ Work Process Analysis Business Information Management
- ✓ Business Planning

Ask the team members to list what they think are the top five most important topics for the team to pursue.

Help the team organize to reach consensus on the priority training needs.

5 minutes *Summary/Close:* Bring this session to an end by summarizing what consensus is and what it is not. Be sure to remind the group that not every decision should be made by consensus—only those that need maximum support. Also state that consensus gets easier as the group matures and practices the helpful hints. Distribute the evaluation and ask the team members for their feedback. Thank everyone for their time.

CONSENSUS IS ACHIEVED WHEN EVERY MEMBER CAN SAY ...

"I have had an opportunity to express my views fully and they have been thoughtfully considered by the group. Even though this solution may not be the one I believe is optimal, I think it will work and I support it."

CONSENSUS INCLUDES/ DOES NOT INCLUDE

Consensus includes:

- ✓ Pooling opinions.
- ✓ Effective listening.
- ✓ Discussing ideas and differences.
- ✓ Not getting all you want.
- ✓ Agreement to the point that everyone "can live with it."

Consensus does not include:

- ✓ Voting.
- ✓ Majority rule.
- ✓ Minority rule.
- ✓ One-person rule.
- ✓ Bargaining.

Each team member:

- ✓ Prepare your position.
- ✓ Express your position.
- ✓ Listen to the opinions and feelings of all other team members.
- ✓ Avoid using "win-lose" techniques.
- ✓ Alter the solution.
- ✓ Take the time you need to listen, consider other views, develop your own perspective, and be reasonable in reaching a group decision. (Decision by consensus is difficult.)

- ✓ Overcome barriers by stressing the possible, not the impossible.

- ✓ Treat each problem as a new one. Solutions that worked before may fail because circumstances are different.

- ✓ Be open to new alternatives. Avoid being closed to ideas that are different.

- ✓ Encourage creative discontent and channel it toward the issue, not toward other group members. Accept responsibility for hearing and being heard.

- ✓ Be sure all participate without allowing any one person to dominate. Silence is not necessarily agreement. Silent members may be an indication the team has not tapped all its resources.

- ✓ Encourage and explore differences. Do not force consensus, even under the pressure of time.

- ✓ While the consensus process values each and every person involved, do not let a single stubborn person hold the team up forever. One organization uses the following criterion to keep things moving: *If you disagree with the proposal, you must offer a viable alternative; that is, one that some members of the group are willing to support. Otherwise, you must allow the process to move forward.*

- ✓ Do not confuse consensus with unanimity. A unanimous decision is one in which everybody supports everything fully (100 percent agree 100 percent). If you allow that to be the definition of consensus, you will never get done. One person at the Saturn Corporation described the consensus process as feeling like "at least 70 percent of yourself can support the proposal." This criterion leaves everybody free to have some feeling that, even if it is not the best possible proposal, it is one with which he or she can live.

REMAINING TRAINING MODULES

- ✓ Overview of the Organization's Business
- ✓ Communication, Listening, and Feedback
- ✓ Mission and Purpose of the Team
- ✓ Creating a Team Vision
- ✓ Resolving Conflict in the Team
- ✓ Team Business Meetings
- ✓ Decision Making
- ✓ Problem Solving
- ✓ Learning Styles
- ✓ Roles in the Team
- ✓ Roles in the Organization
- ✓ High-Performance Business Teams: Quality and Process Improvement Overview
- ✓ Customer Analysis
- ✓ Supplier Analysis
- ✓ Quality and Continuous Improvement
- ✓ Work Process Analysis Business Information Management
- ✓ Business Planning

Module 4

Team Profile

(2 hours)

Objective To provide the team members with baseline data about their team's assets and liabilities as they begin the team development process.

Materials Needed

- ✓ *Flipchart:* Objectives, Key Learning Points, and Topics (copy from this page)
- ✓ *Handouts:* Survey of the Team's Strengths and Weaknesses (page 73)
  Survey of the Team's Strengths and Weaknesses Tally Sheet (page 75)
  Looking to the Future: Strengths and Weaknesses (page 77)
  Evaluation (Appendix)

Key Learning Points

- ✓ To create an accurate picture of the team and its functioning at present.
- ✓ Understanding the relationship between the team's strengths and weaknesses and the team development process.
- ✓ Providing the team with tools and a process for continuous team evaluation.

Topics

- ✓ Team Development: Where You Are
- ✓ Survey of Strengths and Weaknesses
- ✓ Looking to the Future
- ✓ Evaluation

Procedural Outline

Time **Activity**

5 minutes *Introduction:* Open this module by posting and discussing the objectives, key learning points, and topics to be covered. Take a few minutes and explain to the team members this is the first step in the journey of team development. The process has three general stages: determining where you are at present, determining where you want to be, and designing and implementing a plan to get there (see Fig. 4-1).

Further, explain that this module details a process to help team members describe the present state of the team. In the module, an instrument and a process for team assessment are introduced. These are important tools for the ongoing development of the team. Not only should the team pay attention to the outcome of the survey, but the members must also pay attention to the process they use of gathering and processing the data. Be sure to explain to the team

Stage 1	*Stage 2*	*Stage 3*
Determining where you are at the present	A vision of where you want to be	Designing and implementing a plan to get there

Figure 4-1

members they will most likely want to use this assessment process over and over again in the future to measure team progress.

10 minutes *Overview of the Assessment Instrument and the Process*

The Assessment Instrument: Explain to the participants that in a moment they will complete the team assessment instrument called the Survey of the Team's Strengths and Weaknesses, which contains 20 items that describe various aspects of organizational and team functioning. Each team member will individually rate each item on the extent to which they perceive that item to represent a strength, weakness, or both.

The second part of the survey asks team members to identify any additional strengths and weaknesses not mentioned in the survey items (1–20). In addition, each team member is asked to identify what he or she likes best and likes least about the present team.

The Process: After everyone completes the survey, the instructor will collate the individual team member's ratings. Then the entire team, using Looking at the Future: Strengths and Weaknesses, identifies the priority strengths and weaknesses for planning purposes. Finally, the entire module concludes by brainstorming what can be done to reinforce the strengths and overcome the weaknesses.

25 minutes Distribute the Survey of the Team's Strengths and Weaknesses and have each individual complete the survey. Give a specific time for people to have the survey done. (For example, "Be done in 25 minutes at 10:15.") If people finish early, let them take a break. Others may need more time.

20 minutes *Tally the Results:* When everyone has completed the survey, collect the individual team member surveys and tally all the individual answers onto the Survey of the Team's Strengths and Weaknesses Tally Sheet. (*Note:* If you have quick access to a copy machine, make copies of the completed tally sheet for all participants. If there is no quick access, an alternative is to quickly transcribe the answers from the tally sheet onto a flipchart so that all team members can see. Short of both of these options, just have all the team members gather around so they can see how their combined individual ratings were distributed.)

25 minutes *Discuss the Tally Sheet:* Using the best method you can, show the results of the tally sheet to the team. Spend a few minutes to discuss where the individual team members had the same perceptions and where they had different viewpoints. Review the individual perceptions of additional strengths and weaknesses (questions 21–22) and the individual team members' reports about what they liked best and worst about the team (questions 23–24).

30 minutes *Complete Looking into the Future: Strengths and Weaknesses:* After the team has had ample time to discuss individual ratings and trends, distribute Looking into the Future: Strengths and Weaknesses. As a team, use consensus and complete the entire sheet.

5 minutes *Summary/Close:* Remind the team that this module provided baseline data about the team's assets and liabilities as it begins the team development process. Also tell the participants that high-performance teams will go through similar exercises every six months or so to check on how they are doing and to correct any glaring deficiencies. Finally, this module provides the team members with both tools and a process to collect and analyze data about themselves at anytime in the future. Thank everyone for their time. Have participants complete the evaluation.

SURVEY OF THE TEAM'S STRENGTHS AND WEAKNESSES

Rate your team on the following:	Tremendous Strength	Moderate Strength	Strength and Weakness	Moderate Weakness	Tremendous Weakness
1. Clarity of team goals	5	4	3	2	1
2. Commitment to team goals	5	4	3	2	1
3. Work assignment and clarity of roles	5	4	3	2	1
4. Working together as a team	5	4	3	2	1
5. Relationships among team members	5	4	3	2	1
6. Innovation, risk taking, or taking initiative	5	4	3	2	1
7. Team meetings	5	4	3	2	1
8. Team supervision/ leadership	5	4	3	2	1
9. Communication among team members	5	4	3	2	1
10. Feedback to the team on its performance	5	4	3	2	1
11. Ability to get problems solved	5	4	3	2	1
12. Knowledge and skills of team members	5	4	3	2	1
13. Productivity of the team	5	4	3	2	1
14. Quality of the team's work and its product	5	4	3	2	1
15. Recognition for the team's work/efforts	5	4	3	2	1
16. Relationship with team's suppliers	5	4	3	2	1
17. Relationship with team's customers	5	4	3	2	1
18. Resources the team has to do its job	5	4	3	2	1
19. Equipment the team has to use	5	4	3	2	1
20. General attitude of the team	5	4	3	2	1

21. Are there additional strengths not mentioned in the survey?

22. Are there additional weaknesses not mentioned in the survey?

23. What do you like best about this team?

24. What do you like least about this team?

SURVERY OF THE TEAM'S STRENGTHS AND WEAKNESSES TALLY SHEET

HANDOUT 4-2

Rate your team on the following:	Tremendous Strength	Moderate Strength	Strength and Weakness	Moderate Weakness	Tremendous Weakness
1. Clarity of team goals	5	4	3	2	1
2. Commitment to team goals	5	4	3	2	1
3. Work assignment and clarity of roles	5	4	3	2	1
4. Working together as a team	5	4	3	2	1
5. Relationships among team members	5	4	3	2	1
6. Innovation, risk taking, or taking initiative	5	4	3	2	1
7. Team meetings	5	4	3	2	1
8. Team supervision/ leadership	5	4	3	2	1
9. Communication among team members	5	4	3	2	1
10. Feedback to the team on its performance	5	4	3	2	1
11. Ability to get problems solved	5	4	3	2	1
12. Knowledge and skills of team members	5	4	3	2	1
13. Productivity of the team	5	4	3	2	1
14. Quality of the team's work and its product	5	4	3	2	1
15. Recognition for the team's work/efforts	5	4	3	2	1
16. Relationship with team's suppliers	5	4	3	2	1
17. Relationship with team's customers	5	4	3	2	1
18. Resources the team has to do its job	5	4	3	2	1
19. Equipment the team has to use	5	4	3	2	1
20. General attitude of the team	5	4	3	2	1

21. Are there additional strengths not mentioned in the survey?

22. Are there additional weaknesses not mentioned in the survey?

23. What do you like best about this team?

24. What do you like least about this team?

LOOKING TO THE FUTURE: STRENGTHS AND WEAKNESSES

HANDOUT 4-3

As a team, reach consensus about:

A. The top three strengths we need to keep in place for the future:

1. ______________________________

____

2. ______________________________

____

3. ______________________________

____

What can the team do to reinforce these strengths? Or what do you need to ask others to do?

____

____

____

____

____

____

B. The top three weaknesses we need to change or correct in the future:

1.______________________________

____

2.______________________________

____

3.______________________________

____

What can the team do to change or correct these weaknesses? Or what do you need to ask others to do?

____

____

____

____

____

____

Module 5

Overview of the Business

(2 hours)

Objective To help teams understand the overall business of the organization and the relationship of the team to that business.

Materials Needed

✓ *Flipchart:* Objectives, Key Learning Points, and Topics (copy from this page)

✓ *Handouts:* Team Business Profile (page 80)
Evaluation (Appendix)

Key Learning Points

✓ Overview of the business or business unit including mission, goals/objectives, budgets, strategic plans, and political realities.

✓ Understanding the team's relationship and contribution to the overall business.

Topics

✓ Overview of the Business

✓ Team Business Profile

✓ Evaluation

Procedural Outline

Time **Activity**

Prework: The goals of this module are to provide the team an overview of the larger business and its operation, and to explain the team's function in the overall business.

To help the team fully understand the business of your organization, you will have to customize this presentation as much as possible. By "customize" we mean get as much "formal" information as possible that already exists about your business. Some topics to include are:

✓ Mission of the business

✓ Vision for the business

✓ Goals of the business

✓ Products and services

✓ Customers and suppliers

✓ Organizational structure

✓ Financial structure and budgets

✓ Organizational change and improvement strategies

The purpose is to give the team a view of the larger business. Often, team members have never had an opportunity to see the "big picture" and to understand the customer base, products, finances, organizational structure, etc. Once, for example, a team project in a public sector organization revealed that most team members thought the departmental budgets were secret information. In fact, they were public information. Anybody could see them. From that time on, copies of the organization's budgets were on file and available to all teams.

In another case, employees in the iron-producing section of an integrated steel mill (most of whom had been employed in the mill for over 20 years) did not know what happened to the product once it left their division. In fact, it went across the road to another division to be converted into steel and rolled into products for their customers.

Collecting *this prework should not be difficult. Often, much of this information is already contained in a formal report, business document, management* presentation, or newsletter article. Do not be afraid to ask around, to make copies and to bring as much business information as you can to discuss with the team.

5 minutes *Introduction:* Open this session by posting and discussing the objectives, key learning points, and topics to be discussed. Be sure to explain to the team that the goal of this module is to provide the team with an overview of the larger business and its operation and to discuss this team's specific function in the overall business.

55 minutes *Business Topics:* Depending on what formal information you discovered during your prework, hold as in-depth a discussion as possible about the overall business. Post, hand out, or read the mission, vision, and formal goals for the organization. Generate a discussion about the content of these documents. Ask if everyone understands and/or agrees with them. Ask if they are real or consistent with the team members' experience of what it is like to work in the organization. Also, list the major company products and/or services as well as the largest customers and supplies. Generate a similar discussion with the team. See if they agree on how they might adjust their lists. Further, discuss the organizational structure and the financial structure and budget. Does the structure seem to support the mission and vision of the organization? Is it aligned with where the organization wants to be? Finally, present and discuss any organizational change or improvement strategies your company has been through recently. Be sure to discuss the business reasons for those events or processes (i.e., customer relations/satisfaction, cycle time reduction, cost reduction, quality enhancement, etc.).

55 minutes *Team Business Profile:* Once the overview of the business has been discussed, the team's task is to describe its specific place in the business. Distribute the Team Business Profile. Explain that the Team Business Profile is a tool to outline the business of the team. The profile contains the essential information related to what the team does and what it has to do to contribute to the overall success of the organization. Spend as much time as you need and help the team formally complete their business profile.

5 minutes *Summary/Evaluation:* Summarize this module by reminding the team members that they are part of a larger business and that in the midst of the day-to-day work it can be easy to forget about the overall business. It can also be difficult to start thinking of this team in terms of a business. The goal is to always have in mind what the larger organization is trying to achieve and to know how your specific team fits into and aligns with that business. Finally, hand out the evaluation and ask the participants to take a few minutes to jot down their comments.

TEAM BUSINESS PROFILE

HANDOUT 5-1

Team name/location: ______________________________

Team manager/supervisor/coordinator: ______________________________

Annual budget (attach breakdown): ______________________________

Number of employees on the team by job title (attach list): ______________________________

Team's products/services:

Products	Services
______________________________	______________________________
______________________________	______________________________
______________________________	______________________________
______________________________	______________________________
______________________________	______________________________

Key business goals/objectives for this year:

____

____

____

____

____

Module 6

Communication, Listening, and Feedback

(4 hours)

Objective To help team members understand communication and listening strategies and behaviors that will enhance their ability to work together and to achieve their ideal team and business goals.

Materials Needed

- ✓ *Flipchart:* Objectives, Key Learning Points, and Topics (copy from this page)
- ✓ *Handouts:* Communication Strategies to Discourage (page 86)
  Communication Strategies to Encourage (page 87)
  Communication Strategies Exercise (page 88)
  Good Communication (page 89)
  The Ten Commandments for Good Listening (page 90)
  Active Listening Skills (page 91)
  Key Listening Techniques (page 92)
  Feedback Guidelines (page 93)
  Communication/Listening/Feedback Exercise Model (page 94)
  Communication/Listening/Feedback Exercise Recorder's Notes (page 95)
  Evaluation (Appendix)

Key Learning Points

- ✓ Understanding strategies for communication and how the different patterns help or hinder team functioning.
- ✓ Understanding the basic values and behaviors associated with effective listening and how to integrate those behaviors into the team's business functioning.

Topics

- ✓ Good Communication
- ✓ Effective Communication within the Team
- ✓ Communication Strategies
- ✓ Listening
- ✓ Feedback
- ✓ Skill Integration Exercise
- ✓ Evaluation

Procedural Outline

Time	**Activity**
5 minutes	*Overview:* Welcome the participants. Post and explain the objectives, key learning points, and topics of the session.

5 minutes *Effective Communication within the Team:* Explain to the team that interpersonal and team communication is probably one of the most important variables in high-performance team operation. Communication patterns in teams are influenced primarily by:

✓ Individuals' personal histories and learning in communication.

✓ The organizational context including what is valued and necessary to survive.

Consequently, no two teams have exactly the same communication patterns. Each one has its own character and personality.

There are, however, some general patterns of communication. We can use these general patterns as a framework and assess how members of the team communicate under certain conditions.

In the communication strategies exercise to come, there are descriptions of:

✓ Communication strategies to discourage.

✓ Communication strategies to encourage.

Help the team understand that this exercise will allow team members to create a personal profile of their individual communication strengths and weaknesses. In turn, the entire team will discuss what it takes to create different, more effective patterns of communication among team members' communication strategies.

30 minutes *Communication Strategies to Discourage and Encourage:* Distribute Communication Strategies to Discourage and have the team members individually read and mark the two strategies they dislike most. After everyone has completed this task, start a round robin with each team member telling the group which two strategies he/she dislikes. Ask for examples from each person every time a new strategy is mentioned. If at the end of the individual reports some strategies still have not been discussed, briefly mention and define them. The idea is to get the team members to read and digest all ten strategies to discourage.

Once all the "discourage" strategies have been discussed, distribute Communication Strategies to Encourage and have the team follow a similar procedure. This time, however, have participants mark the two strategies they feel they are the best at. As before, after everyone has completed this task, start a round robin with each team member telling the group which two strategies he/she is particularly good at. Ask for examples from each person every time a new strategy is mentioned. If at the end of the individual reports some strategies have not been discussed, briefly mention and define them. Get the team members to read and digest all ten strategies to encourage.

Communication Strategies Exercise: After the team has been exposed to all the communication strategies, distribute and have the team members individually complete the Communication Strategies Exercise.

Explain that the directions for this exercise are to think about how you communicate in a tough or tense situation (at home or at work). In the chart provided, indicate:

1. Which two "discourage" column behaviors you would *most likely* exhibit in the tough or tense situation (put a checkmark in the box next to the two behaviors).

2. Which two "encourage" column behaviors you would be *least likely* to exhibit in the tough or tense situation (put a checkmark in the box next to the two behaviors).

When all the team members have completed the exercise, aggregate the individual answers onto a single flipchart sheet or overhead transparency in front of the group. Ask the team to discuss:

1. What are the patterns of communication we are most likely to see when the going gets tough?
2. What can the team do to increase the chances of "encourage" behaviors and decrease the chances of "discourage" behaviors?

10 minutes Summarize this exercise by reminding the group that we all have strengths and weaknesses in our communication styles and patterns and that those are often magnified on a team. Bring this part of the session to a close by distributing and reviewing the Good Communication handout.

10 minutes *Listening: The Basic Skill:* Explain to the team that, with the emphasis over the years on a quasi-military, hierarchical model of management, we tended to neglect and discourage some skills known to be essential to effective teams. These skills are not, in fact, contrary to the classic top-down management model, but are rarely seen in this model. As a result, members of teams tend to reflect the behaviors of the larger management organization, which means they do not use them.

Leadership and effective decision making are not purely a result of power and position. Among other things they include listening. In the broadest sense *listening* is the ability to demonstrate respect for others, the ability to hear in a caring way what others are communicating, and the ability to understand the emotion and intent of co-workers in the course of conducting business together. In today's organization, listening is critical to effective leadership and to high-performance teams.

For the most part in homes and schools, the skills associated with good listening were neither taught nor rewarded, and, if they were, the practices were often suppressed or forgotten in the context of modern organizations.

Evidence indicates, however, that effective teamwork and high-performance organizations require sophisticated abilities in listening. The skills required for effective listening cannot be learned in a single session. They require practice and reinforcement. This means that, if good listening skills are to be developed, they must be passed on and supported by a strong set of values about the worth and dignity of co-workers as well as a commitment to the overall success of the organization. Committing to better listening and practicing the skills over time help encourage the changes we seek in human systems.

The next section of this module is devoted to the topic of listening and its application to the development of the team.

30 minutes *Ten Commandments:* After you have introduced and given some background on the importance of listening, distribute and discuss the Ten Commandments for Good Listening. Review with the team the ten commandments of good listening. Ask them if they can identify any chronically poor listeners (who are not part of this team). If so, have a discussion regarding what makes those persons poor listeners. During the discussion of what makes for poor listening, write on a flipchart and discuss the five important mental attitudes to possess for effective listening behavior:

1. Interest and attention
2. Respect
3. Openness
4. Tolerance
5. Patience

Be sure to include in the discussion how not possessing these traits can hinder the effectiveness on the listening situation. For example, if the speaker does not perceive the listener to be open or respectful, chances are the speaker will shut down and stop offering valuable information.

15 minutes *Active Listening Techniques:* Although mental attitudes play a big role in good listening, there are some other very helpful skills that lead to effective listening behavior. Distribute the Active Listening Skills handout.

Start a discussion, based on the handout, about how people have seen silence used in effective communication. Also talk about what happens to communication when one person interrupts, argues, passes judgment, or jumps to conclusions. Try to use examples from the team but also be ready to offer your own perceptions.

25 minutes *Key Listening Techniques:* Distribute the Key Listening Techniques handout. These five techniques (natural response, restatement, questioning, summarizing, and reflection), along with the right mental attitude and active listening skills, are the essence of powerful listening.

These techniques are very simple. Have the team practice using these techniques. One easy exercise is simply to have two or three team members start a discussion about anything. The only rule is that, before anyone can respond to anyone else, they must use a key listening technique. Those on the team not participating should observe and act as coaches and judges.

25 minutes *Feedback:* Another very important component of effective team communication is feedback. Explain to the team that feedback is a constant in life. A mirror gives us feedback every morning. We get feedback from people too, either verbally or nonverbally. Most of us are not very skilled at *giving* or *receiving* feedback. Verbal feedback is often given in a way that hurts people instead of helping them. On the other hand, most of us are not very open to receiving feedback even when it is constructive and given in a caring manner.

Distribute the Feedback Guidelines handout and describe each guideline for both giving and receiving feedback. Take your time and try to illustrate each point with a good example from your experiences.

30 minutes *Communication/Listening/Feedback Exercise:* Similar to the quick exercise you may have used with effective listening techniques, this exercise affords the participants the chance to practice using their new listening, communication, and feedback techniques. This exercise also combines the values and skills related to communication, listening, and feedback. The participants focus on one, two, or all three skills depending on their role at the time. Here is how the exercise works:

- ✓ A team is made up of three people; each person eventually plays each role.
- ✓ It takes about 12 minutes to run the cycle of three participants.
- ✓ The exercise involves the Giver providing feedback to the Receiver about behavior he or she would like to see changed.

- ✓ Giver provides exactly two minutes of feedback to Receiver (no interruptions).
- ✓ Receiver (who does not take or look at notes) gives a one-minute summary of (1) what was said and (2) how well it was delivered.
- ✓ Timer/Recorder takes notes during Giver's two-minute delivery, provides a 30-second review of the Giver's message and Receiver's accuracy.
- ✓ When the cycle is complete, participants rotate roles.

Distribute the Communication/Listening/Feedback Exercise Model and the Communication/Listening/Feedback Exercise Recorder's Notes sheet. Explain to the team the preceding instructions and conduct the exercise.

20 minutes *Debrief/Process the Exercise:* After the team completes the exercise, process the learning by asking and starting discussions around the following questions:

1. How did the Giver feel during the exercise?

   Did he or she communicate differently than normal? If so, how?
2. What made the Giver's messages clear?

   What did he or she do to be effective?
3. How well did the Receiver (listener) do?

   What made listening difficult?

   More important, how was the listening in this exercise different than in the normal day-to-day work environment?
4. How well did the Timers/Recorder do?

   What were the quality and accuracy of the feedback? How was the feedback received?
5. Finally, what did you learn in this exercise that you will apply to the communication, listening, and feedback activities in the team?

5 minutes *Summary/Close:* Remind participants that effective interpersonal communication is critical because it is the foundation of team meetings, problem solving and issue resolution, conflict management, supplier and customer interaction, and day-to-day relationships in the team. Thank the participants for their time, distribute the evaluation, and ask the team members to spend a few minutes to give you the feedback (evaluation) that will help you deliver more effective modules in the future.

COMMUNICATION STRATEGIES TO DISCOURAGE

What to Discourage	Description
Twist arms.	Verbal force or coercion. "If we don't come up with an answer at this meeting, we might as well forget the whole thing. Now come on, make up your mind!"
Pull rank.	Status-centered remarks. "I don't care what you say. I'm the boss, and I say we'll never solve that problem!"
Give I'll-get-you-later look.	Staring hard at someone with whom you disagree or dislike. Suggesting that you'll get even with someone.
Hurl sticks and stones.	Verbal abuse or name calling that is intended to "dig" at someone. "I wouldn't trust you any more than a dog," or "That's a dumb idea: just what you'd expect from supervision."
Give the cold shoulder.	Ignoring the opposition. Excluding a particular group member by turning away or ignoring the statement. Talking to someone without looking at them.
Make others pull teeth.	Holding things back. Making others constantly work at pulling out your thoughts or comments.
Create nonverbal drama.	Using gestures instead of words to express opposition. Shaking one's head, turning away from the group, shoulder-shrugging, groaning, rolling eyes, and sleeping are all examples.
Cheerlead.	Vigorous agreement with everyone. The "yes" man. "Yeah, yeah, I like that idea!" "Great, great, great!"
Interrupt.	Constant interrupting and not letting others finish statements or thoughts. Talking so much that it is difficult for other people to say something.
Naysayer.	The eternal pessimist. Always talking about why things won't work instead of helping the group figure out how to plan for success. "Yeah, but…."

COMMUNICATION STRATEGIES TO ENCOURAGE

What to Encourage	Description
Accept opposing views.	Be willing to *accept* and *maintain* opposing points of view. Remember, the fact that not everyone sees the world as you do is an asset, not a liability!
Communicate clearly.	*Clearly communicate* your ideas so that others understand. Ask the group, "Am I making any sense?" or "Do you understand what I am saying?"
Listen completely.	*Listen completely* to the comments of others. Don't be afraid to ask for clarification to be sure you understand. Paraphrasing ("Is this what you mean . . .") and summarizing ("We have two different ideas to think about, specifically . . .") helps good listening occur.
Criticize ideas, not people.	*Criticize the content* of different ideas without criticizing the people behind the ideas. "Your solution could create a safety hazard" is a much different remark than, "Your solution is dumb."
Accept criticism.	*Accept criticism* from others on an intellectual rather than a personal basis. Remember, they are criticizing your idea, not you.
Share your ideas and opinions.	*Share your ideas and opinions.* Sometimes this may feel risky, but have confidence in your contributions and your value to the group.
Invite everyone to participate.	Help your group make *good decisions* by making sure everyone has had a chance to give an opinion and that the group has listened carefully to all points of view.
Stay on the subject.	Keep the group *on track* by not bringing up unrelated topics. If you have a concern that may get the group off the subject, hold onto it until the present discussion is finished.
Thank people.	*Thank* people for their efforts and contributions.
Leave disagreements in the room.	*Leave disagreements* in the meeting room. At the same time, don't bring work disagreements into the meeting unless they are either on the agenda or belong there.

Strategies to Discourage	Strategies to Encourage
*What are you **most** likely to do?*	*What are you **least** likely to do?*
Twist arms.	Accept opposing views.
Pull Rank.	Clearly communicate.
Give I'll-get-you-later look.	Listen completely.
Hurl sticks and stones.	Criticize ideas, not people.
Give the cold shoulder.	Accept criticism.
Make others pull teeth.	Share your ideas.
Create a nonverbal drama.	Invite everyone to participate
Cheerlead.	Stay on the subject.
Interrupt.	Thank people.
Be a naysayer.	Leave disagreements in the room.

Is Goal-Oriented

Is Clear/Understandable

Conveys Respect for Listener(s)

Is Open/Allows Response(s)

Is Consistent with/Uses Emotion

Avoids "Games"/Hidden Agendas

Seeks Mutual Understanding

Includes "I" Statements/Ownership

Avoids Assumptions

TEN COMMANDMENTS FOR GOOD LISTENING*

1. **Stop talking.**

   Polonius (*Hamlet*): "Give every man thine ear, but few thy voice."

2. **Put the talker at ease.**

   Help others feel they are free to talk. Create a "permissive environment."

3. **Show that you want to listen.**

   Look and act interested. Listen to understand rather than to reply.

4. **Minimize distractions.**

   Don't doodle, tap your fingers, or shuffle papers. Attention is a sign of valuing.

5. **Put yourself in the speaker's place.**

   Try to hear to understand the speaker's point of view.

6. **Be patient.**

   Allow plenty of time. Do not interrupt.

7. **Hold your temper.**

   An angry person often interprets the wrong meaning from words.

8. **Go easy on argument and criticism.**

   This puts the speaker on the defensive. In an argument, even if you win, you lose.

9. **Ask questions.**

   This encourages the speaker and shows you are listening.

10. **Stop talking.**

    This is first and last, because all the other commandments depend on it.

*Keith Davis, *Human Relations in Business* (New York: McGraw-Hill, 1951). Reprinted with permission.

Do:

Use silence to:

- ✓ Organize what *the other person* is saying—main ideas, key words, etc.
- ✓ Analyze/compare what is being said with what you think or know.
- ✓ "Hear" feelings/emotions—often they contradict verbal messages.
- ✓ Understand words from the speaker's point of view.

Don't:

- ✓ Interrupt.
- ✓ Argue.
- ✓ Pass judgment.
- ✓ Jump to conclusions.

KEY LISTENING TECHNIQUES

Listening Behavior	Purpose	Examples
Neutral response	To convey that you are interested and listening. To encourage the person to continue talking.	"I see." "That's interesting."
Restatement	To check our meaning and interpretation with the speaker. To show you are listening and that you understand what the speaker is saying. To encourage the speaker to analyze other aspects of the matter being considered and discuss it with you.	"As I understand it then, your plan is …" "This is what you have decided to do and the reasons are …" "If that's the case, what do you think about … ?"
Questioning	To get more information about a subject. To be certain you understand what is being communicated.	"Could you explain more about ... ?" "Do you mean that … ?"
Summarizing	To bring all the discussion into focus in terms of a summary. To serve as a springboard for discussion on a new topic or issue.	"These are the key ideas you have expressed …" "If I understand how you feel about the situation …"
Reflection	To demonstrate that you understand how the speaker feels about the topic.	"So, you're saying that you feel …" "That seems to indicate you were really mad about …"

FEEDBACK GUIDELINES

Giving feedback:

1. Focus on the behavior of the individual or the group, not on the personality or character.
2. Make it specific (what, when, where, etc.).
3. *Describe* the person's behavior; do not *judge* it.
4. Direct it at behavior that can be changed, not at permanent characteristics of an individual.
5. Make it timely, either at the moment the behavior is occurring or as soon afterward as possible.
6. Remember that people are uncomfortable receiving feedback, even if you are handling it the best way possible.
7. Whether the person agrees to continue (positive feedback) or to change (negative feedback), express your appreciation for listening to your concern.

Receiving feedback:

1. Actively listen to the person's description of your behavior and recommendations to continue what you are doing or suggested changes that would be helpful. (This is hard!)
2. Do not get defensive; trust the intent of the feedback is to help, not hurt you.
3. Paraphrase or summarize the feedback to make sure you have heard it correctly.
4. Give the feedback serious consideration. Do not dismiss it as irrelevant or unimportant.
5. Communicate to the person changes in his/her behavior that may be needed to help you change.
6. Whether or not you use the feedback, express appreciation to the other person for caring enough about the relationship to give you the feedback and request that he/she continue to do so.

COMMUNICATION/LISTENING/ FEEDBACK EXERCISE MODEL

HANDOUT 6-9

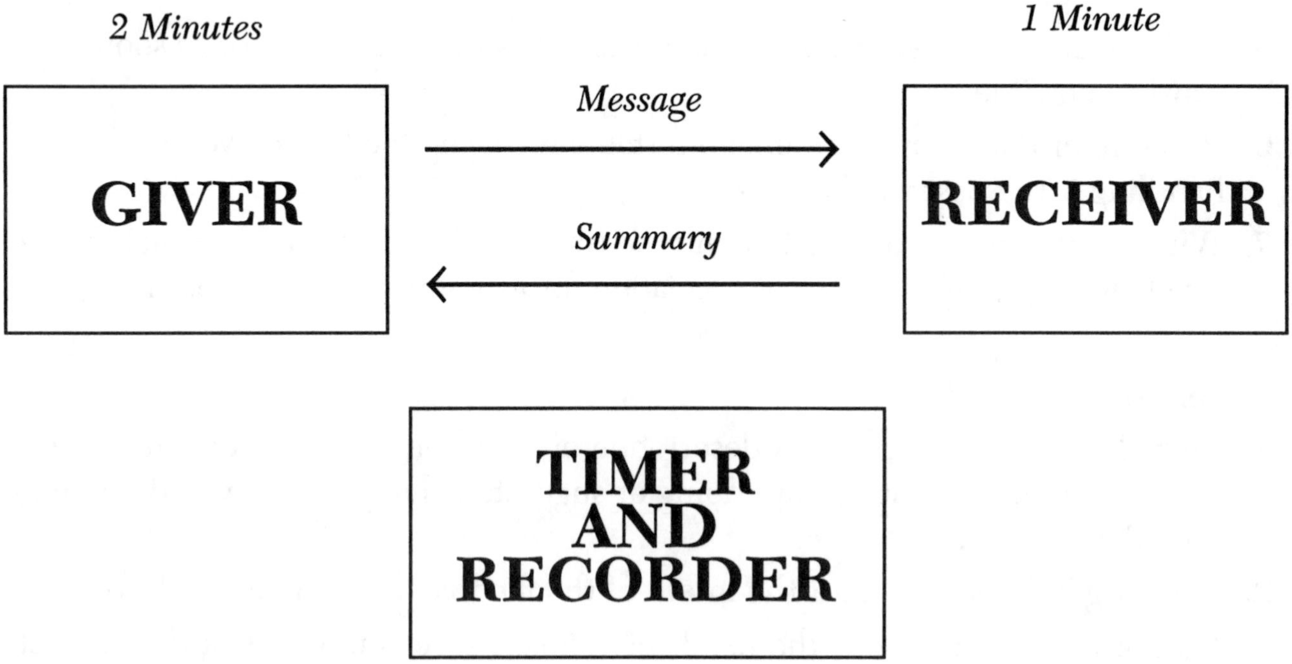
2 Minutes
1 Minute
GIVER
Message
Summary
RECEIVER
TIMER
AND
RECORDER

COMMUNICATION/LISTENING/ FEEDBACK EXERCISE RECORDER'S NOTES

HANDOUT 6-10

Module 7

Conflict Strategies and Integrative Resolution

(3.5 hours)

Objectives

✓ To understand the definition and sources of conflict in organizations and work groups.

✓ To adopt an approach to deal with conflict when it arises.

Materials Needed

✓ *Flipchart:* Objectives, Key Learning Points, and Topics (copy from this page)

✓ *Handouts:* Definition of Conflict (page 101)
Strategic Exercise: Instruction Sheet (page 102)
Strategic Exercise: Planning and Recording Form (page 103)
Strategic Exercise: Process Questions (page 104)
Sources of Conflict (page 105)
Conflict Style Assessment (page 106)
Conflict Style Assessment Scoring Sheet (page 108)
Steps in Integrative Negotiating (page 109)
Integrative Negotiation Exercise: Case Scenario (page 110)
Integrative Negotiation Exercise: Worksheet (page 111)
Evaluation (Appendix)

Key Learning Points

✓ Defining conflict.

✓ Becoming familiar with conflict styles.

✓ Understanding conflict strategies based on personal styles.

✓ Using integrative resolution as a conflict management strategy.

✓ Applying the strategy to a problem.

Topics

✓ Definition of Conflict

✓ Strategic Exercise

✓ Types of Conflict

✓ Sources of Conflict

✓ How You Act in Conflict

✓ Assessing Conflict in the Team

✓ Integrative Resolution Model

✓ Applying the Model to Work Situations

✓ Evaluation

Procedural Outline

Time **Activity**

Preparation: Read through all the integrative negotiation materials. Also, be sure to understand how to play the strategic exercise. Be sure you understand the integrative negotiation model. Also, create at least two personal examples from past experiences that will help to explain the model. Additionally, be sure to read through and to understand the integrative negotiation exercise. Be clear on all the perspectives in both scenarios. Also note that there is a great deal of information in this module but the most important information is about the integrative negotiation model and exercise. As you move through all the module materials with the team, try not to get bogged down with the source, strategy, and style materials. Move through that material as rapidly as possible. Spend the most time with the integrative model and practice exercise.

5 minutes *Introduction:* Begin this session by posting and explaining the module objectives, key learning points, and topics of the session. Also post the definition of conflict and generate a short discussion to see if this definition fits with the experiences of the team members.

30 minutes *Strategy Exercise:* This exercise is played by either two individuals or two small groups. Either is appropriate. Have the team choose. If two individuals play each other, you can run several rounds of the exercise. Have all other team members act as observers and watch the game closely. The other option is to split the team into two groups, who then work the exercise together.

Distribute the Strategy Exercise: Instruction Sheet and review the game rules with the team. Also distribute the Strategy Exercise: Planning and Recording Form. Be sure everyone understands how to play and start the game.

When the exercise has been completed, distribute Strategy Exercise: Process Questions. Have each player (or group) answer all the questions. Hold a discussion about everyone's answers.

This exercise should demonstrate many different perspectives about conflict (and cooperation). Supervise the dialogue by explaining the differences between controversy, conflicts of interest, and conflicts based on style.

- ✓ *Controversy:* One person's ideas, information, conclusions, theories, and opinions are incompatible with those of the other (e.g., disagreeing with one's supervisor about how a job should be completed).
- ✓ *Conflicts of interest:* Incompatible activities are based on differences in needs, values, goals, and competition for resources. These resources include power, time, space, money, position, general rewards, and privilege (e.g., competing with one's co-worker over the availability and use of a word processor).
- ✓ *Conflicts based on style:* Differences arise because two or more people look at the world differently or act on it in seemingly incompatible ways (e.g., one person thinks that it is essential that the rules or procedures be followed to the letter of the law while another thinks that part of the job of the team is to revise rules and apply them as appropriate in the best interests of the business).

10 minutes *Sources of Conflict:* Explain to the team that conflict between people may be generated from as many as four different sources. Distribute the Sources of Conflict handout and convey to the team how important it is to understand the basis of conflict in the workplace. As it turns out, *not all conflict can be managed in the same way.* Refer to the Sources of Conflict handout and explain that conflict may start over values, personality, sources of problems, or solutions.

- ✓ *Values (emotions):* Conflict growing out of deep differences in values is often attached to emotions. Differences over capital punishment, the right to life/abortion, and U.S. involvement in war/armed conflict in various countries result in conflict based on differences over values.

- ✓ *Personality (people):* This conflict arises over differences in people, their styles, personalities, and behavior (e.g., loud, pushy individuals dealing with quiet, retiring people). People who approach tasks in a very organized, systematic, careful way will often be in conflict with those who are more inventive, carefree, and experimental.
- ✓ *Source(s) of problems:* This type of conflict has to do with the definition of the causes of problems. For example, sometimes management attributes productivity or quality problems to workers while workers claim the source of the problem is the equipment or bad materials.
- ✓ *Solutions to problems:* These are disagreements over how goals are achieved or problems solved. The classic debate over how to reduce costs—cut people vs. pursuing nonpeople factors—is conflict over strategies/solutions.

60 minutes *Conflict Styles:* Now that the team has been involved in conflict (the strategy exercise) and has discussed the conceptual basis for conflict, it is appropriate to have each team member complete the conflict styles assessment. This assessment will help to reveal the propensity of each team member when entering a conflict situation.

Distribute the Conflict Style Assessment. Have team members rate each answer and complete the scoring sheet. When everyone is done, go around the team and see which style dominates for each team member. Hold a discussion

		Assertiveness Low	High
Cooperation	Low	Avoid	Complete
		Compromise	
	High	Accommodate	Collaborate

about styles and the combination of styles on the team.

Draw the preceding chart on a flipchart. Explain that another way to view conflict in an organization or work group is in terms of *assertiveness* (one's willingness to act on beliefs, rights, etc.) and *cooperation* (one's need to get along with others and/or to avoid conflict).

The table reflects the *strategies most often employed as a function of the emphasis on assertiveness and the emphasis on cooperation.* If the concern for *assertiveness is low* and the concern for *cooperation is high,* the strategy may be to Accommodate.

On the other hand, if the concern for *assertiveness is high* and the concern for *cooperation is low,* the strategy may be to Compete. The other options play out in a similar manner.

When there is a balance between Assertiveness and Cooperation, Compromise may occur.

25 minutes *Assessing Conflict in the Team:* Explain to the team that all teams have conflict. The basic questions the team should discuss and answer are:

1. What are the major issues over which this team has conflict?
2. What are the primary causes of conflict in the team?

By analyzing the answers to these questions, the team can get a better sense of the nature and causes of conflict in its specific situation.

After analyzing where the conflicts come from, then the team can look at the ways in which its various members handle conflict. For example:

✓ Do some team members "avoid" conflict?

✓ Do others attack or compete?

✓ Are there accommodators in the team? Those are members who tend to give in rather than fight.

Have the team take a look at both the sources of conflict and the ways in which various team members deal with it. Draw the following chart on a flipchart, and have the team as a whole complete the two lists:

What are five kinds of conflict we now have that we could avoid in the future?	*What are five ways that team members could help each other be more effective with conflict?*
1. ______	1. ______
2. ______	2. ______
3. ______	3. ______
4. ______	4. ______
5. ______	5. ______

By creating and discussing these lists, the team should have a head start in dealing with their future conflict situations very successfully.

35 minutes *Steps in Integrative Negotiation:* Understanding where conflict comes from and the conflict styles of others are powerful tools to help a person understand and deal with conflict with another. Yet, in both instances, neither piece of information will actually help a person negotiate through the differences. The integrative negotiation model is designed specifically as an approach to work through conflict. The model consists of five steps, which, when taken together, comprise a very powerful problem-solving conflict resolution tool. Write the five steps on a flipchart (Problem Identification, Setting a Goal or Objective, Generate Solutions, Evaluate Solutions, and Action Planning), and distribute and discuss the Steps in Integrative Negotiating handout.

Note: The best way to explain this model is with one or two excellent examples. The best examples for models like the integrative negotiation model always come from personal experience. Think back on those times when you have been in conflict. Use your personal examples to illustrate how the model works or might have worked if you used it.

35 minutes *An Exercise in Integrative Negotiation:* This is a case scenario exercise designed for four players. Everyone else on the team can act as observers. Explain to the team that all four players will get the same case scenario and that each player will take on a different role in the scenario: plant manager, supervisor, team member, and union steward. The four players then try to work out the conflict using the Integrative Negotiation Model.

Have the team pick their four players and observers and distribute the Integrative Negotiations Exercise: Case Scenario and the Integrative Negotiation Exercise: Worksheet. Tell the players to follow the Integrative Negotiation Exercise: Worksheet as a guideline in trying to resolve the conflict. Run the exercise.

Options for the Exercise: Instead of using the case scenario provided, create your own. Find a situation that mirrors your actual work environment. You can also use a real life conflict situation that was unresolved or resolved unsatisfactorily in the past. Redo the old conflict using the integrative model.

After the exercise is completed, review the five steps to the model and the Integrative Negotiation Exercise: Worksheet as a way to remind the team they can turn to this process for future conflict situations.

5 minutes *Summarize/Close:* Bring this module to a close by reminding the team that conflict can be a positive force for a high-performance team. It can come from many places (values, personality, problem causes, or problem identification), and it may be approached with different styles (compromising, accommodating, competing, avoiding, collaborating). Remind the team members the more they know about conflict sources and styles, the easier it will be to work through the issues and keep the conflict productive. Also, tell the team that the integrative negotiation model is a powerful tool for actually working through and resolving conflict. They should remember and practice those five steps whenever they get the chance. Finally, thank the participants for their time and ask them to complete the evaluation. Distribute the evaluation.

DEFINITION OF CONFLICT

HANDOUT 7-1

con-flict (kən flikt′) *vi.* < L *com-,* together + *flagrare,* to strike to be antagonistic, incompatible, etc. *-n.* **1.** a fight or war **2.** sharp disagreement, as of interests or ideas **3.** emotional disturbance.*

The pursuit of incompatible, or at least seemingly incompatible, goals such that gains by one side come about at the expense of the other.

Derelson & Steiner, 1964

**Webster's New World Dictionary* (New York: Simon & Schuster, 1989).

STRATEGIC EXERCISE: INSTRUCTION SHEET

Introduction. You or a small team will participate in a strategic exercise. In this exercise you will have an opportunity to invest in yourselves and to gain a return on your investment.

Skill is all that is required to be successful with your investment.

Players. This exercise can be played by two individuals or by two small teams. Please decide who will play.

1. You will record your responses on a chart (posted) containing 36 squares.
2. Each individual or group will record his/her/their strategic choices with a felt-tipped marker.
3. Each group's objective is to complete rows (horizontal, vertical, diagonal) of five squares marked with circles of the individual's or group's color or symbol.
4. Each player or group will mark one square per move, and moves will be made alternately by the two players/groups.
5. Each player/group is permitted 30 seconds for each move; the move is lost if not made within that time.
6. Each player/group will be allowed 10 minutes for a strategy session before the marking begins.
7. The activity will be completed when each group has had an opportunity to make 15 moves.
8. The return on the members' investment is based on the number of rows of five consecutive squares filled in by the player/group. (No mark can be counted twice.)

Notes

- ✓ If the activity is done by groups rather than by individuals, each group should select a "marker" to record the move.
- ✓ A coin flip will determine which player/group makes the first mark.

STRATEGIC EXERCISE: PLANNING AND RECORDING FORM

HANDOUT 7-3

NOTES:

STRATEGIC EXERCISE: PROCESS QUESTIONS

HANDOUT 7-4

1. What was the goal of your strategy?

2. Did you achieve your goal?

   If so, why?

   If not, why not?

3. How did you define winning?

4. How did it feel to win? To lose?

5. Now that you've had some time to think about it, what would you do differently the next time?

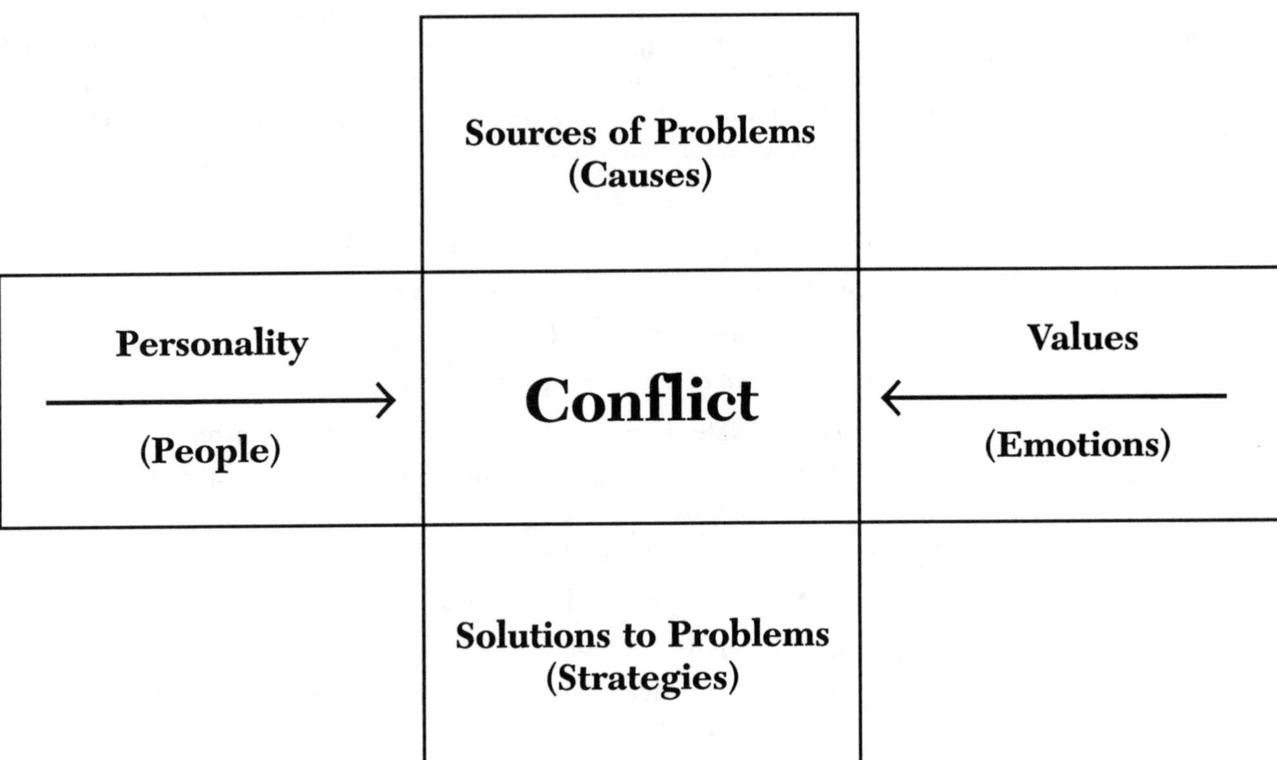
Sources of Problems
(Causes)
Personality
(People)
Conflict
Values
(Emotions)
Solutions to Problems
(Strategies)

CONFLICT STYLE ASSESSMENT*

The following proverbs can be thought of as descriptions of some of the different strategies for resolving conflicts. Proverbs state traditional wisdom, and these proverbs reflect traditional wisdom for resolving conflicts. Read each of the proverbs carefully. Using the following scale, indicate how typical each proverb is of your actions in a conflict.

5 = *very typical* of the way I act in a conflict

4 = *frequently typical* of the way I act in a conflict

3 = *sometimes typical* of the way I act in a conflict

2 = *seldom typical* of the way I act in a conflict

1 = *never typical* of the way I act in a conflict

______ **1.** It is easier to refrain than to retreat from a quarrel.

______ **2.** If you cannot make a person think as you do, make him or her do as you think.

______ **3.** Soft words win hard hearts.

______ **4.** You scratch my back; I'll scratch yours.

______ **5.** Come now and let us reason together.

______ **6.** When two quarrel, the person who keeps silent first is the most praiseworthy.

______ **7.** Might overcomes right.

______ **8.** Smooth words make smooth ways.

______ **9.** Better half a loaf than no bread at all.

______ **10.** Truth lies in knowledge, not in majority opinion.

______ **11.** He who fights and runs away lives to fight another day.

______ **12.** He hath conquered well that hath made his enemies flee.

______ **13.** Kill your enemies with kindness.

______ **14.** A fair exchange brings no quarrel.

______ **15.** No person has the final answer, but every person has a piece to contribute.

______ **16.** Stay away from people who disagree with you.

______ **17.** Fields are won by those who believe in winning.

______ **18.** Kind words are worth much and cost little.

______ **19.** Tit for tat is fair play.

______ **20.** Only the person who is willing to give up his or her monopoly on truth can ever profit from the truths that others hold.

______ **21.** Avoid quarrelsome people as they will only make your life miserable.

*D. W. Johnson and F. P. Johnson, *Joining Together* (New York: Allyn & Bacon, 1987). Reprinted with permission.

______ **22.** A person who will not flee will make others flee.

______ **23.** Soft words ensure harmony.

______ **24.** One gift for another makes good friends.

______ **25.** Bring your conflicts into the open and face them directly; only then will the best solution be discovered.

______ **26.** The best way of handling conflicts is to avoid them.

______ **27.** Put your foot down where you mean to stand.

______ **28.** Gentleness will triumph over anger.

______ **29.** Getting part of what you want is better than not getting anything at all.

______ **30.** Frankness, honesty, and trust will move mountains.

______ **31.** There is nothing so important that you have to fight for it.

______ **32.** There are two kinds of people in the world: the winners and the losers.

______ **33.** When one hits you with a stone, hit him or her with a piece of cotton.

______ **34.** When both give in halfway, a fair settlement is achieved.

______ **35.** By digging and digging, the truth is discovered.

CONFLICT STYLE ASSESSMENT SCORING SHEET

HANDOUT 7-7

Avoid (Withdraw)	Complete (Force)	Accommodate (Concession)	Compromise (Truce)	Collaborate (Integrating)
_____ 1.	_____ 2.	_____ 3.	_____ 4.	_____ 5.
_____ 6.	_____ 7.	_____ 8.	_____ 9.	_____ 10.
_____ 11.	_____ 12.	_____ 13.	_____ 14.	_____ 15.
_____ 16.	_____ 17.	_____ 18.	_____ 19.	_____ 20.
_____ 21.	_____ 22.	_____ 23.	_____ 24.	_____ 25.
_____ 26.	_____ 27.	_____ 28.	_____ 29.	_____ 30.
_____ 31.	_____ 32.	_____ 33.	_____ 34.	_____ 35.
_____ Total	_____ Total	_____ Total	_____ Total	_____ Total

STEPS IN INTEGRATIVE NEGOTIATING

The following five steps comprise a problem-solving approach to conflict resolution.

I. Identifying the problem.

Express your view of the problem and invite the other person to do the same.

- ✓ Deal with the conflict only when there is enough time to discuss it fully.
- ✓ Communicate openly your position and feelings in a non-threatening way.
- ✓ Work hard to understand the position and feelings of the other person.
- ✓ Do not label, accuse, or insult the other person.
- ✓ Try to define the conflict as a *shared* problem, not as a win-lose situation.
- ✓ The goal in this step is to describe the conflict in a clear and precise manner.

II. Set a goal or objective.

Often people want to accomplish the same goal or their goals are complementary. Conflict occurs over *how to accomplish* the goal. If they can identify a common goal or objective, then the conflict over how to accomplish the goal is easier to handle.

- ✓ A goal is an outcome, something that is in the future.
- ✓ Avoid stating methods ("how to," or solutions) as a goal.
- ✓ Each person needs to state what their goal or objective is.
- ✓ Search for what each of you has in common as your goal.
- ✓ Sometimes broadening the goal helps people see what they have in common.
- ✓ Avoid attaching solutions to your goals; stick to discussing the goal at this stage.

III. Generate solutions.

- ✓ Brainstorm as many possible solutions as you can.
- ✓ Be spontaneous in your thinking.
- ✓ Combine alternatives into better solutions.

IV. Evaluate solutions.

- ✓ Use the goals and objectives to evaluate the effectiveness of solutions.
- ✓ Look for a way to cooperate, that is, to help the other person such that the action does not interfere with your goal.
- ✓ Select the solution(s) that maximize joint needs.
- ✓ Compromise only if you can't find an ideal solution.

V. Create an action plan.

- ✓ Develop a detailed plan: who, what, when, where, how.
- ✓ Develop the sequence of steps and time lines.
- ✓ Identify the needed resources: human, material, financial.

INTEGRATIVE NEGOTIATION EXERCISE: CASE SCENARIO

An operations team in Plant ABC is having difficulty agreeing on the daily job assignments related to running their area of the plant. (Plant ABC installed an employee involvement process last year.) The team members, in the spirit of employee involvement, claim that the supervisor is acting like a dictator and telling them what to do (the old way). The supervisor says that some team members are not achieving business objectives and are not cooperating. Therefore, it is his responsibility to give them direction.

The plant manager is getting frustrated with delays and says the team should take action against the team members who are not cooperating. If they don't, he says, he will discipline the team members *and* make the job assignments. The union steward says that the plant manager cannot discipline bargaining unit employees for not being able to reach consensus on the work assignments. "These things take time and they have a right to be able to work them out without interference," she claims.

The Task. Using the information outlined in the situation, try to resolve the difficulty using the five steps in the Integrative Negotiation model. The information on the Integrative Negotiation Exercise Worksheet will help you work through the process.

INTEGRATIVE NEGOTIATION EXERCISE: WORKSHEET

I. Identify the problem.

What is the problem facing the organization? The team?

Is there more than one problem?

II. Set a goal or objective.

After everyone had input, what is the goal or objective of the various members?

Can everyone eventually agree to a single goal?

III. Generate solutions to the problem.

Based on the various persons' interests, can you come up with solutions that have the potential to work for everybody?

IV. Evaluate solutions.

Using the goals and/or objectives developed in step II, select a solution or strategy that maximizes everybody's needs. (*Note:* Compromise only if you cannot find an ideal solution.)

V. Develop an action plan.

Figure out how to make your solution reality. Specify the who, what, when, where, etc.

Module 8

Organizational Mission and Purpose of the Team

(2 hours)

Objectives

- ✓ To reinforce the mission of the business.
- ✓ To have the team develop a purpose statement in support of the organization's mission.

Materials Needed

- ✓ *Flipchart:* Objectives, Key Learning Points, and Topics (copy from this page)
- ✓ *Handouts:* Definition of a Mission (page 115)
  Sample Organizational Mission Statements (page 116)
  Sample Team Purpose Statements (page 117)
  Purpose of the Team Worksheet (page 118)
  Purpose of Our Team (page 119)
  Evaluation (Appendix)

Key Learning Points

- ✓ Understanding the reason for a clear and appropriate mission.
- ✓ Understanding your organization's mission.
- ✓ Developing a team purpose statement.

Topics

- ✓ Definition of Mission
- ✓ Organizational Mission Statement
- ✓ Team Purpose Statement
- ✓ Evaluation

Procedural Outline

Time	Activity
	Preparation: The purpose of this module is to reinforce the mission of the business and to have the team develop a purpose statement in support of the organization's mission. To do this effectively, you will need to find and prepare mission, vision, and value materials specific to your organization and department or unit.
5 minutes	*Introduction:* Begin this session by posting and explaining the module objectives, key learning points, and topics of the session.
30 minutes	*Definition of a Mission:* Distribute the Definition of a Mission and the Sample Organizational Mission Statements handouts. Explain that a *mission* is a *statement of the reason or reasons for the existence of the organization, the ultimate purpose the organization serves in society, and the boundaries within which it operates.* A mission is one of the of the four key building blocks of an organiza-

tional plan. The other three are vision, goals, and strategy. A mission sets direction and defines the boundaries, both of which are critical to the organization's effectiveness and success.

Further explain that without a mission an organization is likely to lose focus and eventually reach a state of decline. For example, what if the United States Postal Service thought its mission was communication? How would that mission affect planning, resource allocation, evaluation of effectiveness, etc. as opposed to a mission of distribution (of parcels and letters)?

One might suspect that a number of organizations in the last decade thought their primary mission was to make a profit. We cannot dispute that a private sector organization must be profitable to survive, but profit is not the *primary mission*; it is a *necessary condition* or a goal of the organization. History may confirm that a number of large corporations got into trouble in the 1980s and 1990s because they lost sight of their missions. The trouble occurred when companies began to acquire other companies that were unrelated to their core business. When they lost sight of the mission and focused strictly on wealth, they set themselves up for difficulties.

The mission of the larger organization should be general, not specific. A general mission of most auto manufacturers is to provide some form of personal transportation. It is *not* a mission to build cars. That is how the companies fulfill their mission. Such a company might also build buggies (if horses were the primary source of locomotion) or bicycles (if located in a society where cars were not affordable or available). So mission does not imply strategy, but it will determine the general direction of the organization. As we move down the corporate "food chain," however, the mission of each succeeding level will be more specific. In fact, some organizations talk about the *purpose* of a unit rather than its mission. In the case of the auto industry, it might be the mission of an assembly plant to "build high-quality, low-cost cars at budget and on schedule." Their mission at the plant depends on the overall mission of the larger organization.

Finally, tell the team that in this module, using your organization's mission, they will write a team purpose statement to guide the planning, resource allocation, and management of the team's business.

25 minutes *Review Your Company's Mission, Vision, and Values:* Distribute your company's mission, vision, and value statements. Have the team review these statements, one at a time, dissecting each for its underlying meaning. Ask the team if they agree with the statements and if there is anything they would like to see different. Further, have the team discuss how these statements were created and if there is companywide ownership of the statements and what they stand for. The purpose is twofold: first, to help the team participants become intimately familiar with the company philosophy, and second, to give them insight about how to create their own purpose statement.

10 minutes *Review of Team Purpose Statements:* Once the team has reviewed the organization's mission, turn to the team purpose statement. Distribute the Sample Team Purpose Statements and explain that some organizations have every team and committee write a mission statement. We believe calling this a "mission statement" is conceptually inappropriate and confusing when one begins to try to figure out which mission statement applies in a given conversation. So we talk about the team's *purpose inside the larger mission. This provides narrower focus and a statement that can be used for planning at the team level.* Review and discuss the sample purpose statements from teams in other organizations.

These statements are designed to demonstrate that every division and department in an organization serves a purpose and, therefore, should have a clear statement of that purpose. Further, when the purpose statements from a number of functional areas are reviewed together, there should not be overlap and/or contradictions. That is one good reason to do the process formally and to make the results public.

The next step, after everyone understands a purpose statement and what it is suppose to do, is to start writing a purpose statement for your team.

60 minutes *Writing the Purpose Statement:* Distribute the Purpose of the Team Worksheet. Explain the instructions on the worksheet and have each team member complete their individual statement of purpose. When all participants are finished drafting their thoughts, have them read their statements. Try to capture the essence of each statement on a blank flipchart. When everyone has read his or her statement, work with the group to combine and refine its purpose until consensus is reached. When the individual statements reflect great diversity, this process may take some discussion and some time. When the individual statements are closer together, the team will take much less time reaching consensus on its purpose.

After the team reaches consensus on its purpose, distribute the Purpose of Our Team handout and have each member fill in the team purpose statement. If possible, the team should consider printing the purpose statement on a poster and posting it in the work area or meeting room.

5 minutes *Summary/Close:* Bring this section to a close by congratulating the team on a job well done. Review any further action steps with regard to publishing the purpose statement. Distribute the evaluation. Ask the team members for their feedback (by completing the evaluation) and thank them for their time.

DEFINITION OF A MISSION

A mission is a statement of the reason or reasons for the existence of the organization, the ultimate purpose the organization serves in society, and the boundaries within which it operates.

A mission is part of the building blocks of the organization.

SAMPLE ORGANIZATIONAL MISSION STATEMENTS

To *help* small businesses and households protect municipal streams, the environment, and human health from the mismanagement of hazardous chemicals.

To be the preferred supplier of engineering, design, system integration, life cycle support, construction, and maintenance products and services for [name the product].

To provide on-time delivery of quality-engineered steels in order to expand market share and to help ensure the future of the company, our customers, our suppliers, and the community.

To provide high-quality, effective, at-the-moment customer service to clients and consumers of the corporation's products.

SAMPLE TEAM PURPOSE STATEMENTS

Maintenance team

To keep equipment running time at a maximum at the lowest possible cost. [Notice the team did not say they were going to repair equipment. Repair is one of the strategies they use to fulfill their purpose.]

Operations team

To process materials in such a way as to meet or exceed permit requirements within resource guidelines. [They might have said that their purpose was to run treatment plants, but they chose to talk about their purpose being the processing of materials.]

Process control

To provide data and statistics on the effectiveness of the treatment process and the kinds of foreign materials in the water. [The actual testing done in the laboratories is not the purpose; it is the strategy to fulfill the purpose.]

Administration

To provide high-quality, cost-effective support services to the operations and maintenance departments. [These services are clearly not mainstream to the operations and maintenance departments, but rather they "support."]

PURPOSE OF THE TEAM WORKSHEET

A statement of the reason or reasons for the existence of a department, program, work group, or team within an organization. The team's purpose should be related to, and supportive of, the overall organization's mission.

After you have reviewed the *mission* of the organization, think about the *purpose of the team* in the context of the mission.

To be clear about the purpose of the team, create a Statement of Purpose. The statement should meet the following criteria:

1. It should be no more than 25–30 words in length.
2. It should reflect the consensus of the team.
3. It should be written so that someone outside the team can understand it.

Draft your individual statement of purpose here:

____

When you are finished drafting your thoughts on the team's purpose, the entire team will begin to assemble a statement that represents your contribution.

PURPOSE OF OUR TEAM

Once the team has reached consensus on its purpose statement, record it in the section following.

Team Purpose Statement

Module 9

Team Vision

(2 hours)

Objectives

- ✓ To define the desired future state of the team.
- ✓ To create team standards by which to live.

Materials Needed

- ✓ *Flipchart:* Objectives, Key Learning Points, and Topics (copy from this page)
- ✓ *Handouts:* Definition of a Vision (page 123)
  12 Characteristics of Effective Teams (page 124)
  Description of Your Ideal Team Worksheet (page 125)
  Team Vision Worksheet (page 126)
  Team Vision (page 127)
  Evaluation (Appendix)

Key Learning Points

- ✓ Understanding the importance of vision in an effective organization.
- ✓ Understanding the organization's vision.
- ✓ Defining an ideal team.
- ✓ Defining a vision for this team.

Topics

- ✓ An Introduction to the Concept of Vision
- ✓ Vision of the Ideal Organization
- ✓ The Ideal Team Exercise
- ✓ Vision for This Team
- ✓ Evaluation

Procedural Outline

Time	Activity
5 minutes	*Preparation:* Go back to Module 8 and pull the company vision statement. Write this on a blank flipchart or make handout copies for the team. This statement will be used as an example during this module.
5 minutes	*Introduction:* Begin this session by posting and explaining the module objectives, key learning points, and topics of the session.
10 minutes	*Definition of a Vision:* Distribute the Definition of a Vision handout. Read the quote aloud to the team. Have a short discussion about vision, who should have a vision, and when and how that vision gets used. Also post or distribute the company vision. Have a brief reminder discussion about how the company vision affects the team.
20 minutes	*Vision and the Ideal Team:* Explain to the team that a vision defines what you want to become. To set the stage for the team vision exercise, distribute the 12

Characteristics of Effective Teams handout.* Create a dialogue with the team around each characteristic. Ask the team members if they agree or disagree with the characteristics and/or how their team rates on each dimension.

✓ *Clear sense of purpose:* All members define and accept their mission or goal, and often push for "stretch" objectives. The team is clear about specifics—meeting agendas, assignments, and milestones—and knows how to focus on the task at hand.

✓ *Informal climate:* Effective teams enjoy being together. They communicate easily and with humor to create a relaxed atmosphere. Members often get together before or after meetings to talk about nonwork subjects. They offer help without being asked and are willing to share the limelight of success with other members.

✓ *Participation:* Each member plays a role in achieving the team's shared goal or task, although not necessarily equally or in the same manner.

✓ *Listening:* The ability of members to listen is the most distinguishing factor of effective teams. They take in what is said without passing judgment. They acknowledge others' contributions and demonstrate interest in what other people have to say.

✓ *Civilized disagreement:* Team members feel free to express opinions. While hostility and denigration are destructive, diversity is a mark of team strength. Effective teams use problem-solving skills to resolve conflicts and increase group cohesion. Team members' flexibility, objectivity, and humor promote a climate that allows civilized disagreement.

✓ *Consensus:* A consensus requires unity but not unanimity. A consensus is reached when all members agree with the decision or have had their "day in court." It is not a majority decision, but rather an agreement by everyone to support the outcome.

✓ *Open communication:* Trust among team members is a requisite for open communication. Team players encourage open communication by being dependable, cooperative, and candid. The leader encourages discussion and offers nonjudgmental responses.

✓ *Clear roles and work assignments:* Effective teamwork involves task interdependence; so agreement on expectations is important. Team members' roles must be clarified, decisions clear-cut, and necessary follow-up actions planned. All members must fulfill their share of responsibilities and help others when possible.

✓ *Shared leadership:* All members must take responsibility for meeting the team's needs because, if the team fails, everyone fails. The leader or coordinator has administrative and bureaucratic responsibilities. Other functions shift among members depending on their skills and the group's needs.

✓ *External relations:* Effective teams communicate their successes to build credibility. They also develop a network of outside contacts with customers or managers of functional departments who provide feedback, resources, or other assistance to the team.

✓ *Style diversity:* The most successful teams have members with different skills and personalities.

*Glenn M. Parker, *Team Players and Teamwork: The New Competitive Business Strategy* (San Francisco: Jossey-Bass, 1990). Reproduced with permission.

✓ *Self-assessment:* Good teams assess their effectiveness, either informally or formally every so often.

40 minutes *Description of Your Ideal Team:* Tell the team members that now, after they have reviewed the *vision* of the organization (Module 5) and the characteristics of effective teams, to think about the characteristics of the ideal team.

Distribute the Description of Your Ideal Team Worksheet and have the team members draft their thoughts about the ideal team in the chart provided. Be sure to explain to the participants not to worry about "getting it right." This is the time to think about what the team members would like a team to be if they could form and develop it any way they wanted.

Have them use the categories provided, but if there is something else they want to add, tell them to simply create a new category. After all the members of the team have drafted their individual thoughts, have them as a team share their thoughts about what is ideal.

10 minutes *Creating the Team Vision:* Now that team members have reviewed the organizational vision and ideal team characteristics, their task is to create a vision for their team. This is not a paragraph of flowery words that is printed and hung on the wall. This vision is a series of statements that represent the team they want to create. If used properly, it will guide how they operate the team and as a baseline against which to measure their team's growth and development.

Distribute the Team Vision Worksheet and read aloud the setting, assumption, the task, and thoughts. After everyone understands the scenario, have the team members individually complete the bottom section on the worksheet (how they would like the team described three years from now).

30 minutes *Team Vision—the Final Version:* After everyone has finished drafting individual statements, have the participants brainstorm their statements onto a list for the entire team to see. Then begin combining, adding, and deleting until you arrive at a final statement.

Note: If you get stuck or run out of time, appoint a subcommittee of the team to draft a statement between this meeting and the next. Then the entire team can review and approve (or revise) the draft. When it is completed, have the final vision statement or statements transcribed on the Team Vision handout.

5 minutes *Summary/Close:* Bring this section to a close by acknowledging the team's good work. Remind the participants that a vision is about long-term change, that it empowers people, and that everyone needs a vision. Recap the team's vision and/or the specific action steps for when the vision will be complete. Thank the team members for their time. Distribute and ask the participants to complete the evaluation.

DEFINITION OF A VISION

Vision is the difference between short-term moves to improve the bottom line (like asset sales or cuts in the R&D budget) and long-term change. Vision translates strategies you might have on paper into a way of life. Vision empowers people to change. Vision teaches the elephant to dance.

Everybody in the organization needs a vision, from the mail room supervisor to the CEO. The success of your organization depends on it. Vision paints a picture of where you want your company to go and what you want it to be.

James A. Belasco
Teaching the Elephant to Dance

12 CHARACTERISTICS OF EFFECTIVE TEAMS

1. **Clear sense of purpose**
2. **Informal climate**
3. **Participation**
4. **Listening**
5. **Civilized disagreement**
6. **Consensus**
7. **Open communication**
8. **Clear roles and work assignments**
9. **Shared leadership**
10. **External relations**
11. **Style diversity**
12. **Self-assessment**

DESCRIPTION OF YOUR IDEAL TEAM WORKSHEET

Characteristic	Description of Your Ideal Team
Productivity	
Quality	
Customers	
Communication	
Relationships with other departments	
Customer service	
Motivation/attitude	
Relationships among team members	

TEAM VISION WORKSHEET

The Setting. It is three years from today. Senior management and the union leaders are hosting a tour of customers (or stakeholders or government officials) through the facility.

Assumption. Assume that your team has the reputation of being the best in the facility.

The Task. Write a series of statements that you would like the tour hosts to make about your team. For example: "This team produces the best-quality product in the corporation." "This team has received more thank-you and recognition letters from our clients than any other team in the organization."

Thoughts. Consider describing some of the following: commitment, quality, relationships within the team, communication, motivation, and so forth. Anything is fair game. *Remember: This is the team you want to become. Be realistic, but also stretch beyond where you think the team will go if you do nothing the next three years.*

Here is how I would like to describe our team three years from now:

- ______________________________
- ______________________________
- ______________________________
- ______________________________
- ______________________________
- ______________________________
- ______________________________

Team Vision Statement

Note: If possible, have your vision statement printed on something that can be displayed in the department and/or provided to everyone on the work team.

Module 10

Team Business Meetings

(2½ hours)

Objectives

✓ To understand a structured approach to team business meetings.

✓ To agree on meeting norms for the team.

Materials Needed

✓ *Flipchart:* Objectives, Key Learning Points, and Topics (copy from this page)

✓ *Handouts:* Team Meetings: Why Bother? (page 135)
Team Meeting Planning Tool (page 138)
Special Meeting Planner (page 139)
Team Business Meetings Goals (page 141)
Team Meeting Model (page 142)
Team Meeting Evaluation Form: Instruction Sheet (page 143)
Team Meeting Evaluation Form (page 144)
Responsibilities of the Facilitator in Team Meetings (page 146)
Responsibilities of the Recorder in Team Meetings (page 147)
Responsibilities of the Members in Team Meetings (page 148)
Team Business Meeting Logistics Worksheet (page 149)
Checklist for Effective Meetings (page 150)
Evaluation (Appendix)

Key Learning Points

✓ Understanding the team meeting model and how to implement the model.

✓ Understanding responsibilities in team meetings.

✓ Establishing team meeting logistics.

Topics

✓ Goals of Team Meetings

✓ Team Meeting Model

✓ Responsibilities in Team Meetings

✓ Logistics of the Team Meeting

✓ Evaluation

Procedural Outline

Time **Activity**

Preparation: Team meetings are more than just a group of people getting together to discuss work. Please read through the Team Meeting Module thoroughly before beginning this session. Familiarize yourself with the reasons for team meetings, the goals of team meetings, the problems with meetings (meeting and organizational pathologies), and the suggested Team Meeting Model. This background information will be very helpful in running this module. Also, you might want to prepare a 5–10-minute lecturette on the Team Meetings: Why Bother? handout to be used in your introduction.

5 minutes *Introduction:* Open this module by posting and describing the module objective, key learning points, and topics for this session. Further, give a short lecturette on Team Meetings: Why Bother? Feel free to distribute the Team Meetings: Why Bother? handout if you think the participants need or desire the detailed information. Also, hand out and discuss Team Business Meeting Goals to set the stage for the rest of the module.

10 minutes *Team Business Meetings Introduction:* Explain that managers spend a great deal of time in meetings. It is not unusual, for example, for meetings to consume 6–8 hours a day. For such managers, the team meeting module is a way to make meetings more productive and efficient. As we move down the organization, team meetings represent a significant step away from the traditional top-down, authoritative, noncommunicative organization toward one in which there is more open and honest communication as well as more involvement in problem solving and decision making. At the level of organizations where the work gets done, team meetings symbolically represent a shift from strictly "doing" to involvement in "thinking."

Further explain that, although the information in this module is useful for teams at any level, there is special emphasis on first- and second-level teams that have not been involved in extensive team meetings. In this framework, teams or work groups meet weekly to receive feedback on performance as well as updates on general business information. In addition, the teams identify issues and make decisions and/or resolve work issues as part of those meetings. The following outlines the goals of the team business meetings and describes the team meeting model.

Describe to the team that effective team meetings are a product of *what is done* in the meeting (task or business orientation) and *how it is done* (process orientation). The best team meetings attend to both task and process. Explain that the following are some general characteristics of effective meetings:

- ✓ The meetings provide a genuine opportunity for involvement of participants in decisions that affect them.
- ✓ Information relevant to participants' roles in their part of the business is shared openly and honestly.
- ✓ The leaders of the meeting listen to participants' needs and input.
- ✓ Cooperation between and among functional areas is encouraged.
- ✓ Participants feel as though they are mature partners in the business and are respected by the leaders.

Finally, explain that this module focuses primarily on the process portion of the meeting, that is, it provides a way to structure and manage the agenda.

We also touch on task issues—the information that needs to be discussed to accomplish the team's goals. But, for the most part, the specific information the team will actually talk about will be generated every week.

30 minutes *Team Meeting Agendas:* The agenda is the team's primary tool for planning and managing meetings. More than a list of topics, it is an outline of what is to be discussed, a definition of what is to be done with what is discussed, a record of who is responsible for what is being discussed, and an estimate of time the team thinks it will take to complete the item.

The module includes two different tools for planning and managing meetings. One is for planning and managing the agenda for a regular team meeting; the other for managing special team meetings.

✓ *Regular Team Meeting Tool:* This tool can be used at the end of a regular team meeting to create a preliminary agenda for the next meeting. Note that the form contains two examples of topics to be covered at the meeting (survey and equipment purchase). And, to remind the planners that they need to be a part of every meeting, the items "Evaluate Meeting" and "Agenda for Next Meeting" appear at the bottom.

Prior to the actual meeting, the topics should be arranged so that the flow of the agenda follows the meeting model described earlier in the module. The agenda should be posted or distributed prior to the meeting so that team members are reminded both of what is to be addressed and of their responsiblities with regard to the various topics.

✓ *Special Meeting Management Tool:* The second tool is provided for use in special team meetings. This might be a meeting related to a special project, a task force meeting, or a multiteam planning meeting. It contains space for different information and a lot more than the standard team meeting agenda form. Some information should be completed ahead of time (time, place, persons invited, purpose, intended outcomes, agenda items, etc.). Other space is provided for recording notes in the actual meeting (notes, action items).

The proper and regular use of agendas is critical to effective team meetings. Simply listing topics and trying to get business done wastes a lot of time and resources. The team should begin using team meeting agenda planning and managing tools at the outset.

In this case, the team might create its own form or the organization may have a meeting planning tool that incorporates the essential information. In any case, the key is to use it to get another step closer to the effective meetings found in high-performance teams.

The Team Meetings Model: Distribute the Team Meeting Model and explain that the model divides team meetings into three basic sections:

1. Business information and performance feedback
2. Listening
3. Problem solving

Using the following detailed information, walk through each part of the model. Be sure people realize this is a very different model than what they are used to. It not only has different components, but the philosophy behind the model is one of employee involvement.

1. *Business information and performance feedback.* The first segment of the team meeting is devoted to giving team members feedback regarding the performance of the business unit and updated business information. The people supplying the information regarding performance feedback need to prepare it in a meaningful, understandable, value-free way for the team. The information should include daily or weekly performance (depending on what is appropriate) as well as trends for the year to date. Terms should be defined and the rationale for performance criteria should be explained.

After performance feedback information is shared and any questions are addressed, the team should take a few moments to discuss other business information. Such information may include schedule and/or resource changes, new business, upcoming tours (e.g., customers), and general announcements.

When the group is finished with the performance feedback and business information portion of the meeting, there should be a clear break to indicate that the team is moving to the next portion of the meeting. For example, tearing off the piece of newsprint you are using and starting with a clean sheet is one way to emphasize the break.

2. *Listening.* The second part of the meeting is designed to promote two-way communication.

Begin the listening portion of the meeting with an update of issues and questions raised at the previous meeting. Have a list of the "open issues" on a piece of newsprint, which you post for the discussion. As questions are answered and information provided, cross the items off the list. If an issue is not resolved, leave it there as a starter for the next meeting's list.

When you finish the open issues from the previous meeting, open the floor to new questions and issues. Team members can talk about what kinds of problems they are encountering that prevent them from doing their jobs effectively, or they can ask questions about things they want to know or do not understand. For this portion of the meeting to be effective, it is critical that all the members, especially the team leader and facilitator, *actively listen* to the concerns or issues raised. Meeting facilitators should be sure that questions and issues are understood by *summarizing* or *paraphrasing* the question or concern. Each question or issue needs to be *recorded* on a flipchart or marker board as it is voiced (sometimes an abbreviated note will do).

Remember: Sometimes, especially in the early stages of implementing a meeting process, tough issues are raised and emotions get intense. At this point, the team leader and/or facilitator should be careful not to let personal feelings get in the way of responding to the issue or deciding whether an issue is important or solvable. Listen, keep the discussion open, and do not dwell too long on any particular item during this part of the meeting.

At the close of this section of the meeting, be sure to summarize the list of issues and unanswered questions that need follow-up. Again, remove this newsprint as part of the transition to the next segment of the meeting.

3. *Decision making and issue identification.* This section of the meeting is designed to give the team and its leadership time to deal with important business issues. The focus of the activity is on both decision making and issue identification. The team is not likely to have or even want to take time in a brief meeting to make a complex decision or to try to solve a complex problem. These often could and should be handled in the listening segment.

Rather, this portion of the meeting is designed to describe and define decisions that have to be made and issues that have to be resolved and to develop a plan for completing them.

Again, the meeting facilitator should be working from a list of issues. The list is a product of:

- ✓ Items left over from prior meetings.
- ✓ Items put there by management, supervision, and business team leaders since the last meeting.
- ✓ Items that came up in earlier sections of the current meeting.

Be sure to start this part of the meeting with the opportunity for team members to add to the list.

A variety of avenues are available to address work issues. Begin by prioritizing the list. One way to prioritize is to put the items into categories. For example, if you want to categorize by "type" of issue, you might use the following categories as a guide:

1. The problem is simple enough to be discussed in the meeting, using problem-solving steps where needed, and can be resolved by someone present in the meeting.

   Team Meeting Strategy: Take care of these items in the meeting or agree to handle it outside the meeting (and before the next meeting).

2. The problem is relatively simple but must be resolved by someone outside the team (not present in the meeting).

   Team Meeting Strategy: Decide who will contact the appropriate person or department and provide the necessary information and request.

3. The problem is complex and resolvable within the team, but needs more time devoted to it than is available in the meeting.

   Team Meeting Strategy: Determine who needs and/or wants to be part of a problem-solving team who meets outside the team meeting to address the issue.

4. The problem is complex and needs to be addressed by people outside the team, perhaps with the involvement of members of the team.

   Team Meeting Strategy: Decide who from the team (it could be a supervisor, team leader, or a couple of members of the team) will contact the appropriate parties to develop a strategy to address the issue. Often a task force or task team, established for the specific purpose of addressing this issue, is appropriate

This is perhaps the most difficult portion of the meeting to manage. First, you have to be certain that you save enough time to address complex issues. Second, remember that only the simplest issues can be resolved in short meetings. The caution is that you not devote all the time to the simple issues because it is likely that the complex ones are the key to team performance improvement.

At the same time, it will be difficult when addressing the complex issues to keep the team focused on *how to go about solving the problem rather than actually trying to solve it.* Keep the distinction in front of the group and use good facilitation skills.

20 minutes *Evaluation of the Meeting:* Explain to the team members that this is an important, but often overlooked, portion of the meeting. First, it is easy to forget because almost no one evaluates their meetings. (Think of the position we would be in if we were asked to tell our bosses about the quality of most of the meetings they hold!) Second, we never seem to have enough time in the meetings to get everything done. So what goes? The meeting evaluation, of course.

How do you assure time for evaluations?

1. Set start and stop times for each segment of the agenda before you start.
2. Manage the agenda to those time lines.
3. Use "quick-shot" evaluations. Set aside two minutes at the end of the meeting for feedback. Take one minute for rapid fire answers to the questions:

   What went well in the meeting?

   What went poorly in the meeting?

4. Take the second minute for the team to brainstorm the question:

What should we do differently the next time to improve the meeting?

The quick-shot approach will provide all the essential data you need to improve the quality of the meeting. Beware, however, that you need to be assertive about this portion of the meeting. Often team members will not seem interested in giving the feedback, especially if it is negative, and will start to leave the room. Keep them there. Make them finish the meeting.

Also explain there is a second and more complex approach to evaluating meetings. This involves the use of a paper-and-pencil instrument. Distribute and review the Team Meeting Evaluation Form: Instruction Sheet and the Team Meeting Evaluation. Further explain this approach to evaluation normally involves:

- ✓ Passing out the instrument to team members, and giving them time to fill it out.
- ✓ Collecting the completed instruments and summarizing the data.
- ✓ Preparing a visual summary to present at the next team meeting.

Often it is helpful to involve someone from outside the team to perform the analysis and reporting of the evaluation such as a member of the training department or an internal coordinator for the participation process. If no such person is available or necessary, the team can select a team member to perform the analysis and reporting function.

Summarize this evaluation section by asking the team members what sort of evaluation they would like to try. Do they want to start with the formal written evaluation? Would they like to try the quick shot approach? Have the team spend a few moments and come to a consensus decision. *Note:* If it's not an easy decision and starts to take too long, ask the team to wait on deciding until the end of the module. Tell them there is still some important information on responsibilities that you would like to cover.

10 minutes *Frequency of Team Meetings:* Start off by asking the team members the question: How often should the team meet? Let them discuss this for a minute and then say the recommended answer is, "As often as you need to get the job done."

Explain that there are all kinds of team meeting patterns. Some teams meet daily at the beginning and end of the work period to plan work and evaluate progress. Other teams meet only at the beginning of the work period. Some teams meet only once a week. And there are some workplaces that hold team meetings only once a month.

Your team has to decide what will work best for your business and your team strategy. You can also suggest our recommendation: Teams have to meet at least once a week for the meeting experience to have any impact on the business. Otherwise, too much happens to keep up with and issues arise that have to be settled in other ways.

Give the team a few minutes to discuss its options and ask the team members to make a plan. Suggest that they try whatever plan they make and revise it if it does not seem to work.

20 minutes *Roles and Responsibilities in the Team Meeting:* Help the team understand that, unlike most meetings they may have attended in business settings, team meetings involve a number of roles and responsibilities. These include facilitator,

recorder, and team member. Hand out and review a summary of the responsibilities of each.

30 minutes *Team Meeting Logistics:* Distribute the Team Business Meeting Logistics Worksheet. If the team is just starting to hold team meetings, the worksheet questions will serve as guidelines for making decisions about the logistics and conduct of the sessions. Have the team answer each question. If you already have discussed an item and have an answer, just keep moving through the questions until the team has all of its logistics planned.

Also distribute the Checklist for Effective Meetings. Remind the team that holding effective meetings is not as easy as it may appear and every team member is equally responsible. As a summary of an effective meeting, quickly review the checklist. This is a good way to make sure everything gets handled and to illustrate a positive model of effective meetings for the team.

5 minutes *Summary/Close:* Summarize this meeting by expressing how hard it is to run great meetings but how you also think this team has a good shot at it. Remind participants that in achieving meeting effectiveness, practices can make perfect, and that they should look at each meeting as an opportunity to get better. Close by summarizing all the formal agreements that had been made in this meeting. Distribute the evaluation. Thank the participants for their time. Have everyone complete the evaluation.

Meetings are not new to the workplace. In fact, most organizations have plenty of them. Meetings are held to communicate (share information) plan, problem-solve, and so forth.

Unfortunately, most people in an organization do not look forward to them. In some places, the meeting is one of the most dreaded events to take place.

Why would that be?

Meetings and Organizational Pathology. Very likely, what is going wrong in the organization is reflected in the organization's meetings. Whether the characteristic is a manager making all the decisions, people's inability or unwillingness to listen, departments publicly administering punishment for mistakes or assigning blame to others for business problems, what goes on in the workplace day to day shows up in its meetings.

In one organization, a division superintendent used the Monday morning production meeting to "beat up" poor performers (supervisors who did not make production). After a bad week, a supervisor who knew it was "his turn in the barrel" spent a miserable weekend anticipating the Monday morning thrashing. In another organization one manager described the top management team meetings as:

> ... the place where we all came to blame the other guy for our business problems. It didn't take long to separate the group into snakes-in-the-grass, fighters, and guys who ran for the hills. Our meetings weren't just a waste of time, they were destructive.

The manager of this team held less and less meetings because he could not tolerate the unproductive behavior of the team.

What's Wrong with Meetings? If meetings reflect the organization's pathology, what specifically do people say is wrong with them?

- ✓ The purpose is not clear.
- ✓ They take too long, waste a lot of time.
- ✓ A lot of irrelevant discussion takes place.
- ✓ Nothing comes of them.
- ✓ All the real discussion goes on out in the hall after the meeting.
- ✓ Someone dominates the meeting; others don't get a chance to say anything.
- ✓ People have to attend who don't need to be there; people are missing who ought to be there.
- ✓ Nobody listens.
- ✓ The real business is done outside the meeting.
- ✓ People are permitted to abuse co-workers in the meetings.

And so on. If we look at the list more carefully, there are three kind of problems with meetings:

1. Those pertaining to the business of the meeting (goal/task/outcome)
2. Those pertaining to how the meeting is conducted (e.g., a few dominate, no listening)
3. Those pertaining to how the real business of the organization gets done

If these characteristics are what constitute ineffective meetings, the reverse are the characteristics of effective meetings.

Team Meetings and Organizational Change. Our premise is that meetings reflect the nature of the organization. Also, we maintain that meetings can be one of the tools to help change an organization. For example, assume an organization says that to improve it must:

✓ Provide better business information to employees.
✓ Listen better to concerns and issues.
✓ Empower people to influence and make decisions to improve the business.
✓ Improve cooperation between and among departments.
✓ Do better problem solving.
✓ Provide a climate of dignity and respect for employees.

Unfortunately, a frequent approach to achieving these conditions is the "mandate" from a top manager or executive and a "program" to improve problem solving, quality, or productivity.

High-performance organizations need a well thought-out, carefully implemented, and coached/supported process to help create these changes. We propose that properly structured, well-conducted team meetings can be a key tool in helping drive and support an organization to new levels of performance and functioning. Here's how it works.

Team Meetings: The Medium Is the Message. The goals, contents, and outcomes of team meetings send a powerful message to employees about what the organization is trying to achieve. For example, if meetings deal only with trivial issues, or do not transmit critical information, or do not result in anything significant, this tells participants that they are not important or that what they are concerned about is not important. Or, if meetings are used to complain about performance but never to celebrate success, employees learn that the meeting will always be a vehicle for bad news and/or punishment.

If you want to tell participants in a meeting that they are important and that their role is important, it is done through the goals of meetings, the content of meetings, and the conduct of the meetings.

What You Do Speaks So Loud. "… I can't hear what you say," is the rest of the statement. In meetings , this means that *how* you conduct meetings is as critical as *what* the meeting is about. Valuing each individual and showing respect for their concerns are reflected in the way meetings are run. If communication is only one-way, if there is a demonstrated lack of listening, or if participants are criticized or humiliated for what they've done in or out of the meeting, these are definite messages about the organization and the things for which it stands.

Thinking vs. Doing. Finally, where and with whom meetings are held reflect the core philosophy of the business. Since historically meetings were primarily *thinking* events rather than *doing* events, they were the domain of the organization's thinkers (managers). This means that a lot of meetings tend to occur at the top of hierarchies, and few or none at the bottom.

On the other hand, numerous organizations have shown that good team meetings uncover talent the organization has buried beneath the hierarchy, encourage higher levels of commitment to the success of the business, and establish new values on the place of people in the organization. As we pursue a major work culture shift to change the historical notions of work at all levels of the organization, it is important that the organization drive and reinforce the shift with real events—not symbolic ones—that both teach and encourage thinking behavior.

The Team Meeting. We believe the team meeting is a key element of a comprehensive strategy to provide employees legitimate, important, and ongoing involvement in the business. The approach to team meetings described in this module is designed to reinforce both the *what* of meetings and the *how* of meetings. Further, the team meeting model can be based at any level of an organization and, we believe, should be replicated in the hierarchy to help align the organization's words with its actions.

Implementing Team Meetings. Effective team meetings require considerable planning, preparation, and support to make them work. Team meetings, as described here, are a minor structural/activity change in the functioning of the organization. Yet they are a major attempt to drive the new culture based on human values and new levels of excellence deep into the organization. To treat team meetings otherwise not only invites, but quite likely encourages, the effort to fail.

TEAM MEETING PLANNING TOOL

HANDOUT 10-2

Topic	Outcome Desired	Responsibility	Time
Example: Employee Survey	Decision about whether to proceed or not.	Harshman	20 min.
Equipment Purchase	Update of task force work.	Phillips	3 min.
Evaluate Meeting	Determine the strengths and weaknesses of this meeting.	Participants	5 min.
Agenda for Next Meeting	Specify topics, outcomes, and responsiblity for next meeting.	Participants	5 min.

Meeting: ______________________________ Date: __________

SPECIAL MEETING PLANNER

HANDOUT 10-3

Special Planner

Subject: ______________________________

Called by: ______________________________ Date: __________

Location: ______________________________

Start Time: __________ End Time: __________ Total: __________

Attendees:

1. ______	5. ______	9. ______
2. ______	6. ______	10. ______
3. ______	7. ______	11. ______
4. ______	8. ______	12. ______

Purpose of Meeting

____

____

____

____

____

Planned Outcome(s)

____

____

____

____

Agenda Items	Time	Person Responsible
1.		
2.		
3.		
4.		
5.		
6.		
7.		

Material and Preparation Needed	Person Responsible
1.	
2.	
3.	
4.	

Meeting Notes

Action Items	Person Responsible

TEAM BUSINESS MEETINGS GOALS

✓ To create a climate of teamwork among managers, supervisors, team leaders, and the members of the team.

✓ To promote effective two-way communication through shared business information.

✓ To provide a setting in which to identify, prioritize, and/or resolve work issues.

✓ To provide a context for collaborative decision making.

TEAM MEETING MODEL

HANDOUT 10-5

Meeting Component (How Time Is Used)	What Occurs During This Portion of the Meeting	Anticipated Outcome in an Effective Meeting
Business Information and Performance Feedback (approximately 1/3 of meeting)	a. Team members receive information about general business issues not provided elsewhere. b. Team members get update on key performance indicators in order to know how they are doing.	Team members are knowledgeable about the business as a whole and about where they stand with regard to business goals and criteria.
Listening (approximately 1/3 of meeting)	a. Team members give supervision and/or facilitators information about unresolved issues in the workplace. b. Team members request information on topics and issues about which they need to know more.	All issues and questions are on the table and are either answered or resolved in the meeting or put on the agenda for the next meeting.
Decision Making and Issue Identification (approximately 1/3 of meeting)	Ideas, issues, and problems presented by management, supervision, other departments, or team members are discussed. Although some decision making may occur in the meeting, usually team members discuss either who decides or how to go about solving a problem.	a. Decisions are made or problems solved. b. Or team members decide how to deal with the issue outside the meeting.
Meeting Evaluation (last 2–3 minutes)	Team members review the quality of the meeting and make recommendations for improvement in the future.	a. Team leader and facilitator(s) have information on what went well and what went poorly in the meeting. b. There are recommendations about how to improve meetings in the future.

TEAM MEETING EVALUATION FORM: INSTRUCTION SHEET

Attached is a short assessment instrument that the team can use to monitor the quality and character of team meetings. The instrument has sections on:

- ✓ Meeting mechanics
- ✓ % team members
- ✓ % meeting facilitators
- ✓ % pluses, minuses, and improvements

The aims are to:

1. Identify strengths and weaknesses.
2. Determine what the team should continue to do and what needs to be done to improve the meetings.

A procedure to use if the team wants to conserve meeting time is to:

- ✓ Distribute the instrument at the end of one meeting

  Ask team members to fill out the instruments and return them to a designated member. (You may choose to have someone outside the team perform the analysis and reporting function)

  The designated team member:

  Tallies team responses to the survey questions.

  Prepares a newsprint summary to use at the next meeting.

- ✓ At the next meeting, the team reviews results as part of the meeting agenda.

  The conclusions should be recorded for review at a future session.

The team should conduct a formal review every three to six months for the first year and at least twice a year thereafter.

TEAM MEETING EVALUATION FORM

Department/Business Team: ______________________________ **Date:** ____________

The Team:	**Always**	**Sometimes**	**Never**
1. Meets regularly.	(1)	(2)	(3)
2. Starts the meetings on time.	(1)	(2)	(3)
3. Ends the meetings on time.	(1)	(2)	(3)
4. Posts the agenda.	(1)	(2)	(3)
5. Has good attendance.	(1)	(2)	(3)
6. Uses resource people as needed.	(1)	(2)	(3)
7. Keeps minutes of the meeting.	(1)	(2)	(3)
8. Evaluates the meetings.	(1)	(2)	(3)
9. Thinks meetings are worthwhile.	(1)	(2)	(3)

Team Members:	**Not True at All**		**Somewhat True**		**Very True**
10. Use resource people as needed.	(1)	(2)	(3)	(4)	(5)
11. Keep minutes of the meeting.	(1)	(2)	(3)	(4)	(5)
12. Evaluate the meetings.	(1)	(2)	(3)	(4)	(5)
13. Think meetings are worthwhile.	(1)	(2)	(3)	(4)	(5)

Meeting Facilitator(s):	**Always**		**Sometimes**		**Never**
14. Is (are) well organized.	(1)	(2)	(3)	(4)	(5)
15. Give(s) the information needed.	(1)	(2)	(3)	(4)	(5)
16. Encourage(s) open communication and listening.	(1)	(2)	(3)	(4)	(5)
17. Manage(s) conflict well.	(1)	(2)	(3)	(4)	(5)
18. Do(es) a good job recording and using visual aids.	(1)	(2)	(3)	(4)	(5)

In your opinion, what is *positive* about your team meetings?

In your opinion, what is *negative* about your team meetings?

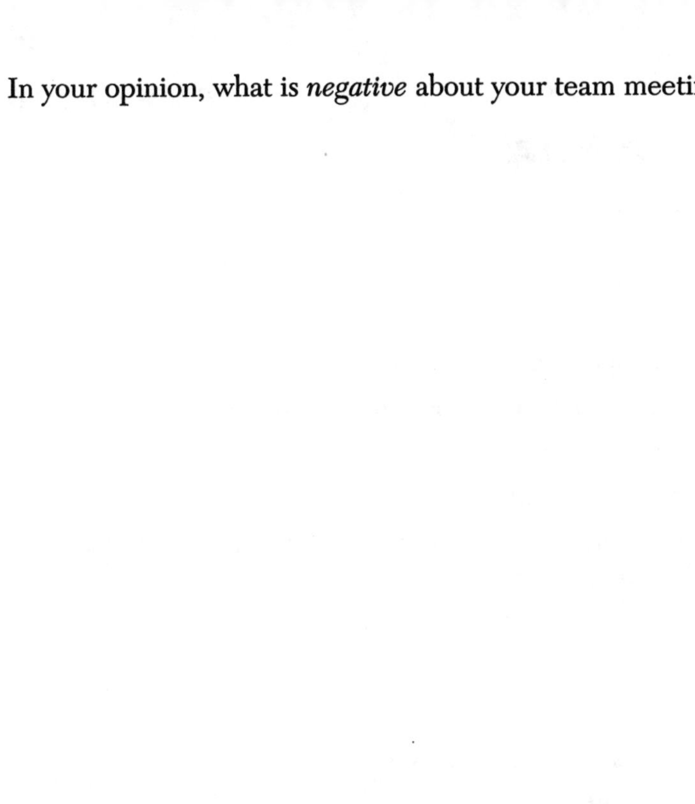

What would you do to *improve* the meetings?

Thank You

RESPONSIBILITIES OF THE FACILITATOR IN TEAM MEETINGS

Before the Meeting

✓ Schedule meeting time, place, date, equipment.

✓ Notify team members and contact appropriate resource persons.

✓ Check on members who have assignments.

✓ Gather information pertinent to meeting.

✓ Discuss any problems (stated or anticipated) with management, staff services, and/or union leadership.

✓ Prepare agenda and forward it to the Recorder.

During the Meeting

✓ Introduce any new members and/or guests to the team.

✓ Review minutes of last meeting.

✓ Identify purpose of the meeting (or outline goals).

✓ Review meeting agenda with group.

✓ Distribute and explain new materials.

✓ Help group communicate effectively:

Encourage listening.

Manage conflicts.

See that the agenda is followed.

Keep communication open.

Clarify ambiguities.

Reach group decisions.

End of Meeting

✓ Delegate follow-up assignments to members.

✓ Restate important points.

✓ Conduct evaluation of meeting.

✓ Help group decide on next meeting date, time, and place.

✓ Make sure the agenda is set for the next meeting.

✓ Close the meeting on a positive note. For example:

Congratulate members on performance.

Recognize important decisions reached.

Express appreciation for group cooperation.

RESPONSIBILITIES OF THE RECORDER IN TEAM MEETINGS

Before the Meeting

✓ Prepare minutes from previous meeting.

✓ Forward minutes to facilitators and coordinator(s).

✓ Distribute minutes to members prior to next meeting.

✓ Post and/or distribute agenda for next meeting.

During the Meeting

✓ Act as the team's memory.

✓ Keep a running summary of meeting on flip chart.

✓ Ask members to comment on notes for possible additions or deletions.

✓ Record group consensus on decisions.

End of the Meeting

✓ Write agenda items for next meeting and record follow-up items.

RESPONSIBILITIES OF THE MEMBERS IN TEAM MEETINGS

Before the Meeting

✓ Submit agenda items to facilitator(s) for the next meeting.
✓ Complete follow-up assignments from the last meeting.
✓ Arrive on time.
✓ Come prepared to contribute to changes through open discussion and cooperation.

During the Meeting

✓ Recognize and encourage members.
✓ Discuss meeting goal(s) and commit to reaching it/them.
✓ Participate by sharing ideas.
✓ Clarify any misunderstandings.
✓ Adhere to agenda.
✓ Avoid unnecessary comments/conflicts.
✓ *Listen* carefully to everyone's ideas.
✓ Ask questions when confused.
✓ Motivate the group.
✓ Reach decisions.

End of the Meeting

✓ Accept follow-up assignments.
✓ Contribute to meeting evaluation by suggesting ways for future improvement.
✓ Reinforce the team culture by recognizing team members for achievements.
✓ Share results with members from other groups ("spread the good word").

TEAM BUSINESS MEETING LOGISTICS WORKSHEET

✓ How often will the team meet?

✓ Where will the meetings be held? Who is responsible for scheduling the room?

✓ How long will each meeting last?

✓ Who will gather business information and update performance measures?

(The Business Information Management module addresses this issue also. When you get to that module, refer to your discussion here, or you may want to wait until after that module to assign this responsibility.)

✓ What form will the visual aids take (e.g., charts with team performance)? Who is responsible for updating them prior to the meeting?

✓ Who will facilitate the meetings? Is there newsprint in the room, or do you have to take it with you?

✓ Who will take the minutes for the meeting? Are they typed up? Who does that? Who is responsible for distribution? Who gets copies?

✓ How will others know what you have done in your meetings? Do they get copies of the minutes? Verbal updates?

✓ Is there anyone beyond the immediate team who needs to attend your meetings on a regular basis? When there are specific issues? Who invites them?

✓ What do we do if people are absent from a meeting and we need to make a consensus decision?

CHECKLIST FOR EFFECTIVE MEETINGS

Team: ______________________________ Date of Meeting: ____________

Several Days Before the Meeting:

______ Confirm that room is scheduled.

______ Review issues from last meeting: Do follow-up.

______ Plan agenda.

______ Post notice; notify team.

______ Invite resource person(s).

Day of the Meeting/Before the Meeting:

______ Set up room.

______ Check audiovisuals.

______ Post newsprint.

______ Post agenda.

The Meeting:

______ Note attendance.

______ Start on time.

______ Cover full agenda.

______ Provide business information.

______ Review performance.

______ Educate/instruct (optional).

______ Hold listening session.

______ Identify problems/issues, select strategies.

______ Take minutes.

______ Make assignments.

______ Have team review meeting (evaluation).

______ Confirm next meeting time and place.

______ Discuss items for next agenda.

______ Stop on time.

After the Meeting:

______ Save critical newsprint sheets.

______ Type, post, and/or distribute minutes.

______ Check on status of assignments.

______ Follow up on questions, issues, or problems.

______ Schedule room for the next meeting.

Module 11

Team Decision Making

(2 hours)

Objective To help the team understand the various influences on decision making, different approaches to decision making, and a method of determining the best approach to making a decision, given the issue and people involved.

Materials Needed

✓ *Flipcharts:* Objectives, Key Learning Points, and Topics (copy from this page)

Influences on Decision Making (page 158)

✓ *Handouts:* Options in Decision Making (page 159)
Analysis of Decision Making at Present (page 160)
Analysis of Decision Making at Present: Discussion Questions (page 161)
Analysis of Decision Making in the Future (page 162)
Thoughts on Decision Making (page 163)
Analysis of Decision Making in the Future: Discussion Questions (page 164)
Critical Factors in Decision Making (page 165)
Final Thoughts on Decision Making (page 166)
Evaluation (Appendix)

Key Learning Points

✓ Surveying decision making in organizations.

✓ Understanding patterns in present decision making and preferred patterns for future decision making.

✓ Identifying key points related to, and pitfalls in, decision making.

Topics

✓ Decision Making in Organizations:

Influences on Decision Making

Options in Making Decisions

Choosing the Best Option

Role of the Team in Decision Making

✓ Five Approaches to Decision Making

✓ Present and Future Decision Making Based on the Five Approaches

✓ A Strategy for Proceeding

✓ Evaluation

Procedural Outline

Time **Activity**

Preparation: Read through this module carefully. Spend some time with the material in the introduction: influences on decision making, options in decision making, choosing the best way to make a decision, and the role of teams in decision making. After you digest all this useful information, you may even want to write an outline or short lecturette to present to the team. Further, be sure to master the process of the exercises and to be clear about the critical factors in decision making. There is a great deal of powerful information in this module. You may want to read through it more than once.

5 minutes *Introduction:* Open this module by posting and describing the module objective, key learning points, and topics for this session. Give a short lecturette to the team. Open by expressing that decision making is one of the most important functions in organizations. Daily, hourly, even minute by minute, everyone in the organization makes decisions that affect the lives of others and the success of the business. The *quality* of these decisions and the *timeliness* with which they are made are measures of the effectiveness of decision making in the organization.

Historically, one benchmark of good leaders or managers is their ability to make good decisions quickly. George C. Scott, in his portrayal of Patton at the height of battle, is one such image who comes to mind. Western culture with its hierarchical structures emphasizes the role of the individual in decision making. The better a person is at making decisions, the better leader that person is judged to be.

Today's business, economic, and social environments bring new dimensions to decision making. The decisions with which we are faced are more complex than in the past and the pace of change requires that decisions be made more quickly. To add to the complexity of decision making, the electronic information age brings with it the potential for having more data than ever to the decision process.

15 minutes *Influences on Decision Making:* To understand decision making, one must understand the influences on the decision making process. Draw Figure 11-1 on a blank flipchart and explain this figure depicts the major variables at work in decision making. The four major forces are:

Culture of the Organization: Your organization's culture is a primary force on decision making. The extent, for example, that the top leadership group is viewed as smarter than the rest of the workforce, and therefore the appropriate group to make decisions, influences to a great extent what decisions are made by whom. Or certain functional groups may have special status in the organization. In one Fortune 100 company in the 1970s, finance had that position; in another, it was engineering. To the extent to which an organization "reveres" certain functions affects how those functions influence decisions.

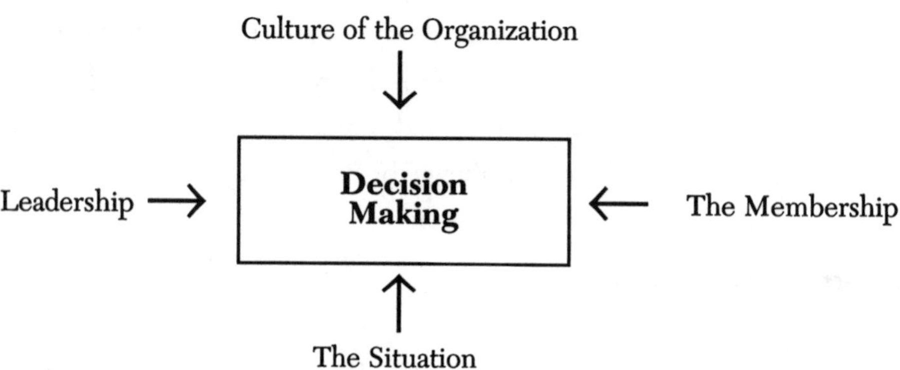

Figure 11-1. Influences on decision making.

The type of organization also influences the role of culture in decision making. Historically, for example, decisions are made differently in the military than in universities, differently in churches than in factories, and so forth. The differences show up in who is involved in the decision-making process and the role of leadership in decision making.

The Leader: Volumes have been written about leadership and leaders. In organizations, the nature and character of the individual leader make a lot of difference in how decisions are made. On the downside, most of us have worked for individuals whose egos depended on their being in charge or who just assumed they were smarter than everyone else (but weren't). On the upside, certain leaders inspire good work; we would do just about anything they asked because of who they are and how they manage. With these examples, one can see that the characteristics of the leader—intelligence, personal style, and experience—influence the leader's role in decision making.

The Membership of Organizations: Various factors come to play in analyzing the role of organizational members (e.g., employees, parishioners, students) in decision making. Of utmost importance is the members' perceptions of their role in the process. For example, college students of the 1940s and 1950s did not appear to believe they had much influence on decision making in the institution. Yet, by the late 1960s and early 1970s, students were demanding a say in hiring, curriculum, and even seats on boards of trustees in some institutions.

In addition to the general perception of role, the membership's capabilities and experience will have an effect on decision making. For example, when workers are young and/or inexperienced, they tend to want a great deal of guidance and leadership. In that case, they do not have strong roles in decision making. As they become more "intelligent" in the sense of knowing how the work is done and what makes for good quality and productivity, they become more able to contribute to planning and decision making.

The Situation: The field of *situational leadership* is based on the premise that the situation is a major influence on the nature of leadership and hence on decision making. For example, if a fire breaks out in a building, the superintendent is not likely to convene tenants to see whether they think everyone should evacuate. The alarm will be sounded and everyone is expected to leave the building. In this case, urgency plays a role in how the decision is made. Employees of a corporation are not asked to vote for the candidate they want to be the new chairman of the board of directors. The legal context dictates how that decision is made.

Historically, business organizations provided few opportunities for employees to be involved in making major decisions because they lacked the knowledge and proper experience to make good decisions. Therefore, the responsibility for making most decisions rested with top leadership. As workers become smarter, gain access to more information, and become more experienced they bring a new resource to the decision-making process and therefore change the context in which decisions are made.

10 minutes *Options in Decision Making:* There are two parts to decision making: (1) the decision and (2) how the decision is made. This section deals with the latter. Hand out Options in Decision Making and explain that this model displays options in how to make decisions. The options are on a continuum. At the left end is decision making in which the leader maintains the authority and makes the decision.

There is very little influence or involvement of subordinates. As we move to the right, the leader uses less authority and the influence of the subordinates increases. The first shift involves asking the team for input on how to implement the decision (that the leader made). From there, we move to a decision process in which the team has the opportunity to provide input *prior* to the decision being made. At this point, however, the leader is still making the decision.

In stage 4 the first significant shift occurs. Here, the team collaborates with the leader to make the decision. Both generally have to agree before a decision is final. As noted, the consensus decision-making process is often employed. In stage 5, the leader delegates the decision to the team. The leader's role in this case is to set the boundaries for the decision (e.g., the budget allowed, the time frame in which the decision must be made, the "rules" that apply, such as no additional staff may be added). Once these are set, the team has the responsibility and the authority to make the decision.

10 minutes *Choosing the Best Way to Make a Decision:* How do leaders and teams decide which way to make a decision? There is a tendency in participative processes for team members to think there should be a radical shift to the right (team involvement in decisions) that is as extreme as the old authoritarian model was to the left.

The best organizations have a balance of decision-making processes based on a set of criteria. Write Information/Expertise, The Time Frame for a Decision, and The Need for Acceptance on a blank flipchart sheet. Explain that these are the key variables in choosing the right decision process:

✓ *Information/expertise:* The amount of information/expertise the potential decision makers have. If the leader of a team, for example, has all the information needed, then consulting someone or a group is a waste of time. [*Note:* A lot of times, leaders think they have all the information and expertise required, but do not. Knowing when to ask for input is critical.]

✓ *The time frame for the decision:* How quickly the decision has to be made. The less time available, the more likely we are to have a single person, usually the leader, make a decision. Getting input and involvement takes time. [*Note:* Leaders sometimes fail to plan for decisions. This results in having little or no time left to get input. Failing to plan is not a valid use of the time criterion.]

✓ *Need for acceptance:* This is perhaps the key variable of the three and the most often ignored. Leaders sometimes think because the decision is correct (their judgment), employees will understand and accept it. (Just, for example, as some employees think that, because they didn't have input, the decision is probably not optimal.) The need for acceptance or "buy-in" is critical if employees will have to implement the decision for it to be successful. The principle is: The more important it is for the team to buy the decision, the more to the right the decision process needs to move. (See Handout 11-1.)

Unfortunately, there is no clear formula for deciding the decision process for each and every decision. All of the variables in Fig. 11-1 interact and mix with these criteria stated. The decision process is a product of all those things (and often the nature and character of leadership in the organization).

5 minutes *The Role of the Team in Decision Making:* Describe to the team how problem-solving and decision-making research tell us that, for complex decisions where

an individual does not possess all the information or expertise needed, two elements improve the quality of the outcome (write the following two items on a blank flipchart sheet and explain):

1. The involvement of the right people in the definition, analysis, and conclusion/implementation
2. The investment of sufficient time in planning/problem solving versus implementing or redoing our solutions/decisions

Unfortunately, neither our traditional business structures (the hierarchy with strong leaders) nor the classic leadership in most large organizations is geared to team-oriented decision making. Our action-oriented culture ("Don't just stand there. Do something—even if it's wrong!") and the focus on the individual-as-hero (reinforced by everything from most valuable player awards to corporate incentive systems) result in decision-making structures and processes focused on individuals rather than on teams.

The process of developing this team says your organization is trying to change the old paradigm. Tell the group that the remainder of this module is designed to begin the process of change. Please understand, however, the historic model of decision making and problem solving is based on centuries of Western culture and reinforced by decades of the American experience in organizing and running complex work systems. Changing those histories will neither be quick nor easy, but we have to start somewhere.

The Remainder of This Module: There are two parts to the remainder of this module. The first is devoted to analyzing the organization's present decision-making patterns with respect to decisions that affect the team. The second is dedicated to proposing how decision making should be done in the future.

45 minutes *Exercise: Analysis of a Decision-Making Process:* Tell the group that the purpose of this exercise is to help the team understand present patterns and modes of decision making in your organization. This provides a basis for analyzing how you think decisions should be made in the future.

Distribute the Analysis of Decision Making at Present handout and explain that the chart lists the five different modes of decision making employed in organizations. Their task is to think about decisions at present and identify the team's relationship to that decision making.

Have the Team

1. Brainstorm a list of important decisions that affect the team and its work. (Put the list on newsprint for everyone to see.)
2. Use a quick selection process (e.g., narrowing) to choose up to five of those decisions for the exercise.
3. List the five in column 1 of the handout. The order does not matter.
4. Now, as a team, analyze each decision and put a checkmark in the column that best describes the team's involvement in, or relationship to, that decision.

When you have completed these steps, distribute the Analysis of Decision Making at Present: Discussion Questions. Have the team work through these questions and their answers together. The answers to these questions should give the team members some idea of what they think about decision making at present.

Next, distribute the Analysis of Decision Making in the Future handout and walk the team though the purpose, task, and procedure. Also distribute and discuss the Thoughts on Decision Making. Finally, distribute and as a team discuss the Analysis of Decision Making in the Future: Discussion Questions. The answers to these questions should give the team some idea about the possibilities and problems related to changing decision making in the organization.

Summarize this exercise by distributing and reviewing the Critical Factors in Decision Making handout. Be sure to review each of the following items.

1. Be clear about the decision to be made and the goals to be achieved. *Do not assume that everyone involved understands either the decision or the goals in the same way.* If you are not clear about both and try to proceed, you will have trouble somewhere along the way.
2. Be clear about:
   a. Who makes the final decision and his or her role in the decision process
   b. Who needs to be:

      Part of the decision-making process

      Consulted during the decision-making process

      Informed of the final decision
3. Be clear about any boundaries related to the decision:
   a. Limitations related to budget, staffing, etc.
   b. Time constraints
4. Be clear about any data and assumptions related to the decision. Thinking you know what is true and/or thinking that everyone has the same data or assumptions is sometimes a precursor to problems in the process or with the final decision.
5. Avoid starting (even implicitly) with a decision or solution and working backward. In problem solving, we call this "solutioning." This means that you know what you want to do before you start and simply use the decision-making process as a showplace for your decision. This is the kind of thinking and action that leads to less than optimal decisions from individuals. Don't let it happen to the team!

15 minutes *Summary:* As a result of this exercise, the team should have a broadened picture of present patterns of decision making in the organization and the roots of those patterns. In addition, the team members have developed a preferred profile for decision making as it relates to the team's involvement.

The big question to pose to the team is: How could you begin to move toward the preferred profile of decision making?

Help the team process this question. Actually, the team could do a variety of things. One idea is to invite the team's boss and boss's boss to the next team meeting. Explain this exercise and your responses to it. Show him or her the results you came up with as a team.

Then ask how you might influence a change in the future with regard to some of the decisions. (Pick two or three you would really like to see change.) This should provide the basis for an interesting discussion about decision making, control, and involvement.

Such an experience will begin to build a path to the leadership of the organization so that the team can begin to influence decision making in the best interests of the business and the people. That's the ultimate goal.

5 minutes *Summary/Close:* Bring this session to a close by distributing the Final Thoughts on Decision Making handout. Tell the group this process is a sure fire way to help the team make sound decisions. Walk through each step and help the team understand its importance. Finally close this session by distributing the evaluation, asking the participants for their feedback and thanking everyone for their time.

INFLUENCES ON DECISION MAKING

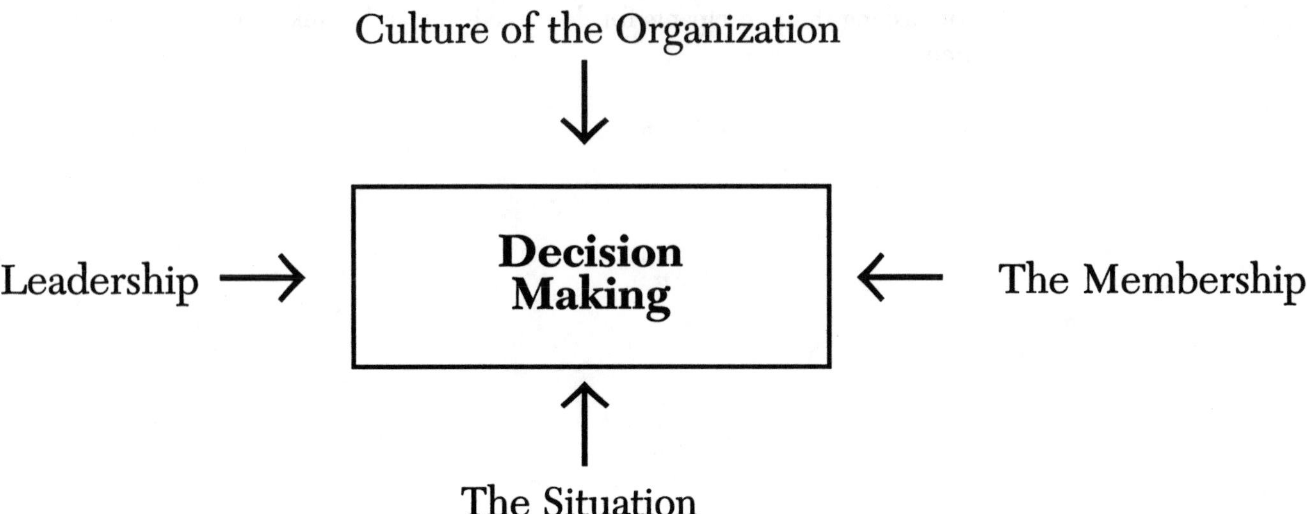

OPTIONS IN DECISION MAKING

Leader-Centered Decision Making				**Team-Centered Decision Making**
← Control and Authority				Participation and Influence →
1	**2**	**3**	**4**	**5**
Leader makes decision and either tells the team or tries to sell the team on the idea.	Leader makes the decision, but consults the team on how to implement it.	The team has the opportunity to give input prior to the leader's making the decision.	Leader jointly makes the decision with the team—*consensus* is a common tool used.	Leader sets guidelines and delegates responsibility for decision to the team.

ANALYSIS OF DECISION MAKING AT PRESENT

Decisions	Team's Relationship to the Decisions				
	The team is informed about a decision made by leadership.	**The team is consulted about how to implement a decision made by leadership.**	**The team provides prior input to leadership on a decision to be made by leadership.**	**The team makes the decision jointly with leadership.**	**Leadership sets guidelines and delegates responsibility for making the decision to the team.**
Example: Layout of work area	✓				
Example: Team meeting				✓	

ANALYSIS OF DECISION MAKING AT PRESENT: DISCUSSION QUESTIONS

- ✓ Is there a pattern in your analysis? For example, are there differences between the kinds of decisions in which the team has a say (✓s in the two right columns) and those in which it does not (✓s in the two left columns)?
- ✓ Is the pattern different in the last year than in the past (say, ten years)? That is, have you seen a significant change since the organization made a commitment to move toward a team environment?
- ✓ How do you rate the quality of decision making in the organization (excellent, good, fair, poor)? What factors contribute to your rating?
- ✓ How, in general, does the team feel about the present pattern of decision making?
- ✓ Does the present process of decision making help or hurt the team's performance? Why?

ANALYSIS OF DECISION MAKING IN THE FUTURE

The Purpose. To get an idea about how the team thinks it should relate to decision making in the future.

The Task. To re-rate the decisions in the prior handout based on how you think these decisions should be made in the future.

The Procedure

1. Return to the table where you analyzed the team's relationship to decisions at present.
2. Using the same list of decisions (column 1), do a second rating based on *how you think the team should relate to those decisions in the future.*
3. Put a circle in the column that represents your opinion.

Decisions	Team's Relationship to the Decisions				
	The team is informed about a decision made by leadership.	The team is consulted about how to implement a decision made by leadership.	The team provides prior input to leadership on a decision to be made by leadership.	The team makes the decision jointly with leadership.	Leadership sets guidelines and delegates responsibility for making the decision to the team.
Layout of work area	✓		0		
Team meeting frequency				✓	0

4. See the Thoughts on Decision Making on the next handout before completing the exercise.

✓ Effective organizations employ patterns of decision making that utilize all of the approaches shown in the scale on the previous handout. Therefore, effective teams will make, and will have made for them, decisions at every point on this continuum.

✓ It is not in the best interests of the business and the people to make all decisions autocratically or participatively.

✓ Ultimately, the effective team needs two kinds of abilities:

The ability to choose correctly the best way to make a given decision

The knowledge, skills, and relationships to make the decision in the chosen manner

ANALYSIS OF DECISION MAKING IN THE FUTURE: DISCUSSION QUESTIONS

- ✓ Is the pattern in your analysis of the future different than your pattern of responses for the present? If so, how?
- ✓ Why do you think the present pattern is as it is?
- ✓ How would changing to the preferred decision-making pattern improve the performance of your business?
- ✓ What would have to change for the decision making of the future to become a reality? In leadership? In the team?
- ✓ What are the barriers to the changes being made?

1. Be clear about the decision to be made and the goals to be achieved.

2. Be clear about who makes the final decision, who needs to be consulted before the decision is made, and who needs to be informed after the decision is made.

3. Be clear about any boundaries related to the decision.

4. Be clear about any data and assumptions related to the decision.

5. Avoid starting with a decision or solution and working backward.

FINAL THOUGHTS ON DECISION MAKING

When you get to the point of making decisions in the team, here are the general steps involved:

1. Define the decision to be made.
2. Be clear about the goal or outcome you want from the decision.
3. Decide the team's role in the decision (consultant, decision maker, etc.). [If the team is involved in the decision, proceed to step 4.]
4. Decide who should be involved in the decision and how.
5. Define and analyze:
   - **a.** The boundaries (limitations) of the decision.
   - **b.** The opportunities and resources available.
   - **c.** The information you need to make a good decision.
6. Develop some tentative alternative decisions.
7. Select the decision most likely to achieve the goals within the given constraints.
8. Develop an action (implementation) plan.
9. Determine how and when you would evaluate the effectiveness of the decision if it were implemented.

Module 12

Problem Solving

(2 hours)

Objective To understand a systematic approach to problem solving and the application of that approach to the resolution of team business issues.

Materials Needed

✓ *Flipcharts:* Objectives, Key Learning Points, and Topics (copy from this page)

Effective Problem Solving in High-Performance Teams (page 172)

✓ *Handouts:* Teams and Problem Solving (page 173)
Problem-Solving Cycle (page 175)
Brainstorming (page 182)
Narrowing (page 183)
Cause and Effect Diagram (page 184)
Polling (Multivote Technique) (page 185)
Sample Polling Sheet (page 186)
Histogram (page 187)
Run Chart (page 188)
Process Flow Chart (page 189)
Problem-Solving Case (page 190)
Sample Process Flow Chart (page 191)
Technique Selection Guide (page 192)
Team Proposal (page 193)
Proposal Tracking Chart (page 196)
Evaluation (Appendix)

Key Learning Points

✓ Understanding a systematic approach to problem solving.

✓ Understanding the synergism of a good problem-solving methodology and effective interpersonal approaches in the team.

✓ Applying the problem-solving/issue-resolution model to team business.

Topics

✓ Teams and Problem Solving

✓ The Problem-Solving Model

✓ Problem-Solving Tools

✓ Integrating Task and Process

✓ Managing Team Proposals

✓ Evaluation

Procedural Outline

Time **Activity**

Preparation: Before you begin this module, become familiar with the problem-solving cycle and all the related tools, techniques, and forms. This helps you facilitate the team toward a deeper understanding of the problem-solving process.

5 minutes *Introduction:* Open this module by posting and describing the module objective, key learning points, and topics for the session. To get started with this module, give the team a brief lecturette on teams and problem solving. Help the team understand the history of team and problem solving by discussing quality circles and the context in which they failed. Also tell them about problem-solving skill and ability and how teams must have the discipline to follow a few simple guidelines. Finally, discuss that, in problem solving, a team must concentrate on both task and process. Use the Teams and Problem Solving handout as the basis for your talk. Distribute the handout if you think the team members need something more concrete than a short talk.

The Problem-Solving Model: The pages in the problem-solving model handout describe the model for the team. Several good problem-solving models and materials are available. If your organization presently uses a different model, feel free to replace this one with it.

Regardless of the model you choose, all problem-solving approaches follow a logical process through a sequence of steps. The process begins with problem identification. Unless the team does this step well, it is difficult to solve the problem efficiently and effectively.

Distribute the Problem-Solving Cycle handout. Overview the problem-solving cycle by explaining that from *problem identification,* you move to *setting objectives.* This step helps the team focus on what it wants to achieve by solving the problem.

The *analysis of the problem* is a key step in isolating the potential causes. Like problem definition, the problem analysis step is key to ultimate success.

The problem definition, objectives, and analysis all serve as a foundation for *generating solutions.* This step provides the team an opportunity to combine their knowledge and skills to create an effective solution to the problem.

Next comes the *evaluation of alternative solutions* and the selection of the one deemed most likely to provide a permanent solution to the problem. The actual *selection of the solution* occurs in step VI.

Once the solution has been chosen, the team creates an *action plan* for implementing the solution.

From there, the team *submits a proposal* for the solution to the problem and, if accepted, oversees the *implementation of the solution.*

Finally, the *evaluation plan* provides the team with not only a set of criteria and tools to assess the extent to which their solution works, but also a process to update the strategy.

Work with the team and review each page of the handout so that each team member understands the purpose of all ten problem-solving steps, the process by which to use each step, the recommendation associated with each step, and when to leave one step and proceed to the next.

Problem-Solving Tools: Now that the team has had a chance to overview the problem-solving cycle, each team member should know how to use a series of tools and techniques to reach the outcome of each step in the problem-solving cycle. The following is an explanation of some of those tools. The list is not exhaustive, but rather is intended as a representative sample containing frequently used tools and techniques.

Also, explain to the team members that the most important technique the team will use to move from step to step is *consensus.* At the end of each step, the team has to reach consensus on the product(s) of that step in order to move on. It would probably be helpful for the team to review the module on consensus (Module 3) before beginning any real life problem-solving process.

For now, we will begin the review of the tools for the problem-solving/decision-making processes. In the following pages you will cover:

- ✓ *Brainstorming:* A tool to encourage creative thinking in the team. Using brainstorming, the team can generate higher-quality and more widely ranging ideas than is possible for the typical individual working alone.
- ✓ *Narrowing:* A technique to reduce a list of options (perhaps generated by a brainstorming process) to a select a few options or just one.
- ✓ *Fishbone:* A technique to organize your data to move toward identifying the root causes of the problem with which you are working.
- ✓ *Polling:* A technique to assess the interest of the team with regard to a set of options for which there is no clear choice or preference.
- ✓ *Histogram:* A visual display tool based on organizing data to assess problem-related factors.
- ✓ *Run chart:* A simple display to summarize trends related to processes.
- ✓ *Process chart:* A listing of the sequence of events in a process or work flow.

Explain that each technique can be used in many different situations and it just takes:

1. Being familiar enough with each technique to have it in your repertoire.
2. Practicing each technique until its application becomes second nature.

Tell the team that we will overview each tool or technique one at a time.

Brainstorming: Distribute the Brainstorming handout and help the team understand its purpose, process, and helpful implementation hints.

Narrowing: Distribute the Narrowing handout and help the team understand its purpose, process, and helpful implementation hints.

Cause and Effect Diagram (Fishbone): Distribute the Cause and Effect Diagram handout and help the team understand what it is, when to use it, and how to use it.

Polling: Distribute the Polling (Multivote Technique) handout and help the team understand what it is, how it works, and what is done after the polling is completed.

Histogram: Distribute the Histogram handout and help the team understand what it is, when to use it, how it works, and other helpful hints.

Run Chart: Distribute the Run Chart handout and help the team understand what it is, when to use it, how to use it, and other helpful hints.

Process Flow Chart: Distribute the Process Flow Chart handout and help the team understand what it is, when to use it, how it works, and other helpful hints.

Technique Selection Guide: As a summary to the tools and techniques section, hand out the Technique Selection Guide. This guide provides some suggestions for matching the problem-solving tools with various tasks in the problem-solving cycle. Work with the team to review each task and its related techniques.

Integrating Task and Process: Tell the team that, after reviewing the problem-solving model, it is time to get some practice at applying the model. Essentially, to be effective at problem solving, you need to combine your knowledge and skills in working through the problem-solving steps (task) with the team relationship skills (process) developed in earlier modules. These include communication, listening, giving and receiving feedback, resolving conflict, running effective meetings, and so forth.

Draw the following model on a flipchart and explain that it describes the combination of both task skills and process skills for effective problem solving.

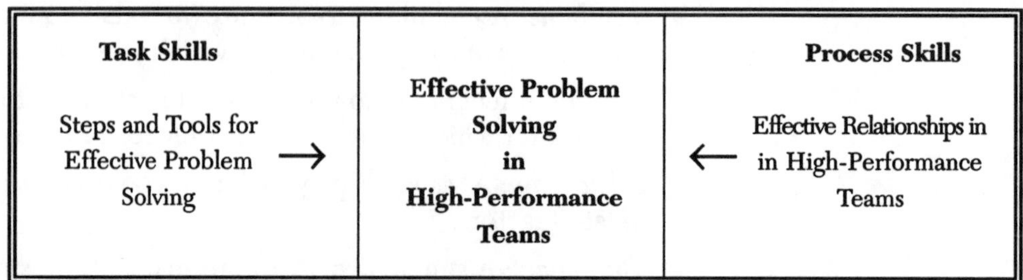

Also explain that some have called the successful combination of the two sets of knowledge and skills "synergy." *Synergy* is thought of as the combination of independent things such that the impact of the total is greater than any individual component would yield alone.

The point is that the extent to which the team is not proficient at, or successful in, using either set of skills is the extent to which the quality of the team problem solving and decision making will suffer.

30 minutes *Problem-Solving Exercise:* Now that the team has had a chance to review the problem-solving cycle and tools, have them practice. The more problem-solving practice team members get using a structured problem-solving process, the easier it gets and the more effective they become. Distribute the Problem Solving Case. Instruct the team to follow the problem-solving cycle and to use any tools they need to come up with a recommended solution. Help them stay on track, use effective tools, and work through any frustration they may encounter.

Note: Special instructions. If asked, it would be possible to allow 3 or 4 people to be gone at the same time if workers are willing to work overtime.

Managing Team Proposals: Once the team has completed work on a project or issue, it is time to enter the decision stream to get some action. The following sections contain two tools for managing team proposals. Distribute the Team Proposal handout. Explain that this form provides an outline for recording the essential components of your problem-solving process as well as the elements of the solution. The team should prepare this form whenever it is dealing with a complex decision. If the decision is within the responsibility of the team, the proposal form is a record of the plan. If the decision responsibility lies outside the team, the proposal form provides a record of the team's best thinking.

The second tool is the Proposal Tracking Chart. Distribute this form and present it is a log of the team's activity. As the team gets more involved in the business and as more and more proposals are submitted, this form provides a record of the team's activity and a way to track progress from proposal to successful implementation.

Explain to the team that the forms are merely suggestions. If you have an alternative you like better or an internal form, use it. The point is to have the team manage its problem-solving and proposal processes as part of its business activity.

5 minutes *Summary/Close:* Wrap up this module by emphasizing how important discipline is in the problem-solving process. For a team to move toward high performance, it needs to stick to the specific steps in the problem-solving cycle, use the tools and techniques presented, make proposals, and track improvements. Encourage the team to try to use the cycle and the tools. Tell them it may be hard at first, but once the team gets familiar with the process and the technique, synergy occurs and problem solving gets easier. Close by distributing the evaluation and asking the team for their feedback. Thank the team members for their time and participation.

EFFECTIVE PROBLEM SOLVING IN HIGH-PERFORMANCE TEAMS

FLIPCHART 12-1

Task Skills		**Process Skills**
Steps and Tools for Effective Problem Solving →	**Effective Problem Solving in High-Performance Teams**	← Effective Relationships in in High-Performance Teams

A great deal has been done in the last 15 years related to problem solving in teams. The entire quality circle movement of the early 1980s placed problem solving at the forefront of team activity. Although this module concentrates on the technology of problem solving—that is, the steps and tools of the process—we would like to frame that technology in the process of change.

The Circle Was Not Unbroken. The decline of quality circles was not a result of the problems with the technology of problem solving. Nor did they disappear because something better came along. In our view, the primary reason for the decline of problem solving and quality circles was the *context in which the quality circles operated.*

Organizations created teams of individuals to improve the quality of the product or service or the process that generated the product or service. Rarely, however, in the early going did the leadership of those organizations ever ask the question: What does it take to create an environment in which team-based problem solving can function and even flourish? The failure to ask and answer this question was, and is, at the heart of having teams involved in problem-solving activity.

Many team-based problem-solving efforts were started inside traditional, hierarchical, nonlistening organizations that often demonstrated the same qualities in response to teams' problem-solving efforts. One problem was that front-line employees were not allowed to work on anything of significance. To paraphrase one management speaker at a recent national conference, "We would redesign a whole workplace and then ask the employees where we should put the water fountain." A second problem was that even when they did get to the "good stuff," the teams were meddling in someone else's territory or were asking threatening questions about why certain things were happening. When this began to happen, the organization's power structure would "lock them out." As a result, teams of interested, committed people soon became frustrated or even angry over an inability to influence things that really made a difference.

The Context Counts for More Than the Process. As your team begins to use problem solving as part of the business strategy for the area, be sure to keep an eye on the larger context. Questions such as: Are we getting the information we need to understand and address issues? Can we get the resources and expertise needed to understand parts of problems and the complexity of certain kinds of solutions? When we make a suggestion or present a proposal, does it get a legitimate hearing? Does the organization implement in a timely and reasonable manner the recommendations it accepts?

If the answer to any of these questions is no on a regular basis or if you find that the organization is generally reluctant to support your problem-solving efforts, then the issue is something larger than the text of this module will solve.

Problem-Solving Ability Counts Too. On the other hand, if a team has the power and license to do significant problem solving, the method and tools you use are important. Sloppy or mismanaged problem-solving processes will yield poor results or consume too much time or too many resources.

Effective problem solving involves a few simple guidelines:

1. Do the problem-solving steps in sequence; do not skip steps or jump ahead.
2. Finish one step before going to the next one.
3. If you encounter new information or run into a wall later in the process, go back to a prior step and rework the content.

Problem Solving Is ... a logical process and a learned skill. It is unlikely that a team will be able to do high-quality problem solving after only the training. Like any complex skill, effective problem solving requires extensive practice. So, while you are implementing the training and model, you are also learning.

To get the most out of your experience, however, you should structure reflective time to examine how you are doing and what you need to do to get better.

Problem Solving Is Task and Process. To be effective problem solvers, your team must develop both *task* and *process* abilities. Your task abilities relate to how you apply the problem-solving technology to business issues. Process abilities pertain to the manner in which you work together as a team. This includes listening, communication, conflict resolution, meeting management techniques, and so forth. Neither ability in and of itself will make you successful. You have to be good at both, and you have to be able to use both sets of skills simultaneously.

I. Identifying the Problem
↓
II. Setting Objectives
↓
III. Analyzing the Problem
↓
IV. Generating Solutions
↓
V. Evaluating Solutions
↓
VI. Making a Decision
↓
VII. Developing an Action Plan
↓
VIII. Submitting the Proposal
↓
IX. Implementing the Solution
↓
X. Evaluating and Updating

I. IDENTIFYING THE PROBLEM

Purpose of This Step. To describe the issue or problem to be addressed.

How to Proceed

✓ Answer the questions:

Why is this a problem?

What specifically is the problem?

What "pain" is occurring?

✓ Where is the problem occurring or not occurring? When did the problem first occur?

✓ How much of a problem do we really have? What are the boundaries of the problem? What is the extent of it?

✓ Who is involved with the problem? Who is not? Look for root or underlying causes; avoid symptoms.

Generate a Preliminary Statement of the Problem

✓ End up with a tight, specific statement of the problem.

Recommendations

✓ Avoid wording the problem in such a way as to dictate the solution.

✓ Deal with one problem at a time. If it is too big, break it down into smaller problems when possible.

✓ Invite others to work with you in complex situations.

Proceed to the Next Step When

✓ The team has consensus on the statement.

✓ Someone outside the team understands the problem statement.

II. SETTING OBJECTIVES

Purpose of This Step. To set objectives for the outcome(s) of the problem-solving process.

How to Proceed

✓ An objective describes the preferred state you want to create in the future. In stating your objective(s):

Identify *what* you want to achieve in solving the problem.

Clarify the level to be achieved, such as:

—20 percent reduction in scrap.

—increase in sales volume of 12 percent in six months.

—increase in problem identification ability by 50 percent.

Indicate by when the objective will be achieved.

Recommendations

✓ Again, avoid attaching solutions to objectives.

✓ A solution is a statement of "how to," an objective is a statement of "what."

✓ If need be, determine a short-term, quick-fix objective and a longer-term, more complete objective. "Put out the fire, but then work on fire prevention."

✓ Include people who might be very important in achieving the objective in writing it.

Proceed to the Next Step When

✓ The team has reached consensus on the objectives.

✓ The objectives are clearly related to the problem statement.

III. ANALYZING THE PROBLEM

Purpose of This Step. To analyze the problem in order to understand its components and to isolate the cause and effect of the problem.

How to Proceed

✓ Identify additional, essential information that is needed to understand the problem and obtain the information.

✓ To do analysis, use tools such as a process flow chart, histogram, fishbone diagram, etc.

✓ Review potential causes by comparing them to the problem.

✓ Select the major cause or combination of causes that, if corrected, will eliminate the problem.

✓ Using your preliminary problem statement as a starting point, and modifying it (if necessary) based on the results of the analysis, create a final problem statement that will guide the remainder of your work.

Recommendations

✓ Use data whenever possible; a lot of people will have opinions, but data are more reliable.

✓ Your final problem statement should be easily understood by someone outside the team. The rule is, "Keep it simple and clear."

Proceed to the Next Step When

✓ The team reaches consensus on the final problem statement.

✓ Others related to the problem both understand and support the statement based on the team's analysis.

IV. GENERATING SOLUTIONS

Purpose of This Step. To generate alternative solutions to the problem.

How to Proceed

✓ Brainstorm (see Tools) as many solutions as possible.

✓ Where appropriate, combine alternatives into more complex solutions.

Recommendations

- ✓ If several people are involved, encourage others to contribute even if they think their ideas might sound stupid.
- ✓ Get the ideas of those who are affected by the problem, involving them directly.
- ✓ Be spontaneous in your thinking; see how many different solutions you can create.
- ✓ Don't be concerned about cost or feasibility at this point.
- ✓ Don't evaluate the worth of each solution; just generate the list.
- ✓ Don't be judgmental of either people or ideas.

Go to the Next Step When

- ✓ The team exhausts the list of new ideas.
- ✓ The team generally agrees that the potential solution is among the alternatives (either by itself or in combination of a number of the alternatives).

V. EVALUATING THE ALTERNATIVES

Purpose of This Step. To select the best solution from among the alternatives generated in the prior step.

How to Proceed

- ✓ Create and carry out an evaluation strategy by:

  Using the objectives to identify important criteria for evaluating alternatives.

  Applying the criteria to the various alternatives.

  Considering each solution thoroughly in terms of positive and negative consequences.

  Seeking information from others to determine adequacy or feasibility.

Recommendations

- ✓ If detailed analysis is needed, start with the simplest analysis and proceed through more complex analyses.
- ✓ Don't make this step more complicated than it needs to be. Sometimes the best solution is obvious.
- ✓ On the other hand, stick to the criteria and the analysis; do not try to manipulate the process to get a predetermined solution.

Proceed to the Next Step When. The team has completed the analysis of alternatives.

VI. MAKING A DECISION

Purpose of This Step. To reach a decision on the best alternative.

How to Proceed

- ✓ Use the results of the prior step and choose the solution(s) that appear(s) to be the best.

- ✓ Test the solution against the criteria of meeting objectives, cost effectiveness, acceptance for implementation, and any other guidelines for the process.

Recommendations

- ✓ Seek advice and input from others whose cooperation or help will be needed to implement this solution.
- ✓ Avoid decisions that may not be accepted by those who are affected by this decision.

Proceed to the Next Step When. The team reaches consensus on the best solution.

VII. DEVELOPING AN ACTION PLAN

Purpose of This Step. To create an action plan for implementation of the alternative chosen.

How to Proceed

- ✓ Identify the steps that will need to occur to implement the solution.
- ✓ Put the steps in sequence.
- ✓ Identify the time each step will take and create a schedule.
- ✓ Identify the human, material, and financial resources required for each step.
- ✓ Determine the decision makers whose approval/cooperation will be sought.
- ✓ Determine how and who will seek this approval/cooperation.
- ✓ Determine accountability for carrying out each step.
- ✓ Create a model to evaluate the proposed solution:

    Develop indicators and measures that will indicate the degree of success in achieving the intended outcome; refer to objectives.

    Develop a plan for gathering the evaluation information and a way to report it to the appropriate individual.

Recommendations

- ✓ Be sure to incorporate experts and implementers in this step.
- ✓ Be careful not to involve valuable team time in detailed planning. Delegate.

Proceed to the Next Step When

- ✓ You have all the elements of the plan in place and the team reaches consensus on those elements.
- ✓ You have a written plan to submit for a decision or to use for implementing the solution.

VIII. SUBMITTING AND TRACKING PROPOSALS

Purpose of This Step. To submit, get approval for, and implement successfully the team's proposal.

How to Proceed

- ✓ Prepare the final version of the written proposal and implementation plan.

✓ Submit the proposal:

Be sure it goes to the right person or persons.

Present it as a team if possible, especially if the proposal is complex; if not, have a team representative deliver it in person and explain the background, process, and outcomes. Try to get a commitment on a date for the decision.

✓ Fill out the Proposal Tracking Chart (see p. 196).

Recommendations

✓ If you are going to deliver the proposal in person or through a presentation, rehearse the presentation and check the room and equipment ahead of time.

✓ If you do not get a response to the proposal in a timely manner, follow up.

✓ If you experience what you consider to be undue delay in getting a response, contact your manager, business team, or steering committee.

Proceed to the Next Step When. You have an affirmative decision on your proposal.

Note: If the proposal is rejected, ask for a live or written critique and rationale. Also request that you be permitted to revise the proposal based on the feedback.

IX. IMPLEMENTATION

Purpose of This Step. To monitor the implementation of a successful proposal.

How to Proceed

✓ Assign a team member or members to oversee implementation. [*Note:* This applies primarily to solutions implemented outside the team. If the solution is implemented by the team, the monitoring updates should be given as part of the team meeting process.]

✓ Track the implementation process to be certain that it conforms to your proposal. If not, notify the implementers and the appropriate manager/team.

Recommendation. Pay attention to this step. Teams sometimes walk away from an approved proposal, especially when it is to be implemented by someone else. However, if the solution does not work, it could be due to the implementation process rather than the solution itself. That is why you need to track implementation.

Proceed to the Next Step When. Your proposal has been fully implemented.

X. EVALUATING AND UPDATING

Purpose of This Step. To monitor, evaluate, and update the solution in the event the outcome is different than projected.

How to Proceed

✓ Implement the evaluation model developed as part of your proposal.

- ✓ If the intended results are not obtained, use the evaluation data to start the problem-solving cycle again.
- ✓ Put any proposed revisions in writing to the person or team who made the original decision.

Recommendations

- ✓ If you are working with a longstanding and/or complex problem, it is highly likely that the first solution will not completely resolve it. This step is extremely important in getting to a permanent, high-quality fix.
- ✓ Retrace your steps through the initial problem-solving process to see where the deficiency might lie. Don't worry about being less than totally successful. This is part of the learning process.

Return to Step IX When

- ✓ You have approval for proposed revisions.

What It Is. A technique to encourage creative thinking. This technique encourages a free exchange of ideas without the fear of criticism or putdowns.

When to Use It. Brainstorming can be used to:

✓ Identify a work issue.

✓ Develop alternative solutions.

✓ Develop and troubleshoot the implementation plan.

✓ Develop any other lists.

How It Works

✓ *A lot of ideas:* Each person is to offer as many ideas as possible. The more ideas offered, the better.

✓ *Anything goes:* Be freewheeling. The wilder the better. Often these wild ideas can be altered to be really usable.

✓ *Rule out criticism:* No one is to comment on the quality of an idea while generating the list. Critical evaluation comes after the brainstorming.

✓ *Everybody participates:* One technique is to keep going around the group until there are no more ideas. A person may "pass" if he/she has no contribution to make at that time.

✓ *Tag on to others' ideas:* Add to and modify others' ideas to expand the list. You can often get a second or third idea out of the original one.

✓ *Record everything:* A person should record the ideas on a board or newsprint as fast as they are given.

Helpful Hints

✓ *Criticism* of an idea should be *stopped.* Time will be provided to evaluate ideas.

✓ Leave a *few seconds between ideas* for other participants to "add on" before going on to the next idea.

✓ The facilitator should *continue to encourage ideas* to flow. Often the most creative ideas come at the end of the process when all the obvious ones have been contributed.

Pitfalls

✓ Failure to describe the scope of the brainstorming task accurately—or making it too broad or too specific.

✓ Failure to warn participants not to be discouraged about "poor-quality" ideas or about the lags in the process.

✓ Failure to distinguish between a freewheeling atmosphere and sheer chaos.

What It Is. The third step in the process of selecting or deciding. In brainstorming (step 1), the team generated the ideas. In polling (step 2), the team collected data on preferred choices. Narrowing provides a way to reduce a number of choices to a single choice.

What It Is Not. Narrowing is *not* a process for counting votes, and it is not a decision-making process or tool.

How It Works

✓ Using the tallies from polling, have the group decide what cutoff should be used (e.g., 5 or less) to eliminate items from the list.

✓ Eliminate items that do not make the cutoff.

✓ Depending on the severity of the issue at stake and/or the number of issues you can:

Use discussion to reach consensus.

Do another round of polling to reduce the list further.

Helpful Hint. Be forward and flexible. That is, set your boundaries to get a cutoff point, but adjust the boundaries if experience suggests it.

CAUSE AND EFFECT DIAGRAM (FISHBONE)

What It Is. A visual aid to help the group analyze a problem or look at issues.

When to Use It. To explore, identify, and display the possible causes of a situation. To explore relationships between an effect and all the possible causes influencing it.

How to Use It

✓ Identify the result or effect to be addressed and write it on the right of the diagram (the head of the fish).

✓ Determine (using brainstorming) the factors that contribute to this effect.

✓ Sort factors into major, minor, and intermediate. There is no rule about how to sort, but typical branches include policies, procedures, people, and plant/equipment.

✓ To get to the root causes (not symptoms), ask "why" four or five times.

✓ Interpret by discussing what it seems to indicate and what additional information is needed.

Helpful Hint. Be careful not to overload the fishbone. There is sometimes a tendency to brainstorm without focusing on the specific problem.

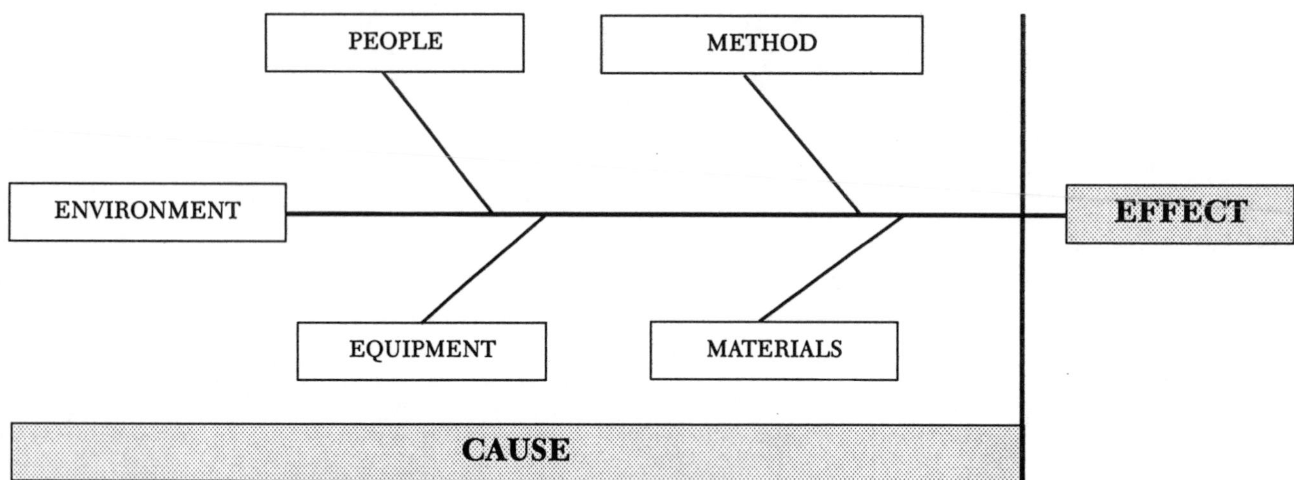

POLLING (MULTIVOTE TECHNIQUE)

What It Is and Is Not

- ✓ Polling is a method used to narrow down a large list and to discover where the interest of the group is and is not.
- ✓ Polling is *not* a way to make a final decision.
- ✓ Polling is *not* a way to create a win-lose attitude within the group.
- ✓ Polling is *not* a tool to establish the majority (voting does that).

How It Works

- ✓ Each person prepares two or three top choices from the list. This is done without consulting others in the group.
- ✓ Each person shares his or her choices with the whole group.
- ✓ Everyone's choices are tallied on a board or newsprint.
- ✓ Ask the group if anyone feels strongly about keeping an item on the list that did not get a tally.
- ✓ Finally, reduce the list to those items where people have indicated a stronger interest. (The number of tallies is not important.)

What Is Done After Polling?

- ✓ Examine your selection standards and delete, alter, or develop additional standards as needed.
- ✓ Test remaining ideas against standards.
- ✓ Ask participants to make a case for or against any of the items left on the list.
- ✓ Work toward consensus to narrow the selection to one item.

Brainstormed List of Ideas for Better Meetings

///	Make the meetings shorter.
	Have more frequent meetings.
//	Have a facilitator.
///	Bring in a stop watch.
/	Invite other non-team-members.
/////	Stick to the agenda.
	Listen to everyone's point of view.
	Do not interrupt each other.
//	Follow the problem-solving cycle.
	Start on time.
///	Rotate scribe duties.
	No zingers.
	No substitutes.
	Put time estimates on all agenda items.
/////	Prioritize agenda items.

Note: Each of the eight team members had three votes.

Narrowed List (cutoff at three votes)

✓ Stick to the agenda
✓ Put time estimates on all agenda items
✓ Bring in a stop watch
✓ Make the meetings shorter
✓ Rotate scribe duties

What It Is. A way to display, at a glance, the distribution of various characteristics of a group of data. A type of bar chart.

When to Use It. In analyzing and finding causes or evaluating the impact of solutions.

How It Works

✓ Collect the data.

✓ Sort data into equal-sized groups. For 30–50 pieces of data, five to seven groups are adequate.

✓ Tally the frequency of data in each class.

✓ Use the frequency table to draw a bar graph with the groups along the horizontal axis and the frequency scale along the vertical axis.

✓ Discuss the distribution the histogram reveals.

Helpful Hints

✓ The number of groups (bars in graph) determine how much of a pattern is visible.

✓ Some processes are naturally distributed and have a bell-shaped curve, but others don't.

✓ Look for twin peaks showing that the data are coming from two or more different sources (e.g., shifts and machines).

NUMBER OF PEOPLE

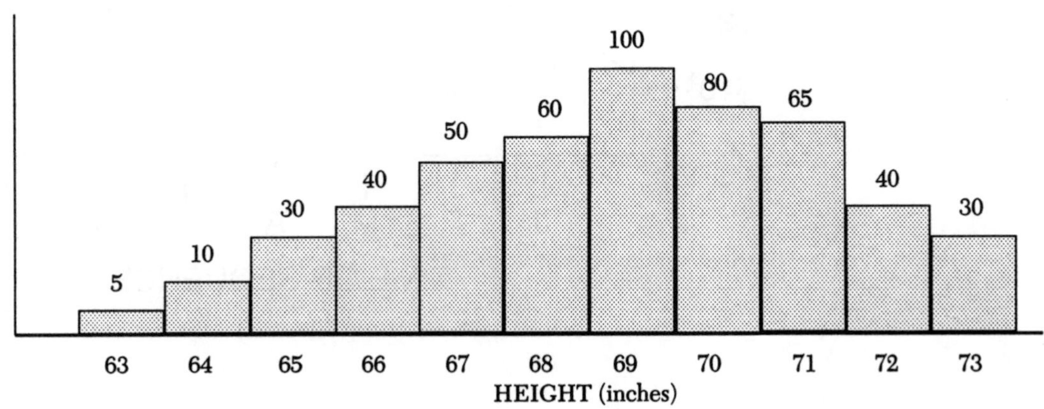

What It Is. A simple display of trends within observation points over a period of time.

When to Use It. To monitor a process to see whether the long-range average is changing, or to focus attention on truly vital changes in the process. (There is a danger in seeing every variation in data as important.)

How to Use It

- ✓ On the vertical axis, identify the units of measurement for item being charted.
- ✓ On the horizontal axis, identify the units of time.

Helpful Hints

- ✓ Pay attention to the divisions on the vertical axis (frequency). Setting them too close or too far apart distorts trends.
- ✓ Mark the data on the chart in the order they are gathered.
- ✓ Connect the data points for easy use and interpretation.

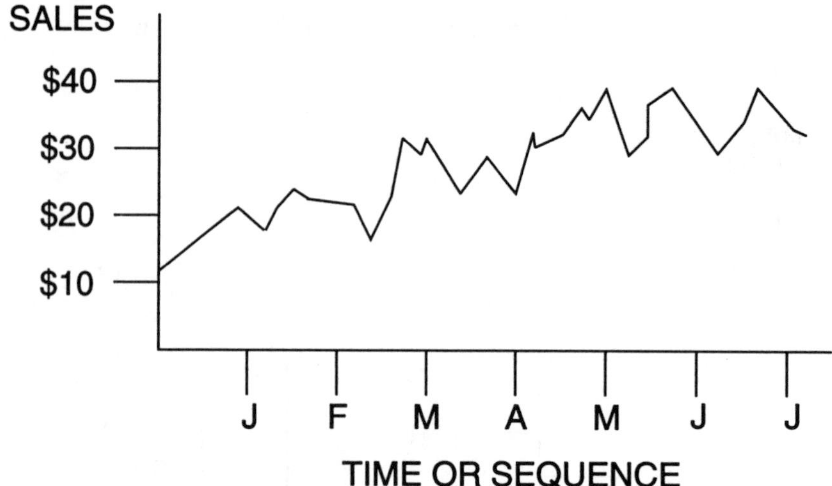

What It Is. A simple display of trends within observation points over a period of time.

When to Use It. To monitor a process to see whether the long-range average is changing, or to focus attention on truly vital changes in the process. (There is a danger in seeing every variation in data as important.)

How to Use It

✓ On the vertical axis, identify the units of measurement for item being charted.

✓ On the horizontal axis, identify the units of time.

Helpful Hints

✓ Pay attention to the divisions on the vertical axis (frequency). Setting them too close or too far apart distorts trends.

✓ Mark the data on the chart in the order they are gathered.

✓ Connect the data points for easy use and interpretation.

Situation. In the Research and Development department of the BRID Corporation, there are 20 members with two supervisors. The tenure of these employees varies from six months to 20 years. There is often a problem scheduling vacation because, given the nature of the work, the company has decided only two people can be gone from the department at the same time. The company has a very liberal vacation policy:

- ✓ All employees employed less than five years have two weeks vacation.
- ✓ All employees employed from five to ten years receive four weeks vacation.
- ✓ All employees employed over ten years receive six weeks vacation.

Also, current policy requires employees to take a minimum of a week at a time, rather than one or two days at a time. There are no other specific guidelines on vacation policy.

Five employees in the R&D department have been there under five years, five have been employed between five and ten years, and all the rest have been employed over ten years. Although these workers are not unionized, the historical practice is that all vacation is scheduled by seniority. Several periods of the year have become real problems, especially the months of June and July, as well as the first two weeks of the hunting season in the fall and the first two weeks of the fishing season in the spring. And almost everyone would like the week off between Christmas and New Year's. Some people know what their vacation schedule is going to be as early as January, while others tend to wait for the last minute to decide what weeks they want. Basically, vacation scheduling is haphazard because a person can request a vacation week any time with at least one week's notice.

Each employee is to give his or her vacation schedule to one of the supervisors. Recently there was a blow-up between four employees who wanted the same week off. The least senior employee had asked for this week six months earlier, while two others had asked a month ahead of time, and the most senior employee had just asked a week earlier, saying he needed to visit his ill mother. The two supervisors have decided to appoint a task force of several people with different levels of seniority to recommend a comprehensive solution.

Your Role and Objective. As a member of this task force, you are charged with the task of using the problem-solving steps to come up with a solution for your team.

SAMPLE PROCESS FLOW CHART

Process. Getting up in the morning.

Objective. To get up in time to arrive at work on time.

Step	Action	Who?
1	Determine time to get up.	Self
2	Check current clock settings; adjust to conform.	Self
3	Set electric alarm.	Self
4	Set manual alarm at +10 minutes.	Self
5	Get into bed.	Self
6	Turn off light on night stand.	Self
7	Electric alarm goes off.	Auto
8	Hit "snooze" bar.	Self
9	Electric alarm goes off at +5 minutes.	Auto
10	Get out of bed.	Self
11	Turn on night stand light.	Self
12	Turn off manual alarm.	Self
13	Go to bathroom.	Self
14+	Continue …	

Getting to Work

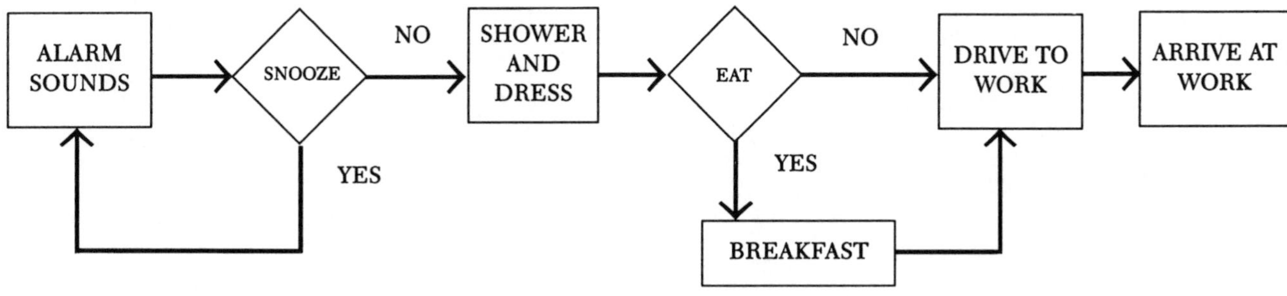

Task	Technique
1. To arrive at a statement that describes the issue in terms of what it is, where it occurs, when it happens, and its extent (problem statement).	Brainstorming Narrowing Polling Run chart Process chart
2. To set goals for the resolution of the issue.	Brainstorming Narrowing Polling
3. To develop a complete picture of all the causes of the issue.	Brainstorming Fishbone (cause and effect) Run chart
4. To agree on the basic cause(s) of the issue.	Narrowing Polling
5. To develop an effective and implementable solution and action plan.	Brainstorming Narrowing Polling
6. To establish needed monitoring procedures.	Histogram Run chart

TEAM PROPOSAL

Issue Number: ______________________________

To: Name: ______________________________

Department: ______________________________

From: Team: ______________________________

Location: ______________________________

Date: ________________

Problem statement: ______________________________

____

____

Cause(s) of the problem:

____

____

____

____

____

____

Proposed solution:

____

____

____

____

____

____

____

TEAM PROPOSAL

Budget	Hours/Number	Rates/Cost	Total
People			
Subtotal			
Materials			
Subtotal			
Equipment			
Subtotal			
Other Items			
Subtotal			
Grand Total			

TEAM PROPOSAL

Evaluation

Expected Outcomes	How Will It Be Measured?	When Will It Be Measured?	By Whom?
1.			
2.			
3.			
4.			

Proposed Schedule

Start date: ______________________________

Completion date: ______________________________

Initial evaluation date: ______________________________

Person responsible: ______________________________

For more information, contact:

Name: ______________________________ Telephone: ____________________

Name: ______________________________ Telephone: ____________________

PROPOSAL TRACKING CHART

Issue No.:	Description	Submitted to:	Date			
			Submitted	Decision	Implemented	Evaluation

Module 13

Roles in the Team

(2½ hours)

Objective To develop and clarify new supervisor/team leader and new member roles.

Materials Needed

✓ *Flipcharts:* Objectives, Key Learning Points, and Topics (copy from this page)
New Roles a Team Should Consider (page 201)

✓ *Handouts:* Role of Leadership Exercise (page 202)
Evaluation (Appendix)

Key Learning Points

✓ Understanding the shift of roles required in leadership by the new team environment.

✓ Reviewing new roles in the team and deciding which apply to this team in this business.

Topics

✓ The Role of Team Leadership

✓ New Roles in the Team

✓ Evaluation

Procedural Outline

Time	Activity
5 minutes	*Introduction:* Open this module by posting and describing the module objective, key learning points, and topics for this session. Explain to the participants that their work group is involved in a major transition from an old paradigm of work to one based on team-oriented planning, problem solving, and decision making. This is a major shift for their organization. It also represents a major shift for the functioning of the team. Historically, most work groups did not need to function as teams to do their jobs. The work was divided such that each employee's role was segmented from every other's. Decisions were made by management and supervision, and reward/recognition as well as disciplinary decisions were made by management (or in collective bargaining processes). As the team changes, so will the roles related to the team. For example, the role of the team's supervisor or leader will be altered to conform to the new model of work being implemented.
15 minutes	*New Roles in the Team:* Help participants understand that the changes in roles in the team take two forms: ✓ Supervisors or team leaders redefine their roles in teaching, leading, and coaching.* ✓ Team members begin to assume part of the role of supervision or team leadership.

*Work in America, New Roles for Leadership.

To assist team leaders and team members in making the shift, this module contains two kinds of activities. The first is devoted to exploring the present and future role of the team's leader. The second proposes new roles within the team. If the team chooses to implement these roles, then team members will be selected to fill them.

The Role of Team Leadership: One of the most significant changes in the American workplace is in the role of leadership. From an era of top-down, authoritarian, take-charge leaders, we are moving to an era defined by leaders who are teachers and coaches as part of a new model of leadership.

How the Role of Leadership Is Changing: Help participants understand that we are moving away from a time when the planning, directing, and controlling of work was the exclusive domain of management leadership. We are moving to roles and relationships that share with, or even assign to, members of the team the functions from traditional management.

The shift is viewed in a number of ways depending on the model or the source. Primarily, however, the role envisioned here involves three major functions: teaching, coaching, and leading. Write these functions on a flipchart and explain them as follows:

✓ *Teaching:* Becoming a provider and promoter of knowledge for the team; beginning to raise the competence of team members so that they can understand the organization and operation of the business, perform the various functions required to help the business be successful, and grow personally and professionally.

✓ *Coaching:* Serving as a mentor and coach for team members, helping them translate new knowledge and skills into effective contributions for the team instead of directing their behavior and punishing mistakes.

✓ *Leading:* Serving as an inspiration to team members to motivate them to perform at their best; creating a work environment that facilitates world-class performance and encourages continuous improvement.

Analyzing the Role of Leadership in the Team: One way for your team to begin to change the historical model of leadership is to look openly at the present management of the team and to talk about how that role will change in the future. This method is more likely to create some movement in the desired direction than would either mandating a change or ignoring the issue.

Next is an exercise in analyzing the role of leadership in the team.

30 minutes *Role of Leadership Exercise:* Distribute the Role of Leadership Exercise handout and facilitate the team as a whole to complete first entry, Past and Present. Tell them to list the present role of leadership in column A and then to place a checkmark (✓) in column B in either the "continue or change" category depending on whether that supervisory behavior should be altered or revised in the future. After the team has completed this section, hold a brief discussion about what the members think needs change and why. Also discuss what should stay the same and why. Next, facilitate the team in completing the second section, The Future. In column A, place the new or revised roles of leadership. Then, in column B, make some notes for the new role to be implemented. After this is completed, have a brief discussion about how to implement this new role.

20 minutes *New Roles in the Team:* Explain to the participants that this section of this module is devoted to identifying and filling new roles in the team. As team members

assume more responsibility for the business and for the operation, and as the leadership of the team shifts from directing and controlling to teaching and coaching, some of the day-to-day functions of the team will need to be provided by members of the team rather than by leaders outside the team or management of the team.

Explain the team should consider filling five roles (write each on a blank flipchart as you explain them):

- ✓ *Team meeting facilitator(s):* This role is responsible for the organization and support of the team meetings. One team member may be responsible for facilitating team meetings or may perform the role in conjunction with another team member, the team leader, or supervisor. [*Note:* See the team meeting module for a full description of meeting facilitator's/leader's duties.]
- ✓ *Team recorder:* This team member is responsible for recording notes and for documenting task commitments and follow-up items in team meetings, task forces, etc. The recorder is also responsible for getting the notes in a form for distribution to key people and other teams. [*Note:* The recorder is not necessarily responsible for typing the minutes and other documents, but must get the material to whoever is responsible and must see that the work is completed according to plan and schedule.]
- ✓ *Communicator:* This team member, working in conjunction with the recorder and team leadership, is responsible for moving information to and from the team. For example, he or she is responsible for getting team minutes distributed. The communicator may also attend meetings to update others on the progress of the team or on its activities. Finally, the team communicator may have some responsibility regarding the acquisition of data for team meetings and problem solving.
- ✓ *Safety representative (only use if appropriate):* This team member is responsible for coordinating activity related to safety. Whether it is safety training, communicating a safety issue to the appropriate company and/or union official, or serving as a resource to a problem-solving team or task force, the safety representative holds an important position in the team.
- ✓ *Training/human resource coordinator:* Human resource functions might include monitoring attendance, sick days, vacation, and so forth (keeping team members' records), coordinating team hiring activities, new team member orientations, and liaison work with the organization's human resource staff.

  This team member is also responsible for training and development activities in the team. These activities may include orientations or training sessions for the entire team, or they may focus on respective teams or individuals. The training coordinator may be responsible for putting together a record system to track individual growth and development plans and for seeing that opportunities are available to help team members meet those objectives. This team member may also serve as a trainer, providing training services as needed and available, or simply monitor training needs and requirements and acquire the training when needed.
- ✓ *Other roles:* Because of the nature of the business or the history of the team, there may be other roles that are appropriate. If so, define the other role(s) before proceeding to the next section.

45 minutes *Adopting New Team Roles:* After each of the new roles have been discussed, the next step is for the team to decide whether it wants to adopt any of these new

roles. Help the team work through the following screen questions as a means for deciding which new roles to adopt, who should adopt them, and how to deal with the expanded responsibilities.

A. Does the team want to add some or all of the roles (facilitator, recorder, communicator, safety representative, and training/human resource coordinator) to the official team plan?

B. If you will add the roles, which ones?

______ Team meeting facilitator

______ Team recorder

______ Team communicator

______ Safety representative

______ Training/human resources coordinator

______ Other: ____

C. If you choose *not* to add roles to the team, who has responsibility for the new or expanded duties?

D. How will the team member who fills each function be chosen?

E. How long will team members serve? Six months? One year? Two years?

F. How will their performance be evaluated? Who will give them the feedback? When? Based on what?

G. If someone does not work out or wishes to resign, how will he or she be replaced?

30 minutes *Filling the New Roles:* After the team has answered these questions, if appropriate, go ahead and choose team members to fill the new roles identified. Be sure the team does not take this task lightly. New roles require team members to take on added responsibilities. In the beginning, this may seem like a new burden. Reassure the team that taking control of itself will eventually be a freeing exercise that will allow the team members to make decisions about their destiny, as opposed to having a boss or supervisor making decisions that affect everyone.

5 minutes *Summary/Close:* Summarize this module by reminding the team that, when the organization shifts to a more team-centered approach, so do the roles, goals, and daily activities. This module should help team members understand and choose their new roles. Distribute the evaluation, ask team members for their feedback, wish them well in their new roles, and thank them for their time.

NEW ROLES A TEAM SHOULD CONSIDER

- ✓ Team Meeting Facilitator(s)
- ✓ Team Recorder
- ✓ Communicator
- ✓ Training/Human Resource Coordinator
- ✓ Other Roles

ROLE OF LEADERSHIP EXERCISE

Section 1. Past and Present

✓ *Step 1:* List the present roles of leadership of your team in column A.

A. Present Roles of Leadership	B. Decision on the Role	
	Continue	Change
Schedule and assign work.		✓
Track attendance.		✓
Create and oversee budget.		✓
Communicate with upper management.	✓	✓

✓ *Step 2:* After completing the list, indicate with a checkmark ✓ in column B, whether you think the role should "Continue" or "Change" (be altered or eliminated) in the future.

Section 2. The Future

✓ *Step 1:* List the revised roles of leadership in the team in column A.

A. Future Roles of Leadership	B. What Needs to Change?
Remove barriers to problems.	Work with other supervisors to change policies or remake systematic issues.
Coach team members in development areas.	Help to assess each team member's development needs.
Administer employee discipline.	Nothing: Do the same.

✓ *Step 2:* After completing the list, make some notes in column B about what needs to change in the leader and/or the team for the new role to be implemented.

Module 14

Roles in the Organization

(2 hours)

Objective To help the team clarify its new roles in various aspects of the business.

Materials Needed

✓ *Flipchart:* Objectives, Key Learning Points, and Topics (copy from this page)

✓ *Handouts:* New Roles for the Team (page 205)
Role Clarification Exercise Instructions (page 206)
Role Clarification Exercise Role Description Chart (page 207)
Evaluation (Appendix)

Key Learning Point Developing team role statements oriented to a high-commitment/high-performance workplace.

Topics

✓ Understanding Traditional Organization vs. Team-Based Organization Roles

✓ Developing Team Roles Statements

✓ Evaluation

Procedural Outline

Time	Activity
5 minutes	*Introduction:* Open this module by posting and reviewing the module objective, key learning points, and topics to be covered. Explain that this module is a major step forward for the team. By completing this module, the team will define its role for the future.
45 minutes	*New Roles for the Team:* Distribute the New Roles for the Team handout, and spend some time reviewing and discussing the traditional and team-based roles associated with each function. Help the team members understand that the team-based process is designed to shift the roles described in the center column toward an alternative such as that represented in the right column. The exercises that follow are designed to help the team define its roles for the future as related to key functions in the business.
65 minutes	*Role Clarification Exercise:* Distribute the Role Clarification Exercise Instructions and Role Clarification Exercise Role Description Chart [*Note:* This exercise can be completed either by each individual team member and then combined for a simple team response, or by the team as a whole as facilitated by the instructor. Either option works well.] Work with the team to understand the instructions and then have the team follow steps 1–5 on the instruction sheet.
5 minutes	*Summary/Close:* Summarize this session by reminding the participants that their team must now think of itself as part of a bigger picture. This module should have helped the team understand how it plays an important role as connected to the larger organization. Moreover, with new team member roles and new roles for the entire group, team members should start to feel the shift toward a more team-based organization. Distribute the evaluation, ask participants for their feedback, and thank them for their time and hard work.

NEW ROLES FOR THE TEAM

Function	Traditional Role	Team-Based Role
Leadership	Separate from workers; provides direction and oversight; leader thinks, team does.	Team works with leadership of organization and shares or assumes the leadership functions in the team.
Work processes	Designed by functional specialists; modified with the specialists' approval.	Controlled and adjusted by the team in conjunction with content experts who consult to the team.
Decision making	Done by management or organizational leadership; team is informed if necessary.	Team becomes a part of the decision-making process for those items that affect them and the success of the business.
Quality	Controlled by functional areas; inspected at best.	Controlled by the team using state-of-the-art tools and continuous improvement processes.
Customers	The sole responsibility of sales, customer service, or other special areas; teams often did not even know who the customers were.	Front-line teams have direct responsibility for understanding and meeting customers' satisfaction criteria.
Training	Team members received minimal training to perform their stated duties.	Team members write developmental plans and engage in continuous learning for personal and team growth.
Rewards	Controlled by management; often directed toward individuals.	Team has a role in the definition and application; rewards are directed toward the team rather than individuals.

ROLE CLARIFICATION EXERCISE INSTRUCTIONS

In the Role Clarification Exercise Role Description Chart (other handout), the left column contains a list of Organizational Functions such as:

Planning/Goal Setting
Customer Relations
Quality

✓ *Step 1:* Read through the list of functions and decide in which ones your team has a role. For example, your team may have a role in quality, but may *not* have a role in customer relations.

✓ *Step 2:* Leave blank the functions in which your team does not have a role.

✓ *Step 3:* If your team has a role in a particular function, write a statement that describes what you think the team's role should be *in the box to the right.* Example:

Quality: "The team should have total responsibility for maintaining and assessing the quality of its work."

✓ *Step 4:* After all members of the team complete the form, compare your responses and reach consensus about the statement you would like for the team. If time does not permit this to be completed in this training session, you could proceed in one of two ways:

1. Continue the discussion as a team at a subsequent session.
2. Or appoint a subgroup in the team to review everyone's statements and compile a team statement for review at a future session.

Either way, you will get a working product for the team.

✓ *Step 5:* Take the completed roles statement to your manager or business group, and ask if it fits the overall plan for the organization. By getting confirmation (or clarification), you also get endorsement and support for your actions.

ROLE CLARIFICATION EXERCISE ROLE DESCRIPTION CHART

Role Description Chart	Date:	Team:
Organizational Function	**Role Description**	
Planning/goal setting		
Work assignments		
Processing procedures		
Quality		
Rejects/scrap/error		
Customer relations		
Budget		
Equipment/maintenance		
Communication		
Performance evaluation		
HR: Training, discipline, etc.		
Other:		
Other:		
Other:		

Module 15

Personal Styles and Team Effectiveness

(2½ hours)

Objectives

- ✓ To introduce the team to the concept of similarities and differences in personal styles.
- ✓ To discuss the impact of the similarities and differences on the functioning of the team.

Materials Needed

✓ *Flipcharts:* Objectives, Key Learning Points, and Topics (copy from this page)
Michael Schrange Quote (page211)
Impact on the Individual (page 212)
Impact on the Team (page 213)

✓ *Handouts:* Personal Style Assessment (page 214)
Styles Chart (page 215)
Style Descriptions (page 216)
Four Letters (page 217)
Evaluation (Appendix)

Key Learning Points

- ✓ Communication and influence styles are a critical component of team development and functioning.
- ✓ People have different but identifiable styles of communicating with and influencing each other.
- ✓ Understanding your personal style and how different styles relate to one another is the key to better communication and influence patterns.

Topics

- ✓ Introduction to Personal Styles and Team Effectiveness
- ✓ Personal Assessment of Style
- ✓ Personal Style and Style Indicators
- ✓ Style Descriptions
- ✓ Personal Styles and the Team
- ✓ Implications
- ✓ Evaluation

Procedural Outline

Time **Activity**

Note: Many other style assessments on the market may be more powerful, but may also be more expensive and more time-consuming. Two we have often substituted in the past are the Myers Briggs Type Inventory and the Social Styles. If you are certified and/or more comfortable with a different style assessment, replace this module with a similar inventory of your choice.

10 minutes *Introduction:* Open this module by posting and explaining the objectives, key learning points, and topics to be covered. Post and review the following quote.

> ... it's the relationships—the formal and informal networks of people that really govern how the organization runs and how value is created.
>
> *Michael Schrage*[*]

Help them understand the power of relationships and differences in style by explaining that central factors in defining business relationships are the communication and influence processes that occur between and among people. These communication and influence patterns inform, persuade, negotiate, attach, and reposition in the course of doing business.

Although context, circumstances, and training all affect communication and influence patterns and behaviors, one of the most powerful forces in determining how people behave and react to the behavior of others is *personal style.* Each of us has a unique way of communicating. These communication modes and patterns apply to thoughts, feelings, beliefs, and actions.

We assume that one key to a successful organization is teamwork. This module is based on the assumption that one element of effective teamwork is how team members relate to each other in the course of conducting business. As such, we believe that:

- ✓ Although every individual is unique, differences can be categorized to identify different style and interaction preferences among people.
- ✓ Employees want to be successful and to have good relationships with each other as part of their work experience.
- ✓ Understanding similarities and differences among and between people is essential to building effective teams and productive working relationships.
- ✓ Failure to understand and acknowledge critical differences in personal style and to manage the team on the basis of the diversity of styles within it will result in lost productivity and potentially harmful relationships among team members.

20 minutes *Personal Style Assessment:* Distribute the Personal Style Assessment handout. Ask team members to complete this assessment by placing a checkmark (✓) next to each word that is a good descriptor of their behavior, thoughts, or actions. Tell the team members not to spend too much time on any single item but simply to go with their initial responses. When each participant completes the assessment, have them total the number of checks in each column.

10 minutes Next, distribute and review the Styles Chart handout. This chart contains words that describe the basic characteristics that fit the various styles.

20 minutes *Style Descriptions:* After everyone gets a feeling for each of the four styles, distribute the Style Descriptions handout. This handout goes into more depth and detail for each style. Tell the team that each of the quadrants provides a general description of the four styles for the letters. Also tell them that these are not mutually exclusive descriptions. Some individuals may have a strong orientation to one style, although many people reflect a mixture of two or more styles depending on the situation and the people involved.

After all four styles (T, F, L, and P) have been explored, have the participants answer the following questions:

[*]Michael Schrage, "Manager's Journal," *The Wall Street Journal* (March 19, 1990). Reprinted with permission of *The Wall Street Journal* (Dow-Jones Company, Inc., 1990). All rights reserved.

1. Which style (letter) is most like you? Least like you?
2. Do your answers correspond to the outcomes of the checklist exercise?
3. If not, what are the differences?

45 minutes *Personal Styles Exercise:* Distribute the Four Letters handout. To do the exercises, each member of the team should tear the sheet into four squares, one for each letter.

Then have each team member arrange the four letters in order of "most like me" on top to "least like me" on the bottom.

Next, have team members gather according to preferred style (based on the card on top). In pairs or small groups, have the team members of a given style discuss the strengths and limitations of their style. The discussion should last 10–15 minutes. (If there are individuals without a pair, work with them to answer the questions.) Each group then presents a 2–3-minute summary of their discussion.

After the groups have discussed and presented their strengths and limitations, regroup the members of the team according to the style that they are least like (the bottom card).

In this group, have the team members focus on the following questions:

1. What do we admire about this style?
2. What do we have to do differently (than if we were communicating with someone of a style similar to our dominant one) in order to communicate with and influence people of this style?

Each group should present a summary of their responses to these questions.

40 minutes *Implications:* After the exercise is complete, generate a discussion about the implications of styles on individuals and on the team. Post the Impact on the Individual flipchart and facilitate the team members to answer each of the following three questions:

1. What do you now understand about personal differences that you did not understand prior to the module?
2. How will what you have learned change your behavior?
3. How could you help others understand how to be more effective in communicating with you?

Next, post the Impact on the Team flipchart and facilitate the team members in answering all four of the following questions:

1. How can your knowledge of personal styles and differences affect your functioning as a team?
2. Where are the team's strengths in terms of styles?
3. What are the advantages and disadvantages of (a) all the members of a team having the same style? (b) All members having a different style?
4. If you were putting together a task force to work on a major project, what kinds of styles would you want on the team? What strengths would differing styles bring to the various aspects of the project?

5 minutes *Summary/Conclusion:* Conclude this module by summarizing how important it is for people to recognize and encourage differences in style. Also, remind the team that acknowledging differences leads to better relationships and more productive teamwork. Finally, thank the team members for their time and distribute the evaluations.

"... it's the relationships—the formal and informal networks of people that really govern how the organization runs and how value is created."

Michael Schrage*

*Michael Schrage, "Manager's Journal," *Wall Street Journal* (March 19, 1990).

IMPACT ON THE INDIVIDUAL

1. What do you now understand about personal differences that you did not understand prior to the module?

2. How will what you have learned change your behavior in the future?

3. How could you help others understand how to be more effective in communicating with you?

IMPACT ON THE TEAM

FLIPCHART 15-3

1. How can your knowledge of personal styles and differences affect your functioning as a team?

2. Where are the team's strengths in terms of styles?

3. What are the advantages and disadvantages of (a) all the members of a team having the same style? (b) a member having a different style?

4. If you were putting together a task force to work on a major project, what kinds of styles would you want on the team? What strengths would various styles bring to the various aspects of the project?

PERSONAL STYLE ASSESSMENT

HANDOUT 15-1

To create a profile of your preferences, place a checkmark (✓) by each word that is really like you.

T	F	L	P
____ take charge	____ fun	____ loyal	____ planner
____ implementer	____ spontaneous	____ giving	____ logical
____ responsible	____ flexible	____ sentimental	____ creative
____ leader	____ dramatic	____ team-oriented	____ analytical
____ strong-willed	____ stimulating	____ sensitive	____ theoretical
____ traditional	____ flashy	____ supportive	____ precise
____ prepared	____ enthusiastic	____ relater	____ serious
____ results-oriented	____ gestures	____ asks	____ probing
____ saving	____ flamboyant	____ emotional	____ skeptical
____ practical	____ fast	____ willing	____ thinker
____ accountable	____ excitable	____ dependable	____ predicts
____ being in control	____ performer	____ agreeable	____ history
____ dutiful	____ action	____ loving	____ exacting
____ impatient	____ freedom	____ harmonious	____ innovative
____ powerful	____ rapid reaction	____ listening	____ budgets
____ bottom line	____ don't like routine	____ sympathetic	____ orderly
____ law and order	____ like change	____ honest feelings	____ cautious action
____ status	____ zestful	____ friendly	____ questioning
____ tells	____ future focus	____ people-centered	____ mastery
____ authority	____ impulsive	____ being accepted	____ organized
____ efficient	____ spurt worker	____ romantic	____ conceptual
____ decisive	____ exciting	____ feelings first	____ prioritizes
____ tough	____ playful	____ helps others	____ perfectionist
____ direct	____ spends	____ present focused	____ strategist
____ do it now	____ lighthearted	____ avoids conflict	____ detail oriented
____ achievement	____ originality	____ amiable	____ accuracy
____ discipline	____ adventurer	____ warmth	____ works best alone
____ structure	____ mover	____ considerate	____ careful
____ driver	____ risk taker	____ conforming	____ patient
____ demanding	____ challenge authority	____ link together	____ quality
____ Total T	____ Total F	____ Total L	____ Total P

When you are finished with the checkmarks, add the total number of checks in each column. The four numbers at the bottom of the chart are your style indicators.

STYLES CHART

The following chart contains words that describe the basic style characteristics that fit the various letters.

P			T		
Prudent Planning Requires Patience, Precision and Preparation.			*Tried and True in Two minutes Turn-around Time!*		
Planner	Precise	Patient	Tangible	Today	Top dog
Prudent	Probe	Prepared	Targets	Task-oriented	Take charge
Prove it	Pattern	Predictability	Tough	Tactical	Time
Practice	Prioritize	Prefers logic	Tiger	Tenacious	
Pace	Programs	Past-focused	Tackle	Titles	
Place	Projections	Probabilities	Traditional	To do lists	
L			**F**		
Let me Lighten your Load.			*Fun-loving, Free, and Fast-moving.*		
Love	Lamb	Languish	Fast	Free wheel	Fresh
Loyalty	Link together		Fearless	Formless	Flashy
Look after	Likes others		Funky	(un)Fettered	Fun
Lasting	Listening		Forward	Finder	
Lend a hand	Let alone		Fascinating	Flexible	

STYLE DESCRIPTIONS

T	F
A person with a T style is often a leader. He or she is direct and tends to want to take charge, to get things moving. T's tend to be organized and strong-willed with a respect for tradition. This style of person is dependable, down-to-earth, and likes structure. Tradition and following the rules are important to the T's.	F's like to be where the action is. They value freedom and fun. They often behave impulsively, acting on the spur of the moment. They tend to live in the here and now, breaking loose from the past quickly and not worrying about tomorrow. The F's will be risk takers with an orientation toward adventure in what they do. They will be easily bored by routine.
L	**P**
The L's are the people persons. Building relationships and keeping them healthy are at the heart of their style. They like being around people and value the quality of emotional life involved. Honesty, harmony, and being open with feelings are at the core of their concerns. L's believe that consideration for others is the foundation of all that follows.	P's tend to focus on logic, fact, and reason as the basis for action. They focus on details and want to be sure they have all the facts before decisions are made. A person with a P orientation will tend to be cautious, intuitive, creative, and stable. They will be concerned about how to improve things and about the ability to do things right based on information and fact.

P	T
L	F

Module 16

High-Performance Business Teams: Quality and Process Improvement Overview

(2 hours)

Objective To help the team understand the critical components of planning and managing a high-performance business.

Materials Needed

✓ *Flipcharts:* Objectives, Key Learning Points, and Topics (copy from this page)
System Diagram (page 221)

✓ *Handouts:* Components of Quality and Process Improvement (page 222)
Team Customer Worksheet (page 223)
Supplier/Input Specification Worksheet (page 224)
Success Indicator Worksheet (page 225)
Evaluation (Appendix)

Key Learning Points

✓ Building a basic understanding of the business practices of high-performance teams.

✓ Identifying the team's customers, suppliers, and success indicators.

Topics

✓ The System View

✓ High-Performance Team Functions

✓ Identification of Customers, Suppliers, and Success Indicators

✓ Evaluation

Procedural Outline

Time	Activity
	Prework: This module is the overview of the quality and process improvement portion of the training. It is helpful at this point to read through Modules 16–22 to grasp the entire concept of quality and process improvement.
5 minutes	*Introduction:* Open this session by posting the objectives, key learning points, and topics to be covered. Be sure to explain that this module is only the beginning of a much larger quality and process improvement process. The notion is to overview all the components in the process and take the first step by learning about systems thinking and identifying the team's major suppliers, customers, products, and services.

Moreover, explain to the participants that this portion of the business team development process requires that the team start thinking of its work as a business. As a business, the team makes something that it delivers (or "sells") to another individual, group, department, or external customer. Or it performs a service that an individual, group, or department consumes or external customer

INPUTS (Suppliers)	→	TRANSFORMATION (Work Processes)	→	OUTPUTS (Customers)

Figure 16-1.

purchases. So, in every sense of the word, the work team represents a business involved in production and/or service.

We suggest that you think of your business in terms of a system. Draw Fig. 16-1 on a blank flipchart. Explain that a system has three basic, interrelated components: *input, transformation,* and *output.* As a business, the team takes things in (raw materials, equipment for repair, information) and transforms them into output—a finished assembly, completed part (product), a piece of equipment that is no longer broken, or a customer who has a problem solved or a question answered (service).

In this module, the team defines its supplier(s) (who provide critical input) and customer(s) (consumers of output) as well as the primary indicators of success in converting inputs to outputs (the work in your business).

10 minutes *Components of Quality and Process Improvement:* Once the team starts thinking of itself as part of a system with suppliers, a transformation process, and customers, we move into six in-depth modules to help everyone understand how to build quality into the system and to improve the system continuously. Distribute the Components of Quality and Process Improvement handout. Briefly discuss each of the six components to give the team an overview of the entire process and what the next six modules will cover.

30 minutes *Team Customer Exercise:* The first step in this process is to identify the team's major customers and what they buy or consume. Distribute the Team Customer Worksheet. Have the team work together to identify who follows them in the work flow process. This can be a tricky proposition if the team has never thought like this before. Often there are multiple customers for any given team. Have the team discuss this notion. A powerful process question to ask is: Who uses what we [the team] produce? Brainstorm as many users as possible. These users may be considered the team's customers. Additionally if there are many customers, try to narrow the focus to just the major customers, those who use 80 percent or more of the team's output.

After the customers have been identified, have the team describe what they consume and then label that as a product or service.

30 minutes *Team Supplier Exercise:* The next step for the team is to identify who supplies the team with the information or materials to start its transformation process. Supplier identification asks the team to think of itself as a customer. Distribute the Supplier/Input Specification Worksheet and have the team work together to identify all their inputs and who supplies those inputs. Just like the customer identification exercise, have the team identify all its inputs and suppliers, and then note the major inputs and suppliers (those who account for 80 percent or more of the process).

30 minutes *Success Indicators:* Now that the team has identified its major suppliers and customers, the next step is to identify the major success indicators of high performance. How does the team know when it is successful? What targets does the team have in place, for which it is currently shooting? Success indicators often, but not always, take the form of measurable performance targets such as quali-

ty, cost, schedule, down time, cycle time, customer satisfaction, rejects, rework, etc. Distribute the Success Indicator Worksheet and have the team identify its success indicators and its current targets.

5 minutes *Summary/Close:* Remind the team members that thinking like a business may be a different way to think about their work. It offers a new perspective to what they do. The first step is to understand the systems nature of the work and then to identify the other major players and pieces in the system. Customer and supplier identification is only a start. In the modules to follow, the team will work the entire quality and process improvement cycle. Thank the team members for their time, distribute the evaluations and ask for feedback about the training.

INPUTS (Suppliers) → **TRANSFORMATION** (Work Processes) → **OUTPUTS** (Customers)

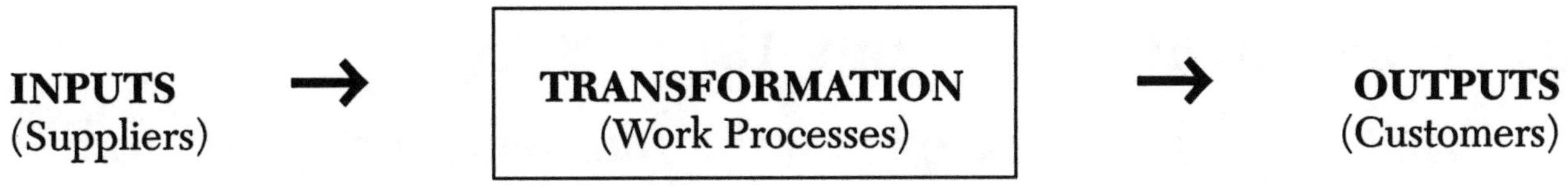

COMPONENTS OF QUALITY AND PROCESS IMPROVEMENT

1. **Customer Analysis (Module 17)**
   Who are your major customers?
   Do they get from you what they need?
2. **Supplier Analysis (Module 18)**
   Who supplies you with what you need to do your work?
   Is what you get what you need?
3. **Process Analysis (Module 19)**
   What steps do you take from the moment work starts to the moment you deliver your product or service?
4. **Quality Improvement (Module 20)**
   What are the basic principles of quality in a high-performance system?
   What practices are characteristic of teams doing high-performance work?
5. **Quality and Productivity Improvement Strategies (Module 21)**
   Tools and techniques you can use to improve.
6. **Business Information Management (Module 22)**
   What information do you need to ensure your success?
   Where do you get the information? How often?
   How do you want to display this information?

TEAM CUSTOMER WORKSHEET

In the following chart, identify your team's customers and what they "buy" or "consume."

Who are our customers?	What do they buy/consume?	Product (P) or Service (S)

Note: If you produce a single product or service that goes to a number of customers, there is no need to repeat the listing. Group them all together.

SUPPLIER/INPUT SPECIFICATION WORKSHEET

HANDOUT 16-3

In the following chart, identify your team's suppliers and what they "sell" or provide to your team.

Who are our suppliers?	What do they sell\provide?	Product (P) or Service (S)

Note: If you produce a single product or service that goes to a number of customers, there is no need to repeat the listing. Group them all together.

SUCCESS INDICATOR WORKSHEET

In the following chart, list (a) the major indicators of the success of your team's business and (b) the current target for that indicator.

Success Indicator	Current Target
Example: Quality of our Product	Less than 1:1000 rejects

Module 17

Customer Analysis

(3 hours)

Objectives

- ✓ To develop a customer focus in the team.
- ✓ To define customer standards for the team.
- ✓ To get feedback on how well the team is meeting those standards.

Materials Needed

- ✓ *Flipcharts:* Objectives, Key Learning Points, and Topics (copy from this page)
  Supplier-Customer Model of Doing Business (page 231)
- ✓ *Handouts:* Customer Principles in an Era of Quality (page 232)
  Employee Principles in an Era of Customer and Quality Improvement (page 233)
  Customer Relations: Strengths and Weaknesses Assessment (page 234)
  Customer Rating and Feedback Form (page 235)
  Team Customer Worksheet (from Module 16) (page 223)
  Examples of Customer Expectations and Standards (page 236)
  Customer Standards Form (page 237)
  Evaluation (Appendix)

Key Learning Points

- ✓ Identifying the team's internal and external customers' standards.
- ✓ Conducting an analysis of customer satisfaction.
- ✓ Creating a customer feedback loop for the team.

Topics

- ✓ Customer Principles in an Era of Quality
- ✓ Employee Principles in an Era of Quality
- ✓ Customer Relations
- ✓ Customer Standards
- ✓ Customer Assessment and Feedback
- ✓ Evaluation

Procedural Outline

Time **Activity**

Prework: Review all the phases and steps in this module. In several instances the team will be required either to meet with their customers or to meet again to discuss their customers' ratings. When these circumstances occur, help the team understand the process and plan to complete the exercise. In many cases the team will have to meet two or three times to complete this entire module.

Additionally, in this module we will be reviewing the team's customers. Make sure you have—or one of the team members brings—a completed Team Customer Worksheet from Module 16. It is best if all team members have a copy of this worksheet. You may want to make copies for everyone if you don't think participants will bring theirs with them.

10 minutes *Introduction:* Open this session by posting the objectives, key learning points, and topics to be covered. Explain that fully understanding your customer is the next phase of building a high-performance team. The foundation of most high-performance organizations today lies in outstanding quality, exceeding customer expectations, and value pricing.

Moreover, to work effectively as a business team, you have to think of the team as a vendor or supplier for others in your organization. As such, the team is moving to an era in which a key definition of the success of your business is: *satisfying your customer's needs.*

Why is the customer important? In writing about quality management, Bruce and Suzanne Brocka say that you must focus on satisfying customer needs and expectations. Specifically, their principle is:

> The Customer is King. The customer must rule, whether this is an internal customer (a customer is the next person in the process—internal customers are peers and supervisors) or external customer (the traditional customer). Every worker has a customer of some sort. Customers or users must be identified, and their needs, wants, expectations and desires clearly delineated and served. Customers and their needs are the only reason a business exists.*

The relationship between customers and quality was emphasized by Tom Peters in *Thriving on Chaos*:

> With high quality products and services being provided by new, especially foreign, competitors; and with quality being increasingly demanded by industrial and individual customers, every firm must:
>
> ✓ Mount a quality improvement revolution.
>
> ✓ Ensure that quality is always defined in terms of customer perceptions.
>
> A quality revolution means eating, sleeping, and breathing quality. Management obsession and persistence at all levels are essential. But the passion must be matched with a detailed process. And always, the customer must be present—as the chief definer of what's important.**

The message is clear: Satisfying the team's customers is key to your long-term success. This module provides a number of steps and tools to move in that direction and builds on the customer definition that the team completed in Module 16.

20 minutes *Principles in the Era of Quality:* Distribute the Customer Principles in an Era of Quality handout. Work with the team to come up with examples of each of the principles in action. These examples can be either within the organization or from other team member experiences.

20 minutes Next, distribute the Employee Principles in the Era of Customer and Quality Improvement. Work through each principle with the team. Ask them what each principle means, whether it is currently in force, and, if it is not currently in force, how things would be different if it were now implemented.

*B. Brocka and M. S. Brocka, *Quality Management: Implementing the Best Ideas of the Masters* (Homewood, IL: Richard D. Irwin, Inc., 1992), p. 10. Reprinted with permission.

**Tom Peters, *Thriving on Chaos: Handbook for Management Revolution* (New York: Harper & Row, 1988), p. 78. Reprinted with permission.

40 minutes *Customer Relations:* Now that the team members have had a chance to understand some of the new principles in operation, distribute the Customer Relations: Strengths and Weaknesses Assessment. Ask the team members to take a moment and individually complete both parts of the assessment. When they have all written a few responses, have them share and explain their responses one at a time. This should generate some good initial thoughts on where they are strong and where they can improve their customer relations. (*Note:* If you feel pressed for time or prefer, you can complete this exercise as a single group by brainstorming each category and capturing the team members' thoughts on a blank flipchart.)

15 minutes *Customer Analysis:* Help the team members understand as part of the new orientation to the business, we are redefining business relationships with each other. One way to do this is to define team-to-team, department-to-department, and organization-to-organization relationships in terms of suppliers and customers (just as companies or agencies define their buyers or constituents as customers).

A primary goal of a business is to satisfy our external customer's needs in terms of quality, on-time delivery, cost, etc. These are the same goals we have for our relationship with internal customers.

Draw Fig. 17-1 on a blank flipchart and explain:

1. Supplier.
2. Products or services produced.
3. Customers.
4. Standards on each product or service.
5. Agreement on the standards from the supplier and customer.
6. Feedback from the customer about the products and services received.

The supplier-customer model of doing business is only effective if:

✓ Both the supplier and the customer *understand* and *agree* on *what is required* and on the *standards* that are set.

✓ There is regular and meaningful *feedback* on supplier performance.

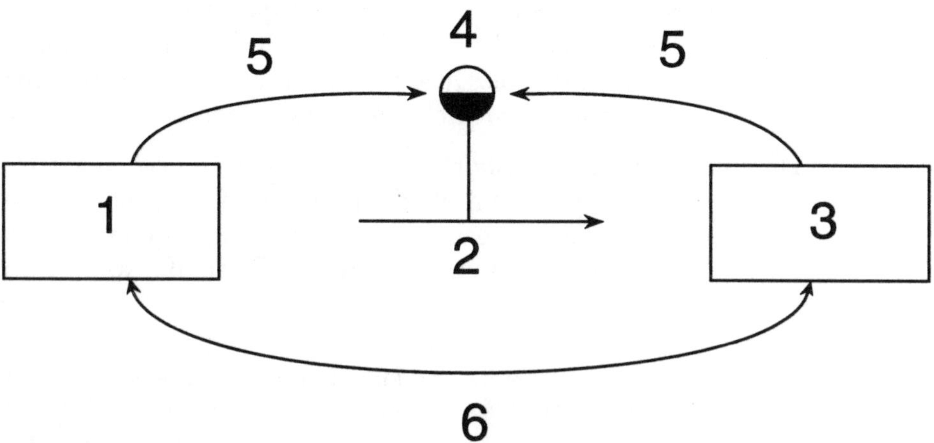

Figure 17-1.

✓ There are commitments to and plans for *continuous improvement* of the quality, reliability, and efficiency of products or services provided.

The purpose of this section is to provide a structured format within which to discuss the information and actions required to make the supplier/customer relationship work well.

Now with a background of customer and quality principles and a model illustrating the supplier customer relationship, the next series of exercises will actually help the team identify the standards on its products and services and to create feedback loops with its customers.

40 minutes *Phase I: Customer Definition Exercise: Identifying the customers' standards (needs):* Tell the team members our approach to the change in the way we do business is based on seeing yourself as a supplier for a variety of products and/or services used or "consumed" by other departments or groups in the organization.

Step 1: Ask the team members to turn to/or distribute the Team Customer Worksheet (from Module 16). Have the team review the products and/or make additions or corrections as necessary.

Step 2: Distribute and review the Examples of Customer Expectations and Standards handout. Help the team understand 1) What a general standard is; 2) What a general standard means; and 3) How it will be measured. Next, obtain one Customer Standard Form for each customer listed in the Customer/Output Definition chart from Module 16. Have the team members fill out the "Customer" blank at top and write their team's name in the "Supplier" blank. Then:

✓ Fill out the chart for each customer

✓ Identify whether they are providing a Product (P) or Service (S)

✓ Describe the Product or Service

✓ Identify the customer's standard(s) (have them contact the customer if you do not know the standards)

15 minutes *Phase II: Customer Ratings:* In this phase, your customers will rate how well you are doing in meeting their standards.

Step 1: Fill out the "Customer" and "Supplier" blanks at the top of the form (Customer Rating and Feedback Form).

Step 2: Enter the Customer Standards.

Step 3: Tell the team members the next step is to give the form to customers (or to make a plan to give the form to their customers). Ask them to rate how well you (the supplier) are doing in meeting each standard. Have them record their rating by entering a grade in Column (3). Use the following grading system:

A = Excellent

B = Good

C = Acceptable

D = Below Standard

E = Unacceptable

[*Instructor Note:* Be sure you identify who on the team will deliver the forms to each customer and when you want to get the forms back. You may even want the team to schedule another meeting specifically to discuss each rating.]

Step 4: *Basis for the Rating (4):* Ask the customer to make some notes about the factors that contributed to the rating. That is, what made the customer give a high rating (e.g., "Always delivered parts to us on time") or a low rating (e.g., "Currently reject over 12% of the material supplied—goal is 5%")?

Step 5: *What to Do to Improve (5):* Ask the customer to identify what you (the supplier) can or should do to maintain (good) or improve (poor) the rating assigned.

20 minutes *Phase III: Customer Meeting and Feedback:* Explain to the participants after the customer completes the rating and documentation (Phase II), the team moves to the feedback phase. This phase involves an actual discussion and feedback process with the customer. The aim of this phase is to get feedback about your performance, including explanations about the basis for judgments and indications of what could be done to improve.

Step 1: Arrange a meeting with the customer. Take as many or few members of the team to the meeting as necessary.

Step 2: Have the customer provide a copy of the Customer Rating Feedback Form. Ask the customer to go over the information with your representative(s).

Step 3: If you agree with the customer ratings and data, reinforce their accuracy and work on a plan (or time to discuss a plan) for changing the areas which need to improve. (Perhaps you could discuss some possibilities in this meeting.)

Step 4: If you and the customer do not agree on the ratings and/or data, explain possible changes to satisfy both groups' needs *and* interests. (Adjustments may be required on both sides to get agreement.)

Step 5: If you are unable to agree, you have two choices:

1. Decide who should decide and ask them for help in the situation (e.g., a manager over both departments); or
2. Get someone, preferably from outside the two groups, to act as a facilitator for a problem-solving/integrative negotiation session aimed at reaching mutual agreement.

Step 6: Schedule a date for the next review and feedback session.

10 minutes *Summary/Close:* End this session by reinforcing how important it is to understand your customers' needs, expectations, and desires. Review the action plans the team has put in place. Distribute the evaluation and thank the team members for their hard work.

SUPPLIER-CUSTOMER MODEL OF DOING BUSINESS

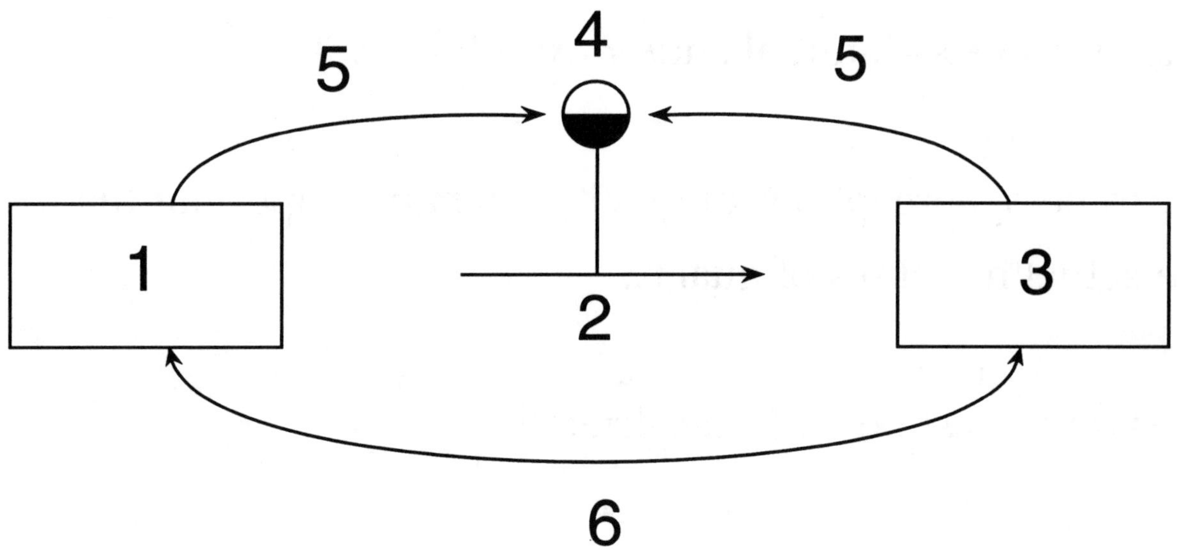

1. Supplier
2. Products or services
3. Customers
4. Standards on each product or service
5. Agreement on the standards from the supplier and customer
6. Feedback from the customers about the products and services received

CUSTOMER PRINCIPLES IN AN ERA OF QUALITY

HANDOUT 17-1

- ✓ The customer—internal and/or external—is #1.
- ✓ Customers' perceptions of quality are *more* important than the actual measures of quality.
- ✓ Everyone must be customer-friendly.
- ✓ Customer service is more important than boss or budget service.
- ✓ Customer relations reflect employee relations.
- ✓ External customer satisfaction will *not* exceed internal customer satisfaction.
- ✓ Customers want you to fix the problem, not the blame.
- ✓ If it weren't for the customer, we wouldn't exist.

EMPLOYEE PRINCIPLES IN AN ERA OF CUSTOMER AND QUALITY IMPROVEMENT

- ✓ Employees and teams hold the key to quality and customer satisfaction.
- ✓ Control of employees is an illusion; commitment of employees is a must.
- ✓ Employees should be invited to contribute to innovation and decision-making related to customer satisfaction.
- ✓ Empowered employees will foster innovation and customer satisfaction.
- ✓ Employees who experience trust and respect contribute more than those who do not.
- ✓ Employees are appreciating assets; equipment and technology are depreciating assets.
- ✓ For employees, communication is more important than commands.
- ✓ A machine, or a part, or a process never had a good idea or cared one iota about the customer.

CUSTOMER RELATIONS: STRENGTHS AND WEAKNESSES ASSESSMENT

Internal Customers

Given the customer and employee principles previously discussed and your general awareness of the relationship between your business and your *internal* customers, list what you think are the team's current strengths and weaknesses in satisfying your *internal* customers.

Strengths

1. ______________________________
2. ______________________________
3. ______________________________
4. ______________________________
5. ______________________________

Weaknesses

1. ______________________________
2. ______________________________
3. ______________________________
4. ______________________________
5. ______________________________

External Customers

Strengths

1. ______________________________
2. ______________________________
3. ______________________________
4. ______________________________
5. ______________________________

Weaknesses

1. ______________________________
2. ______________________________
3. ______________________________
4. ______________________________
5. ______________________________

CUSTOMER RATING AND FEEDBACK FORM

(1) No.	(2) **Standards** (Copy your customer standards from the customer definition form.)	(3) **Grade** A = excellent B = good C = acceptable D = below par E = unacceptable	(4) **Basis for Your Rating** (Cite the data or actions on which you based your grade for this supplier.)	(5) **What to Do to Improve** (Give some examples of what needs to happen to maintain or raise performance.)
Example	Downtime not to exceed 1% month	D	Downtime is over 4% per month	Need better parts supply on hand

EXAMPLES OF CUSTOMER EXPECTATIONS AND STANDARDS

HANDOUT 17-5

On the next page you will prepare a customer standards form. Following are some examples of standards your internal customers might have.

Example 1

General standard	A quality product
What the general standard means	A product they can depend on A product that meets their needs
How the standard will be measured	Less than .5 percent rejection rate Field test failure rate 1:10,000 or less

Example 2

General standard	Fast, dependable service
What the general standard means	If there is a problem, they want to know that you will do something about it and what you do is correct.
How the standard will be measured	Respond to repair call within 30 minutes Repair is correct the first time—no recalls.

Example 3

General standard	Customer wants to feel appreciated.
What the general standard means	To feel that we sincerely want and appreciate their business
How the standard will be measured	Customer problems or complaints are handled promptly and courteously 100 percent of the time.

CUSTOMER STANDARDS FORM

Product (P) or Service (S)	**Product or Service Description** (List the product or service provided.)	**Customer Requirements** (Write a description of the customer's requirements for this product or service. Include as many standards for each product or service as the customer provides)
S	Equipment Repair	Equipment downtime not to exceed 2% per month

Module 18

Supplier Analysis

(3 hours)

Objective To create a solid relationship with the team's suppliers through supplier and input assessment, the development of input standards, and the creation of a team supplier feedback loop.

Materials Needed

✓ *Flipcharts:* Objectives, Key Learning Points, and Topics (copy from this page)
Supplier-Customer Model of Doing Business (page 241)

✓ *Handouts:* Principles in the Supplier Relationship (page 242)
Guiding Questions in Developing Supplier Relationships (page 243)
Supplier Identification Chart (page 244)
A Completed Supplier/Input Specification Worksheet from Module 16 (page 224)
Sample Supplier Standards Worksheet (page 245)
Defining Requirements/Standards for Suppliers (page 246)
Identifying Supplier Standards Worksheet (page 247)
Assessing Supplier Standards (page 248)
Evaluation (Appendix)

Key Learning Points

- ✓ Identifying the team's suppliers.
- ✓ Defining work group inputs and supplier standards.
- ✓ Conducting an assessment of supplier input.
- ✓ Creating a supplier loop.

Topics

- ✓ Principles in the Supplier Relationship
- ✓ Guiding Questions
- ✓ Supplier Identification
- ✓ Defining Requirements
- ✓ Assessing Standards
- ✓ Evaluation

Procedural Outline

Time **Activity**

Prework: In this module you will need to work with the team members to create a high-performance relationship with its suppliers. In Module 16 the team has already identified its major suppliers in the Supplier Specification Worksheet. Make sure you bring copies of that worksheet to the session if you feel the team members won't have their originals with them.

30 minutes *Introduction:* Open this module by posting and explaining the objectives, key learning points, and topics to be discussed. Explain to the team members that, after assessing and working with their customers, it's time to think of themselves as a customer to work with their suppliers to ensure quality inputs. Distribute the Principles in the Supplier Relationship handout and discuss each point.

Next, help the team understand that working with suppliers is a joint effort and that several guiding questions help in developing their relationship. Distribute the Guiding Questions in Developing Supplier Relationships handout. Work with the team to understand the importance of each question.

15 minutes *Supplier Identification:* The next step in the process is to identify your suppliers and what they supply to the team. The team has already done this in Module 16. Either distribute copies of the completed Supplier Specification Worksheet or have the team members find their completed copies. Also distribute the Supplier Identification Chart and have the team use the supplier information from Module 16 to fill it out. Tell them to list (in the right column) all the products and services supplied to their team. (Or simply use the form you completed in Module 16.)

75 minutes *Identifying Supplier Standards:* The next step in the process is to identify the minimum acceptable performance standards that each team input should meet. These standards not only help the team do a better job in the transformation of inputs to outputs, but they also act as a baseline for giving productive feedback to the team's suppliers. Draw the diagram in Fig. 18-1 on a flipchart, point to numbers 4 and 5. Explain that, just as with the team's customers, supplier input standards should be mutually agreed on by the team and the supplier.

Distribute the Sample Supplier Standards Worksheet handout. The sample worksheet gives the team an idea what supplier standards may look like. Have the team members read through the worksheet. Discuss the sample until all team members understand the nature of supplier standards. Next distribute Defining Requirements/Standards for Suppliers. This worksheet can be used both with your suppliers to generate agreement and, alone, for team planning purposes. In this module, we will use the worksheet as a planning tool to establish clarity and team consensus about supplier requirements. Have the team members read through all eight questions. Then facilitate the team as a whole to answer each question.

Distribute the Identifying Supplier Standards Worksheet and have the team complete the worksheet for each major input supplier. Remember to use

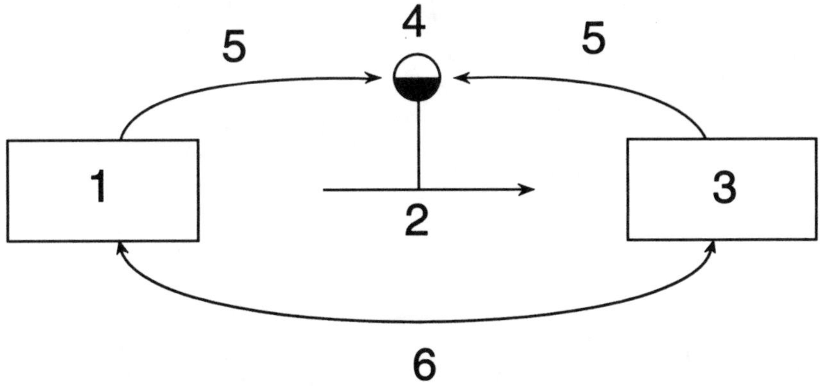

Figure 18-1. Supplier–customer model of doing business.

the 80/20 rule and to avoid getting bogged down in too much detail. It should hold that about 20 percent of your suppliers account for about 80 percent of the team's most important inputs. For now, just have the team concentrate on the major or most important inputs (those most critical to the team's success).

45 minutes *Assessing Supplier Standards:* After the team members have worked to identify the most critical supplier standards, the next step is to collect data on those standards. Data collection is an important step in the feedback and improvement process. By collecting data on the team inputs (according to standards), the team can give very specific, fact-based feedback to its suppliers. Without the data, the feedback is simply opinion and can easily be denied or rejected. Moreover, by collecting specific data, the team can easily decipher whether its problems stem from faulty inputs (i.e., their suppliers need to give them better-quality materials or information) or from faulty processes (i.e., the team needs to rethink the way they do their work). Either way, data collection is very powerful.

The process for collecting data may go beyond this meeting. Distribute Assessing Supplier Standards. Have the team use this form as a guide for collecting and feeding back data. Use the time in the training session to make sure everyone understands what is expected, to clarify everyone's role, and to establish the specific action steps for collecting, analyzing, and feeding back the data.

15 minutes *Summary/Close:* Bring this session to a close by reviewing the supplier–customer model of doing business. Be sure to emphasize how important it is for a business team to understand:

1. Who their suppliers are.
2. What they supply.
3. What standards those inputs need to measure up to.
4. Collecting data on inputs.
5. Analyzing that data.
6. Feeding back that data for the purpose of improvement.

Additionally, summarize the team action plan for collecting, analyzing, and feeding back the data to their suppliers. Finally, thank the team members for their time and hard work. Distribute the evaluation.

SUPPLIER–CUSTOMER MODEL OF DOING BUSINESS

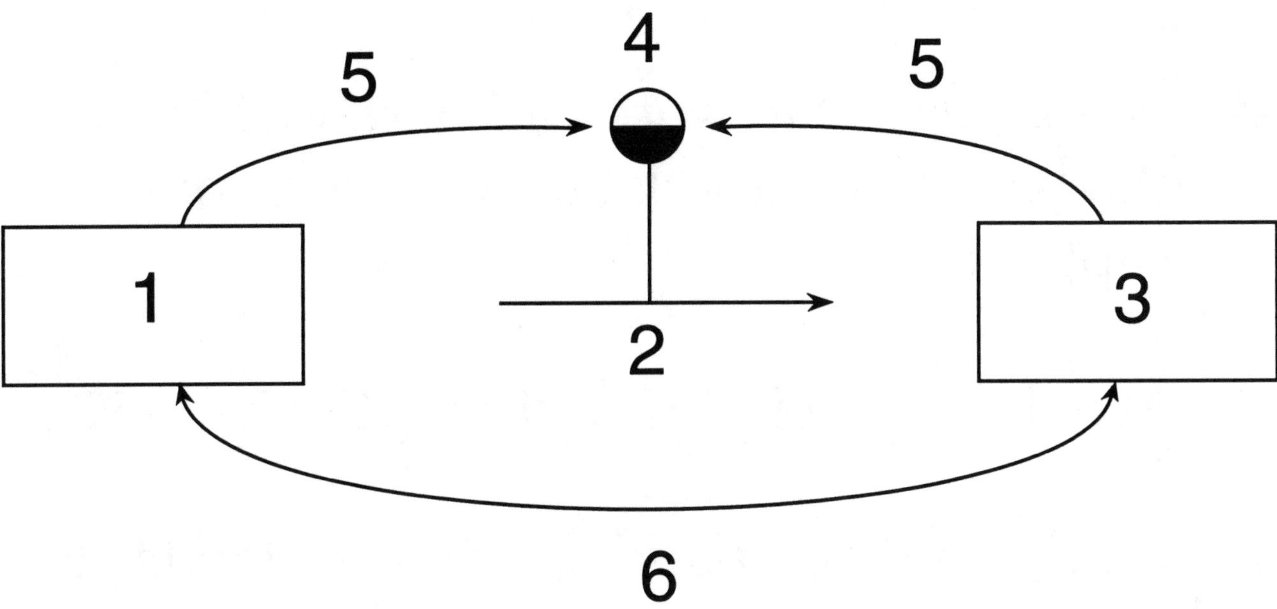

1. Supplier
2. Products or services
3. Customers
4. Standards on each product or service
5. Agreement on the standards from the supplier and customer
6. Feedback from the customers about the products and services received

PRINCIPLES IN THE SUPPLIER RELATIONSHIP

- ✓ Emphasize teamwork and partnership as the bases for the relationship with your suppliers.
- ✓ Avoid fingerpointing and negative criticism.
- ✓ Work jointly on the definition of standards and on plans for meeting them.
- ✓ Provide clear, open, and low-threat lines of communication.
- ✓ Reinforce supplier success.

GUIDING QUESTIONS IN DEVELOPING SUPPLIER RELATIONSHIPS

1. Who are your suppliers?
2. Do your suppliers know exactly how you use their products/services? If not, how can you communicate this information to them?
3. Do your suppliers know your needs, expectations, and standards?
4. Do your suppliers agree with your expectations and standards?
5. Are your suppliers meeting your expectations and standards?
6. Do they know how well they are doing in regard to your expectations and standards?
7. If there is a discrepancy between your standards and the supplier's performance, is there a plan to reduce it?

SUPPLIER IDENTIFICATION CHART

Who are Your suppliers?	What do they sell/provide?	Product (P) or Service (S)

Note: If you produce a single product or service that goes to a number of customers, there is no need to repeat the listing. Group them all together.

SAMPLE SUPPLIER STANDARDS WORKSHEET

Paper Airplane Company

Input	Source/Supplier	Standards
Engineering drawing	Engineering Department	1. Readable: No question 2. Up-to-date 3. Available: In file
Paper	Purchasing	1. Available when needed 2. Lowest cost: Does not exceed budget 3. Good quality: .01% scrap

DEFINING REQUIREMENTS/ STANDARDS FOR SUPPLIERS

HANDOUT 18-5

Together with each major supplier, describe the product/service needed by you, as clearly as possible using the following as guidelines:

1. What products/services/other input does the team require?

2. When is delivery expected? How much variance is allowable in the delivery time? At what point does the team need to be informed of changes in delivery time?

3. What materials (fabrics, reports, diagrams) are required? What substitutions are acceptable? Does the team need to be informed if substitutions are used?

4. What information does the team need to have with the product or service? What form should it be in? Can the team get by without it?

5. What level (or margin) of error will be allowed? Under what circumstances?

6. What standards and indicators will the team use to measure its supplier's performance?

7. How, when, and how frequently will the team provide feedback to suppliers on how well they are meeting expectations?

8. How will the team communicate changes in the agreed-on standards and expectations?

IDENTIFYING SUPPLIER STANDARDS WORKSHEET

In the chart below, list:

1. All major inputs to your business.
2. The source/supplier for each input.
3. The standard or standards you have for each input.
   Use measures such as:
   Delivery
   Cost
   Quality
   Accuracy (information)
   Etc.

(1) Inputs	(2) Source/Supplier	(3) Standards

Using the Identifying Supplier Standards chart as a guide, structure an analysis of the most important standards.

Proceed as follows:

1. Collect data on a specific standard.
2. Display the data in a way the team or work group can compare the standard to actual data.
3. If the data indicate that inputs meet or exceed the standards, let your suppliers know; that is, give them positive feedback.

   If, however, the data indicate that inputs are not meeting standards, you should arrange a session with the source/supplier to discuss strategies for improvement.
4. If you have a meeting focused on improvement, develop a "contract" with your supplier. The contract should indicate:
   a. The goal(s) to achieve.
   b. The measures of that achievement.
   c. A plan for achieving the goals.
   d. The date by which the plan will be implemented.
   e. When you will get feedback (follow up on) the improvements.

Module 19

Process Analysis

(3 hours)

Objectives

✓ To help the team analyze and understand how it gets work done.

✓ To identify the critical points that affect the quality of the business.

Materials Needed

✓ *Flipcharts:* Objectives, Key Learning Points, and Topics (copy from this page)
Benefits of Mapping (page 254)
Guidelines for Mapping (page 255)

✓ *Handouts:* Business Process Flowchart (page 256)
Process Analysis: Paper Folding Department Example (page 257)
Sample Process Analysis Paper Airplane Company Department: Paper Folding (page 258)
Mapping Symbols (page 259)
Process Map: Paper Folding Department (page 260)
Mapping Questions (page 261)
Critical Impact Points for the Paper Folding Department (page 262)
Evaluation (Appendix)

Key Learning Points

✓ Mapping the key internal processes in the team's business.

✓ Identifying the critical impact points (CIPs) in the team's business processes.

✓ Creating a foundation for continuous improvement processes.

Topics

✓ Process Analysis

✓ Process Flow Chart

✓ Work Flow Mapping

✓ Mapping Symbols

✓ Mapping Questions

✓ Critical Impact Points

✓ Evaluation

Procedural Outline

Time **Activity**

Prework: Read through the module and become familiar with the process-mapping symbols and technology. Make sure you understand the examples and practice the mapping process. Your familiarity with process mapping will greatly help the team in learning the technique.

Additionally, you will need to make sure the team members bring with them Modules 16 through 18. You will be reviewing your initial process steps from each of those analyses.

15 minutes *Introduction:* Open this session by posting and reviewing the objectives, key learning points, and topics to be covered. Also tell the team that by this time you have already identified your primary suppliers and customers and are well on your way to establishing some agreed-on standards for your inputs and outputs. In Module 16, High-Performance Business Teams: Quality and Process Improvement Overview, you also started to identify your major throughputs or processes. Have the team members review that module if they have not already done so.

Explain that, in this module, the team will learn how to "map" the work flow of its business. The module offers tools and techniques that should help the team describe how work gets done from the instant an input comes into the team until the moment the team passes along the output it has created.

Mapping can be as simple or complex as the team wishes. The important points are to:

- ✓ Identify the most critical and time consuming processes.
- ✓ Analyze these processes in enough detail to find issues and opportunities for improvement.
- ✓ Take action on the improvement opportunities that give the team the most benefit.

Some teams may resist the mapping process. If this is the case, help the team understand this entire series of quality improvement modules, from High-Performance Business Teams: Quality and Process Improvement Overview to business information management, depends totally on three assumptions:

1. The desire of people to do the best job possible
2. The commitment to keep getting better
3. A sense that "we are all in this together," that is, we are not separate and unrelated parts, either in a team or in the organization

Unless those three assumptions are true, nothing in the modules can make a difference. The concepts and procedures in these modules do not make up for a lack of caring, commitment, or cooperation.

Help the team members remember that this process is an attempt not to take advantage of the team, but rather to give the team a structure and process within which to change the system and procedures that get in the way of the team trying to be the best it can be. Explain that the first several of the productivity improvement modules—Productivity Improvement, Customer Analysis, Supplier Analysis, and Process Analysis—are designed to define the business: That is, the team describes what it does, with whom, and the quality of those exchanges and interactions. In this module, the team will learn how to map its internal work flow processes. The improvement strategies module will give the team some techniques to improve the quality and/or efficiency of those processes.

40 minutes *Business Processes:* Distribute the Business Process Flow Chart handout. Have the team complete the chart by using the other quality and process improvement modules (16–18). This acts as a solid systems review and prepares the team to move more deeply into operations mapping.

Next, distribute the Process Analysis: Paper Folding Department Example. Spend some time with the team working through and digesting this example. This should act as a bridge between talking about process analysis and beginning the mapping process.

20 minutes *Work Flow Mapping:* Offer the team an overview of the mapping process. Explain mapping provides a picture of the internal processes of a team. Mapping helps the team examine where to establish internal measures of performance that will contribute to meeting customer requirements and improving internal processes.

Moreover, a map is a diagram of the flow of processes through the work group showing the linkages between inputs and outputs. Post the Benefits of Mapping flipchart and describe that mapping can be beneficial because it:

- ✓ Graphically displays the way a team works as a system.
- ✓ Examines how the team gets work done or should get work done.
- ✓ Demonstrates how the major inputs flow through the team to their customers.
- ✓ Communicates to others what is happening and/or what should be happening.
- ✓ Gives team members an understanding of the work processes and responsibilities of others in the system.

After the team has an understanding of the benefits and general concepts of the mapping process, post and review the Guidelines for Mapping flipchart.

30 minutes *Guidelines for Mapping:*

- ✓ Think about the major steps your work group goes through to convert its inputs into outputs (see your worksheet from Module 16).
- ✓ Start with a basic input to the work group and trace that input through the system, designating the major activities required to process the input.
- ✓ Use boxes to designate functions (subsystems) and arrows to designate inputs and outputs.
- ✓ In general, keep a left-to-right or top-to-bottom sequence of converting inputs to outputs.
- ✓ Inputs and outputs should not intersect, but should pass over and under one another.
- ✓ Your team map should track only the processes that play a major role in converting inputs to outputs.

Next distribute the Mapping Symbols handout. Demonstrate how to use these symbols with a short example. Then hand out the Process Map: Paper Folding Department. This example demonstrates how to take a written process and turn it into a process flow map. Spend as much time as you need with the team to help them understand the mapping process in the example.

35 minutes *Mapping the Team's Work Process:* After the team has an understanding of mapping and has worked through several examples, pick a major team process and map all the major steps. Have the team pick a major process to map and distribute the Mapping Questions handout. Facilitate the team in answering these questions. Work as the mapping scribe, and draw on a blank flipchart the process steps undertaken.

Mapping is rarely, if ever, a clean process. Do not be afraid to get ahead of the team and to draw a step and ask if it's correct. Sometimes team members need to see the step to know if it's accurate or not. All in all, mapping is an art that takes both time and practice to get good at. In the beginning, do not worry about initial accuracy. Just keep revising until the map resembles the real process. Over time, however, you and the team will become proficient in mapping and process flow analysis will take much less time.

The final outcome of this step is to generate an accurate picture of the true steps the team takes in trying to get its work done.

30 minutes *Critical Impact Points:* Once the team has created the picture of the entire work (business) system, the next step is to analyze *critical impact points* (CIPs).

> Critical impact points (CIPs) are the places in the work system where the business team can make a difference in success indicators such as quality, cost, or productivity.

Explain that there are three steps in assessing CIPs:

1. Identify the point(s) in product flow or service that the team can impact success indicators. In general, there are three areas:
   - **a.** Input stage (suppliers and inputs)
   - **b.** Operations stage (where the team does something)
   - **c.** Output stage (customer satisfaction)
2. Determine the standards for performance at the critical impact point. (Standards should be measurable.)
3. Assess the level of performance against the standard.

Next help the team understand that the discrepancies between standards and performance should be the basis for adjusting inputs or processes. Distribute the Critical Impact Points for the Paper Folding Department as an example. Work with the team and point out how each of the critical impact points are measurable with the specific standards.

Because the team has already looked at supplier inputs and standards and customer requirements and standards, it is time now to focus on what the team can do differently to improve its performance.

Have the team members go back through their process flow and identify internal areas where performance is critical. At those critical points, the team should create a performance indicator from which to measure and assess performance. Each performance indicator may be further defined by specific criteria for making assessments (as in the airplane company example).

Once the team members decide where to put those indicators, they need to decide who collects and analyzes data about their own performance. This is a very important step that many teams resist. If the team members do not want to collect and analyze data about themselves, explain how fact-based decisions actually give a team more freedom and better performance than waiting to discover problems later in the process (e.g., when the customer rejects its inputs). The sooner the team detects flaws or problems in the process, the less work needs to be done to correct the problem.

10 minutes *Summary/Close:* The outcomes of this module are (1) a comprehensive process flow map with critical impact points identified; (2) an action plan for collecting and analyzing data; and (3) an acknowledgment that, based on the data, the team will work to improve the system.

Remind the team members that mapping technology can be used in all types of work and problem solving. Also tell them that, the more they try to use mapping, the easier it becomes and the better they get at it. Encourage them to use mapping as much as they can. Finally, thank the participants for their time and distribute the evaluation.

BENEFITS OF MAPPING

Mapping is beneficial because it:

✓ Graphically displays how a team works as a system.

✓ Examines how the team gets work done or should get work done.

✓ Demonstrates how the major inputs flow through the team to their customers.

✓ Communicates to others what is happening and/or what should be happening.

✓ Gives team members an understanding of the work processes and responsibilities of others in the system.

- ✓ Think about the major steps your work group goes through to convert its inputs into outputs (see your worksheet from Module 16).
- ✓ Start with a basic input to the work group and trace that input through the system, designating major activities required to process that input.
- ✓ Use boxes to designate functions (subsystems) and arrows to designate inputs and outputs.
- ✓ In general, keep a left-to-right or top-to-bottom sequence of converting inputs to outputs.
- ✓ Inputs and outputs should not intersect, but should pass over and under one another.
- ✓ Your team map should track only the processes that play a major role in converting inputs to outputs.

BUSINESS PROCESS FLOWCHART

HANDOUT 19-1

Suppliers	Inputs	Operations	Output(s)/Products	Consumer/Customer

PROCESS ANALYSIS: PAPER FOLDING DEPARTMENT EXAMPLE

I. Who is/are the department's supplier/s?

Supplier(s):		*Supply (Input):*	
	Engineering		Airplane drawings
	Purchasing		Paper

II. What do they supply? (See above.)

III. What operations does the team perform on inputs to create outputs?

1. Receive the order and process (style and number).
2. Assign team jobs.
3. Get proper drawing from engineering.
4. Get paper from purchasing (warehouse).
5. Fold paper; make the airplane.
6. Check the final product:
   a. Style vs. order
   b. Number vs. order
   c. Quality
7. Complete production paperwork.
8. Send product to shipping.
9. Send billing information to accounting.

IV. What are the team's outputs (products)?

Product:	*Consumer/Customer:*
Paper airplanes	Shipping
Billing information	Accounting department

V. Who are the team's customers/consumers? (See above.)

SAMPLE PROCESS ANALYSIS PAPER AIRPLANE COMPANY DEPARTMENT: PAPER FOLDING

Suppliers	Inputs	Operations	Output(s)/Products	Consumer/Customer
Purchasing	Paper	Receive and process order.	Paper airplanes	Shipping department
Engineering	Airplane drawings	Send billing information to accounting.	Billing information	Accounting department

MAPPING SYMBOLS

Symbol	Description	Example
Box	Show a process activity or function with a box sized according to need.	
Decisions	Define a decision with a diamond and label showing a "Yes" and a "No" alternative.	
Line	Shows inputs and outputs throughout the mapping area. Label if possible. Use an arrow pointing to the next process.	
Crossover	Show a line crossing another line with a crossover.	
Connector	Mark the connection of a process flow to another area, page, or point of interest with a connector.	
Performance indicator	Identify with a meter the specific junctions on the map where performance indicators should be set.	

PROCESS MAP: PAPER FOLDING DEPARTMENT

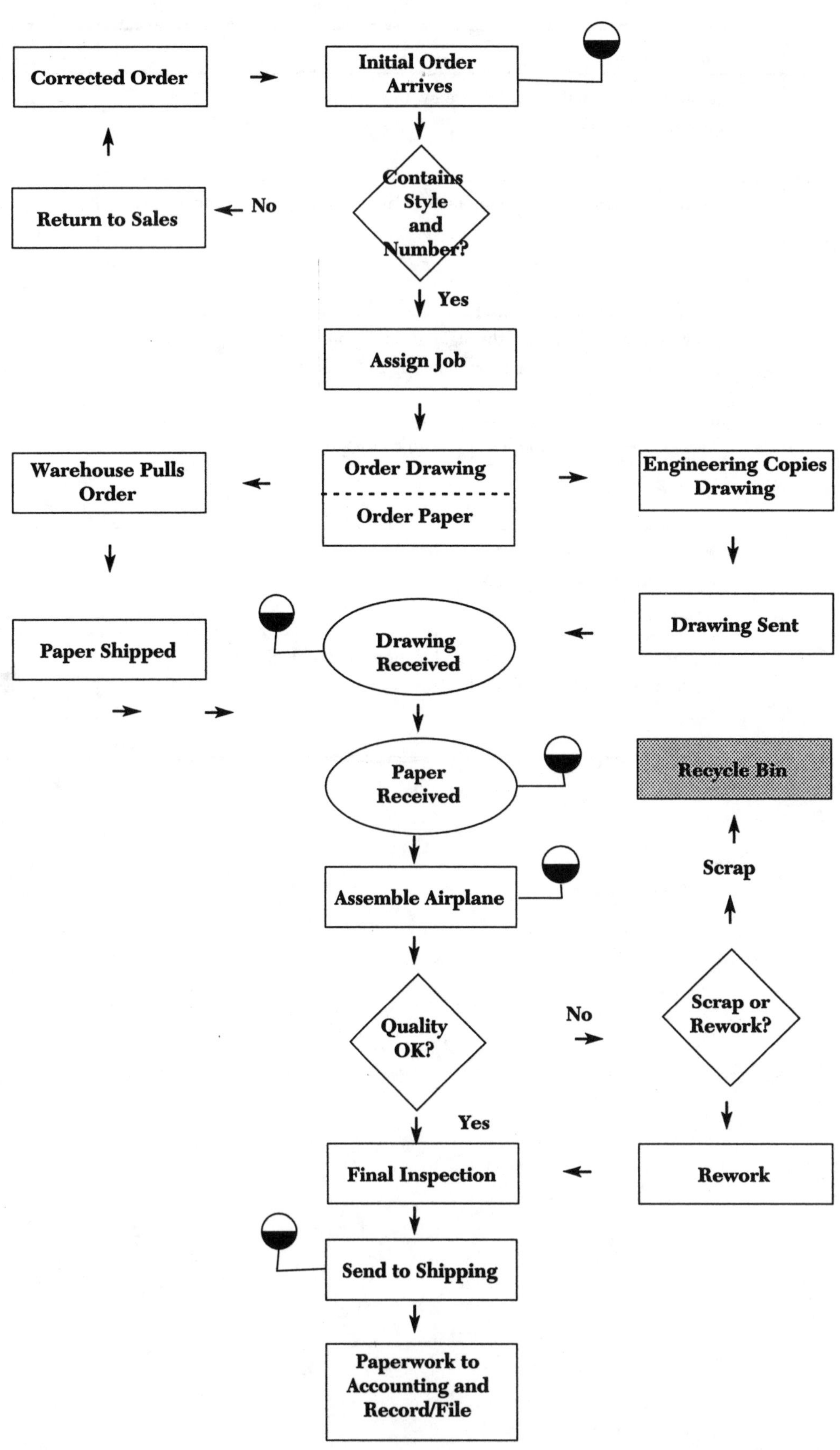

MAPPING QUESTIONS

1. How does our work get started?
2. How do we know when to start our job?
3. What usually occurs first?
4. And then what happens?
5. What happens after that?
6. Does that always happen or is it just a one-time occurrence?
7. If it doesn't occur, what happens?
8. What decision had to be made for that to occur?
9. What if it went the other way?
10. Are there any other steps in the process?

Using these questions and the sample map on the prior page, create a map (or maps) of your team's work processes.

CRITICAL IMPACT POINTS FOR THE PAPER FOLDING DEPARTMENT

No.	Critical Impact Point	Criteria to Assess
1.	Order receipt	a. Contains correct information b. Legible for data input
2.	Drawing received	a. Correct drawing b. Legible c. On time
3.	Paper received	a. Correct type and amount b. Good condition c. On time
4.	Assemble	a. Plane meets quality standards b. Done on time c. Completed within budget
5.	Product to shipping	a. Packed properly b. Labeled properly c. On time
6.	Billing information	a. Correct information sent to accounting dept. b. Information is legible c. Information goes out on time (within 8 hours)
7.	Order disposition	a. Material filed in correct file b. Completed within 48 hours of completion

Module 20

Quality and Continuous Improvement Strategies

(3 hours)

Objective To help participants understand the concept of total quality and continuous improvement and their application to the business of the organization and to the work of the team.

Materials Needed

✓ *Flipcharts:* Objectives, Key Learning Points, and Topics (copy from this page)
Misconceptions about Quality (page 267)
Definition of Continuous Improvement (page 268)

✓ *Handouts:* Quality Definitions (page 269)
Quality Exercise (page 270)
Defining Quality Exercise (page 271)
Factors That Affect Quality (page 272)
Deming's Fourteen Management Principles (page 273)
Continuous Improvement Exercise (page 274)
Evaluation (Appendix)

Key Learning Points

✓ Defining quality and continuous improvement.

✓ Understanding the meaning of quality and continuous improvement.

✓ Knowing when you have quality.

Topics

✓ Definitions of Quality

✓ Misconceptions about Quality

✓ Quality Exercise

✓ Defining Quality Exercise

✓ Continuous Improvement

✓ Deming's Fourteen Points

✓ Continuous Improvement Exercise

✓ Evaluation

Procedural Outline

Time	Activity
5 minutes	*Quality and Continuous Improvement Strategies:* Open this session by posting and reviewing the objectives, key learning points, and topics to be covered. Next introduce the topics of quality and continuous improvement by explaining that most of us grew up in an era when quality was not a major concern. If it sold, it was good enough. Today it seems as if nothing else matters. That does not mean that productivity and cost are unimportant; it means that, unless you produce quality, the other factors will be irrelevant. Further, our world competitors and

some American organizations have shown us that if an organization has a certain attitude about quality and approaches it in certain ways, the other critical factors fall in line.

Although there are a number of different definitions of quality, world-class organizations—public and private—know that as one vice president said, "Better than we were, ain't good enough." Increasingly over the last decade, quality has been defined by the consumer, customer, or taxpayer, not by the producer. This means that the high-performance organization must pay attention to different signposts than they were watching a decade ago.

Finally, quality is no longer viewed as a "you have it" or "you don't have it" phenomenon, but rather as a product of efforts at continuous improvement. You can always get better at what you're doing. And if quality reaches a point beyond which it need not go for the time, efforts can be directed at achieving it more quickly or less expensively.

Consequently, the concept of quality and the business practices related to it are among the most important topics you will address in moving toward becoming a world-class, high-performance business organization.

5 minutes *Different Ways of Looking at Quality:* Like most concepts, quality can be viewed in many different ways. Distribute the Quality Definitions handout and briefly cover each perspective.

- ✓ *Quality:* Meeting the customer's requirements. Quality is defined by the internal and external customers. Quality requirements change as customer requirements change.
- ✓ *First-time quality:* Doing it right the first time. It means doing the work without generating waste and satisfying the customer the first time every time.
- ✓ *Quality first:* Cost and schedule should be achieved through quality. If there is a question of priorities among the three, quality should be the driver of cost and schedule.
- ✓ *Total quality:* The focusing of all organizational functions on quality.

25 minutes *Quality exercise:* After the team has a sense of the four different perspectives on quality, distribute the Quality Exercise.

After each team member has had a moment to jot down some ideas, start a discussion about each category. Be sure to use the team member examples to illustrate each type of quality. Further, if the team has no examples, ask them to think outside their current work to past experiences or to other companies.

10 minutes *Misconceptions about Quality:* Explain to the team members that quality is often misunderstood. Just as there are several different perspectives on quality, there are also several misconceptions. Write the following misconceptions on a flipchart and work with the team to understand the fallacy in each statement:

- ✓ Quality is only conformance to standards/specifications.
- ✓ Quality can and should be assured by inspection.
- ✓ Quality increases cost.
- ✓ Quality is providing more value or features than customers require.
- ✓ Quality is the responsibility of the quality assurance or quality control department.

30 minutes *Defining Quality:* Now that team members have some exposure to the various natures of quality, have them define what quality means in the team's business.

Distribute the Defining Quality Exercise handout and facilitate the team as a whole to answer questions I and II.

After the team has defined their notion of quality and listed their quality standards, review the instructions for question III. Then have the team as a whole complete the Factors That Affect Quality chart.

Be sure to facilitate any discussion the team has while trying to complete the chart. The idea is to look at the factors influencing quality and to rank them by importance. This work is the perfect precursor to the next section on continuous improvement.

10 minutes *Continuous Improvement:* A different but related topic is continuous improvement. This concept is at the core of quality and process improvement. Write the following three definitions on a blank flipchart, and ask the team to take a moment to ponder their nature:

- ✓ *Productivity:* A measure of *how much* we produce.
- ✓ *Quality:* A measure of *how well* we produce it.
- ✓ *Continuous improvement: How much we improve* how well we produce it

Further explain:

- ✓ Continuous improvement is a systematic approach to managing quality and quality problems and to improving the level of quality in the organization
- ✓ Everyone who contributes directly and indirectly to the product or service has a continuing stake in quality and its improvement
- ✓ Quality can always be improved—"good enough" is not acceptable
- ✓ In an environment of continuous improvement, problems are welcomed and viewed as opportunities to *improve.*

45 minutes *Dr. Deming:* The idea of continuous improvement can generally be traced back to a single person and his system for producing quality products.

Dr. W. Edwards Deming was an internationally known authority on quality and the processes involved in continuous improvement. In the late 1940s, Dr. Deming predicted the decline of quality and the loss of American market share. Unfortunately, the Japanese listened; American business and industry did not. As a result, Japan recruited Dr. Deming to teach his methods. The results were astounding, and within 20 years the world was clamoring for Japanese products.

As America comes to grips with our decline of dominance in some world markets, they often turn to Dr. Deming's proven quality principles and system. His system is not difficult to understand and has been boiled down to fourteen points. Distribute and review Deming's Fourteen Management Principles. Have the group take one principle at a time and try to understand why it is so important. Also, tell the team that, although there are fourteen principles, Deming was very clear in suggesting that all fourteen must be in operation together to get results. They should be considered a total system.

45 minutes *Continuous Improvement Exercise:* Distribute the Continuous Improvement Exercise handouts and help the team complete section A. Next, move to section B and help the team problem-solve to develop a plan to improve the "inside factors" that affect quality.

If a variable is controlled "outside" your business, it may be impossible to influence it directly within the confines of the team. You can, however, bring pressure to bear—in the form of information, requests for help, and the like—

on those responsible for the area. Help the team complete section C by listing influence strategies for the factors "outside" the team's control.

Finally, have the team discuss and answer section D.

5 minutes *Summary/Close:* Summarize this section by reinforcing the power of continuous improvement. Further remind the team that continuous improvement is what being a business team is all about. The goal is to always get better. In traditional organizations, work groups were just told what to do. In high-performance organizations, teams take control of their environment and continuously try to get better. Thank the participants for their time. Distribute the evaluation.

MISCONCEPTIONS ABOUT QUALITY

- ✓ Quality is only conformance to standards/specifications.
- ✓ Quality can and should be assured by inspection.
- ✓ Quality increases cost.
- ✓ Quality is providing more value or features than the customers require.
- ✓ Quality is the responsibility of the quality assurance or quality control departments.

DEFINITION OF CONTINUOUS IMPROVEMENT

✓ **Productivity**

*A measure of **how much** we produce*

✓ **Quality**

*A measure of **how well** we produce it*

✓ **Continuous Improvement**

*How much **we improve** how well we produce it*

Quality: Meeting the customers' requirements. Quality is defined by the internal and external customers. Quality requirements change as customer requirements change.

First-time quality: Doing it right the first time. It means doing the work without generating waste and satisfying the customer the first time every time.

Quality first: Cost and schedule should be achieved through quality. If there is a question of priorities among the three, quality should be the driver of cost and schedule.

Total quality: The focusing of all organizational functions on quality.

QUALITY EXERCISE

HANDOUT 20-2

Think of an example of each type of quality in your business. Write the example (or examples) in the space below.

Quality: Meeting the Customers' Requirements:

____

____

____

First-time quality:

____

____

____

Quality first:

____

____

____

Total quality:

____

____

____

DEFINING QUALITY EXERCISE

I. How would you define quality in your team's business?

____

____

____

II. How would you measure quality in your business? That is, what are your standards or specifications to achieve the quality you defined in section I?

	Standard	Measure
A.	____________	____________
B.	____________	____________
C.	____________	____________
D.	____________	____________
E.	____________	____________

III. On the next handout is a list of factors that could affect quality in your business.

A. Review the list of factors in column 1.

B. In column 2, identify the top five items inside your business (team) that presently influence your quality;

In column 3, rank the top five items outside your business.

C. Rank the items based on:

1 = *Most important* factor in achieving quality

2 = *Second most important* factor in achieving quality

3 = *Third most important* factor in achieving quality

4 = *Fourth most important* factor in achieving quality

5 = *Fifth most important* factor in achieving quality

FACTORS THAT AFFECT QUALITY

(1) Factor	(2) Inside Your Business Rank	(3) Outside Your Business Rank
Management/supervision decisions		
Employee attitudes		
Training		
Cooperation between departments		
Cooperation between divisions		
Cooperation between sections/crews/teams		
Equipment		
Administrative support areas/staff		
Scheduling		
Parts and materials availability		
Maintenance		
Employees' suggestions/ideas		
Labor agreement/employee policies		
Technical support		
Quality of parts and materials		
Other:		

DEMING'S FOURTEEN MANAGEMENT PRINCIPLES*

1. Create constancy of purpose toward improving products and services, allocating resources to provide for long-range needs rather than short-term profitability.
2. Adopt the new philosophy for economic stability by refusing to allow commonly accepted levels of delays, mistakes, defective materials, and defective workmanship.
3. Cease dependence on mass inspection by requiring statistical evidence of built-in quality in both manufacturing and purchasing functions.
4. Reduce the number of suppliers for the same item by eliminating those that do not qualify with statistical evidence of quality; end the practice of awarding business solely on the basis of price.
5. Search continually for problems in the system to constantly improve process.
6. Institute modern methods of training to make better use of all employees.
7. Focus supervision on helping people do a better job; ensure that immediate action is taken on reports of defects, maintenance requirements, poor tools, inadequate operating definitions, or other conditions detrimental to quality.
8. Encourage effective, two-way communication and other means to drive out fear throughout the organization and help people work more productively.
9. Break down barriers between departments by encouraging problem solving through teamwork, combining the efforts of people from different areas such as research, design, sales, and production.
10. Eliminate use of numerical goals, posters, and slogans for the workforce that ask for new levels of productivity without providing methods.
11. Use statistical methods for continuing improvement of quality and productivity, and eliminate work standards that prescribe numerical quotas.
12. Remove all barriers that inhibit the worker's right to pride of workmanship.
13. Institute a vigorous program of education and retraining to keep up with changes in materials, methods, product design, and machinery.
14. Clearly define top management's permanent commitment to quality and productivity and its obligation to implement all of these principles.

*Originally published in W. Edwards Deming, *Out of the Crisis* (Cambridge, MA: MIT Center for Advanced Engineering Study). Copyright © 1986 by W. Edwards Deming. Revised by W. Edwards Deming in January 1990. Reprinted by permission of MIT and The W. Edwards Deming Institute.

A. Now, go back to your quality ranking exercise. Transfer the top five items "inside" and the top five "outside" items that affect quality to the chart below.

Quality Factors

Inside Your Business

Rank	Factor	Improvement Strategy
1		
2		
3		
4		
5		

Outside Your Business

Rank	Variable	Influence Strategy
1		
2		
3		
4		
5		

B. Using the "inside" list, use a planning/problem-solving strategy to develop a plan to improve the factor's impact on quality.

____

____

C. If a variable is controlled "outside" your business, it may be impossible to influence it directly within the confines of the team. You can, however, bring pressure to bear—in the form of information, requests for help, and the like—on those who are responsible for the area.

List some influence strategies for the factors "outside" the business team.

____

____

D. To affirm the concept of continuous improvement, if you were able to improve quality by reducing or eliminating the negative impacts on the chart, what would you do next in your efforts related to continuous improvement?

____

____

Module 21

Business Information Management

(2½ hours)

Objectives

- ✓ To understand the process of team business information management.
- ✓ To identify critical measures for tracking progress.
- ✓ To create a plan for managing information.

Materials Needed

- ✓ *Flipcharts:* Objectives, Key Learning Points, and Topics (copy from this page)
  Stable Business Information (page 278)
- ✓ *Handouts:* Why Is Business Information So Important? (page 279)
  Principles Underlying High-Performance Business Information Management (page 280)
  Business Performance Indicators (page 281)
  Business Team Information Needs Survey (page 282)
  Sample Safety/Housekeeping Awareness Checklist (page 283)
  Evaluation (Appendix)

Key Learning Points

- ✓ Identifying the importance of business information and its management.
- ✓ Identifying critical information.
- ✓ Identifying sources of information.
- ✓ Creating a business information management plan.

Topics

- ✓ Principles of Business Information Management
- ✓ Business Performance Indicators
- ✓ Evaluation

Procedural Outline

Time	Activity
5 minutes	*Introduction:* Open this session by posting and reviewing the objectives, key learning points, and topics to be discussed. Further, help the team understand there is no more important variable in an era of quality and continuous improvement than business information and its management. In many traditional organizations, little or no information was available to middle and lower levels of the organization because information was configured for, focused at, and given only to those in the organization with major authority. As such, information became part of the arsenal of power wielded by the top of the hierarchy.

The lack of information not only kept a critical tool (information) out of the hands of people managing and doing the work, but also eliminated an essential element of adaptive, high-performance systems—the feedback loop. In these settings, business units knew how well they were doing only when and where the keepers of the information were ready to tell them. The era of business teams bring with it a need for relevant immediate and usable business information.

The first stage of the process of business information management is identifying what kind of information the team members need and how often they need it. Second, the business team must identify both the source of the information and the responsibility for obtaining it. Finally, the information will be recorded and displayed in a form that the team can understand and use to plan, monitor performance, and drive continuous improvement.

This module provides the structure and methodology to help the team design and manage the information critical to its business.

Note: You may also want to tell the team that a problem in many organizations is that information is not available or, at best, is in a form that is of no value to the team in terms of its business. In such cases, someone must take responsibility at upper levels of the organization for reassigning information systems to support a business team organization. This is often done in the organizational steering committee. If you know anything about this process, be sure to inform the team.

15 minutes *Importance of Business Information:* Now that the team has been introduced to the nature of business information, distribute the Why Is Business Information So Important? handout and spend a few minutes discussing each of the bulleted items.

20 minutes *Principles of Business Information:* Distribute the Principles Underlying High-Performance Business Information Management handout. Help the team understand each item in the handout. Further, and more importantly, emphasize to the team that business information must be worth the time and effort it takes to collect and analyze the data. Consequently, the bulleted points on the handout must be lived, not just understood. As you help the team understand the business information principles, you can also ask them if the information must live up to any other standards or criteria.

30 minutes *Business Performance Indicators:* To start looking at what business information the team needs, have the team assess its own performance indicators. Distribute the Business Performance Indicators handout and have the team as a whole complete items 1–10. If other indicators are not listed, have the team write them in the open slots 11–13. This exercise gets the team thinking about what is the most important and valuable information needed.

35 minutes *Business Information Needs:* After identifying the critical performance measures, the team members are now ready to assess and design their own business information. Distribute the Business Team Information Needs Survey, with the following instructions. "To complete the survey, answer the following questions:"

A. What information do you need to monitor your performance measures?

B. What (who) is the source of the information?

C. How often do you need the information (daily, weekly, monthly, or quarterly)?

D. Who on the team is responsible for obtaining the information and for updating team charts?

Facilitate the team as a whole in completing the survey.

30 minutes After the team has completed the survey, help them create a plan for obtaining, charting, and updating the information. Distribute the Sample Safety/Housekeeping Awareness Checklist handout as a sample.

10 minutes *Other Forms of Business Information:* Express to the team that, in addition to the changing information (e.g., daily quality measures) used for managing the business, some kinds of information tend to be stable and ongoing. This information is important to know or to reference on occasion, but does not require daily or weekly updating. (Updates of this kind of information are normally done on an as-needed basis.)

Write the following on a flipchart and explain that these are the primary examples of more stable information:

- ✓ Organization (team) mission (purpose) and vision
- ✓ Organization charts
- ✓ Business plans and team goals
- ✓ Work flow documentation
- ✓ Work assignments
- ✓ Safety standards
- ✓ Customer list
- ✓ Team budgets

Have the team members decide which of these they want and/or need to keep visible to help the team perform better. Often, a group of teams agree on the information and posting that serves all of them (e.g., the organization's mission or safety standards). In other cases, the team posts its own enduring information (e.g., the team business goals).

Make sure the team members understand that, once they have the information, to post it in an area easily accessible to the team or put it (e.g., team proposals) in a storage location convenient and accessible to all team members.

5 minutes *Summary/Close:* Summarize this session by reminding the team that business information is a necessity for continuous improvement. It may also take some hard work in the beginning to get the information they need. Because traditional organizations have been set up only to generate information for those at the top, the team may have to overcome some initial barriers to get the data they desire. Moreover, they may not know exactly what they need. This session is about getting started and about the power of information. Remind the team members that they should be able to get any information they need to continually improve their business. Finally, thank the team for its time and distribute the evaluation.

STABLE BUSINESS INFORMATION

- ✓ Organization (team) mission (purpose) and vision
- ✓ Organization charts
- ✓ Business plans and team goals
- ✓ Work flow documentation
- ✓ Work assignments
- ✓ Safety standards
- ✓ Customer list
- ✓ Team budgets

WHY IS BUSINESS INFORMATION SO IMPORTANT?

HANDOUT 21-1

✓ It is critical to business planning.

✓ It provides a common language for talking about performance and improvement.

✓ It provides data and information for problem solving and decision making.

✓ It is the key element in the feedback loop of an adaptive, high-performance organization.

✓ It is part of the definition of power in the organization.

PRINCIPLES UNDERLYING HIGH-PERFORMANCE BUSINESS INFORMATION MANAGEMENT

HANDOUT 21-2

✓ The information must be relevant to the team's business.

✓ The information must be seen as useful by the team.

✓ The information must be timely, accurate, and up-to-date.

✓ The information must be updated regularly.

✓ The information must be in a form that is easily understood by the team.

✓ The information must be used in business activities—team meetings, decision making, and problem solving.

✓ The information must not be used to punish individuals or teams.

BUSINESS PERFORMANCE INDICATORS

What are the primary indicators of how well your business is doing? In the chart below, indicate whether the performance indicator is:

E = Extremely important
R = Reasonably important
S = Somewhat important
N = Not important

Peformance Indicator Ratings

Indicator	Importance			
	Extremely	**Reasonably**	**Somewhat**	**Not**
1. Quality levels—rework, purity, customer rejects	E	R	S	N
2. Workload factors—input, output, backlog, etc.	E	R	S	N
3. Performance indicators—productivity, cost, etc.	E	R	S	N
4. Attendance, on-time, absenteeism, etc.	E	R	S	N
5. Training—certifications, etc.	E	R	S	N
6. Overtime	E	R	S	N
7. Inspection data (in process)	E	R	S	N
8. Problem-solving activity—charts, lists, plans, etc.	E	R	S	N
9. Customer feedback	E	R	S	N
10. Employee morale	E	R	S	N
11.	E	R	S	N
12.	E	R	S	N
13.	E	R	S	N

BUSINESS TEAM INFORMATION NEEDS SURVEY

HANDOUT 21-4

Team: ______________________________ Date: ______________

A. What type of information is needed?	B. What is the source of of the information?	C. How often do you need to receive it? D = Daily W = Weekly M = Monthly Q = Quarterly	D. Who is responsible for obtaining it?

SAMPLE SAFETY/ HOUSEKEEPING AWARENESS CHECKLIST

HANDOUT 21-5

Team: ______________________ Week Ending: __________ Building: __________

Factory										
Personal protective gear										
Aisles										
Posted signs										
Unprotected heights										
Cranes/lift devices/stands										
Chemical and solvent use										
Storage										
Appliance plugs										
Tripping hazards										
Cleanliness/litter										
Spillage/leaks										
Furniture										
Computer office equipment										
Traffic										

S = Satisfactory *U = Unsatisfactory* *M = Marginal*

Module 22

Business Planning: Part I

(2 hours)

Objective To establish the framework for and initial portions of a team business plan.

Materials Needed

✓ *Flipcharts:* Objectives, Key Learning Points, and Topics (copy from this page)
Business Plan Analysis Questions (page 287)
Business Planning Definition (page 288)

✓ *Handouts:* Business Plan Examples 1–3 (page 289)
Business Planning: Critical Elements (page 295)
Preparing to Develop a Business Plan (page 296)
Evaluation (Appendix)

Key Learning Points

✓ Understanding the philosophy underlying the business planning process.

✓ Understanding the components of, and steps in, a good business plan.

✓ Preparing sample business plans.

Topics

✓ Definition of a Business Plan

✓ Elements of a Business Plan

✓ Sample Business Plans

✓ Preparing to Develop a Business Plan

✓ Evaluation

Procedural Outline

Time	Activity
	Prework: The goal of this module is to inform the team about business plans and to prepare them to write their own plan. Review and become familiar with the three business plans in this module. It will help facilitate the team's understanding.
10 minutes	*Introduction:* Open this session by posting and reviewing the session objectives, key learning points, and topics to be covered. Further, help the team grasp the notion of business planning. Explain that the business-planning process is one element of the growing "empowerment" of the business team. As a result of participating in the business planning, the team will better understand the dynamics of the process and ultimately improve the team's effectiveness. Business plans are a way of keeping focused on the important elements of the job ahead. With such a focus, the team can set priorities and allocate resources—budget, people, and time—in the best way possible to achieve business goals. Business planning, like other elements of the business team development process, is a complex activity. As such, the business team should have confidence

that the quality and effectiveness of planning will improve with time and practice.

Also explain that today's session is only the first part of the business planning training. The idea is to get a sense of business planning, its critical elements, and the format the team likes best. The team will be asked to try to create a first draft plan. (Often business plans take many revisions.) Today, the team takes its first cut.

45 minutes *Business Plan Analysis:* Distribute the Business Plan Example 1: Department 600, and have all team members read and digest the plan. Once they are familiar with the example, have them assess the plan. Post the Business Plan Analysis Questions flipchart and ask the following questions, recording their answers on a blank flipchart. (*Note:* Do this with all three plans):

Business Plan Analysis Questions:

- ✓ What is the overall impression of the plan?
- ✓ What are the major elements in the plan (purpose, vision, baseline data, business goals, etc. ...)?
- ✓ Is the plan easy to read and follow?
- ✓ Do they think the team will achieve their goal? Why or why not?
- ✓ Is this plan suitable to show to the next two levels up in the organization? Why or why not?
- ✓ Would you be happy with a plan that looked like this? Why or why not?

After the first example plan has been assessed, distribute Business Plan Example 2: Department XYZ, and do the same assessment. Do the same for Business Plan Example 3: Department ABC. The purpose of the analysis is to familiarize the team with the critical elements and different formats of a business plan, and to get the team members thinking about what format works best for them.

20 minutes *Business Plan Definition:* As a summary to the team's analysis, write the following business planning definition on a flipchart:

> *A process that uses baseline information to determine the necessary action items and specific responsibilities required to achieve goals as well as a way to chart progress toward the goals.*

Suggest to the team that any good business plan contains at least seven critical elements. Review the elements you captured from their earlier analysis, and then distribute the Business Planning: Critical Elements handout. Compare these elements with the ones the team has already discovered. Reinforce that each business plan may be a little different but that any effective plan will have at least the seven sections listed in the handout.

40 minutes *Preparation to Develop a Business Plan:* The next major step for the team is to develop their own business plan. This is never as easy as it seems. Data have to be recollected, improvement goals have to be made, people have to commit to doing things differently, etc. Distribute the Preparing to Develop a Business Plan handout. Work with the team to answer all the preparation questions. Spend as much time as you need, and get as specific as possible answering questions C (What does the team need to do in preparation for developing a business plan?) and D (What is your schedule for completing the plan?). Detailing

the answers to these two questions helps the team get ready for writing their final plan.

5 minutes *Summary/Close:* Reinforce that the creation of a business plan helps the team stay focused and helps the organization make better decisions about resources. Business planning is a skill that takes practice, and in the next module the team members will have their chance to write their first formal team plan. Close the session by reviewing any action items the team has made, distribute the evaluation, and thank the team for their hard work.

BUSINESS PLAN ANALYSIS QUESTIONS

- ✓ What is the overall impression of the plan?
- ✓ What are the major elements in the plan (purpose, vision, baseline data, business goals, etc.)?
- ✓ Is the plan easy to read and follow?
- ✓ Do they think the team will achieve their goal? Why or why not?
- ✓ Is this plan suitable to show to the next two levels up in the organization? Why or why not?
- ✓ Would you be happy with a plan that looked like this? Why or why not?

A process that uses baseline information to determine the necessary action items and specific responsibilities required to achieve goals as well as a way to chart progress toward the goals.

BUSINESS PLAN
EXAMPLE 1: DEPARTMENT 600

Proposed Business Operating Plan

Purpose. The purpose of the team is to assemble high-quality widgets for XYZ Company. The widgets should be assembled per the schedule from production planning and within the budget established by the finance group.

Vision. To achieve a partnership of the business team, management, and coworkers to ensure shared ownership and mutual accountability.

To become a world-class assembly operation known for quality and the ability to deliver product on time.

Business Category	Baseline Data	Business Goal
Quality	✓ 93% acceptance ✓ Parts are scrapped on the line as needed	✓ 98% by 12/31 ✓ Parts to be scrapped immediately when damaged
Performance	✓ 1.4% down time	✓ 0.4% down time
Cost	✓ 3% over budget	✓ At or below budget
Attendance	✓ 8% absenteeism	✓ 2% absenteeism

ACTION PLANS

Category	Action/Requirement	Responsibility	Contact	Deadline
Quality	✓ Team achieves one-day turnaround from laboratory.	Jones	Porter	TBD
	✓ Review corrective action investigation process to propose plan for linking quality to customer.	Duffey	Sales	8/15
	✓ Team charts its quality performance.	Team	Team	4/1
	✓ Team completes certification classes.	Bethel	Training	TBD
	✓ Link is established between team and vendors to set policies on unacceptable or late parts.	Smith	SFC OM/PUR	TBD
Performance	✓ Monthly meetings are held with maintenance.	Team	Aaron	1/15
	✓ Chart downtime.	Team	Team	3/15
	✓ Create "uptime" task force.	Miller	Training	6/1

Vision. To create a work environment and level of performance that exceeds any on record.

Goals

Goal Category	Requirement	Currently	Team Goal
Quality (scrap parts)	5	20 per week	0
Cost	315	Avg. 385	300
Shared ownership	100%	80%	100%

Action Steps

Quality

A. Initiate weekly quality meetings with team.

B. Team will call a meeting when they see a problem with quality and develop a way to resolve it.

C. Identify and discuss all scrapped parts and develop a cure for the problem.

D. Plot all tags and scraps on a chart and discuss the chart daily.

Cost

A. Hold a monthly team budget review to monitor costs.

B. Create a task force on cost reduction.

Shared Ownership

A. "Trust the team members" to take care of problems.

B. Let the team members account for their own destiny, such as:

1. Job assignments.
2. Line moves.
3. Tool needs.
4. Safety meetings.

I. Responsibilities and Team Commitment. It is our responsibility to provide first-time quality ailerons, shrouds, and leading edge flaps to the wing shop and final assembly at a cost at or below our budget and on a schedule that allows our customers to meet their deadlines.

To do so we must operate as a team. Each member of our team will be treated fairly and with respect, and will be given every opportunity to expand his or her knowledge. Every member can and should participate in deciding how we can test our long-range and weekly goals.

II. Goals and Accountability. Our long-range goal and the goal of our company are to strive for continuous improvements in the areas of quality and productivity. Our noncompliance with set procedures and unplanned rework in our department, or in our customer's departments, will be recorded as affecting quality. Productivity will be measured and recorded as cost versus budget.

Progress toward our goals of zero rework, and a cost that is at or below budget, will be shown in graph form. These graphs will be posted in our department and will be updated weekly to show our long-range goal status.

The charts will include information on our past and current performance, as well as our goals for future performance. Our current performance level of 79 percent with four hours of rework gives our department a cost of 229.5 hours, which is 9.5 hours over our current budget of 220. Our goal for a performance level of 85 percent and no rework will result in a department cost of 201.6, which is one hour below our budget of March 22, 19X7, and 17.4 hours below our current budget. Charts will be posted and updated daily to show our daily status toward reaching our goals.

Our weekly goals will be established first to meet the quality and schedule requirements of our customer. Second, we will compare the available parts and resources with the number of hours we expect to expend. This will establish where we need to be at the end of the week to effectively meet our productivity goal.

III. Team Versatility. To reduce the effect that parts shortages and absenteeism have on achieving our goals, we need a versatile team. Each member of our team will be encouraged to learn more than one job. This will allow us to maintain high levels of quality and productivity when it becomes necessary for a person to work an alternate job. Knowing more than one job will also allow for some variety in our day-to-day work. (All this must be done within the labor agreement. First, we must consult with human resources and the union representatives.)

IV. Suggestions for Improvement. Suggestions for continuous improvements and innovations will be recorded and forwarded to the proper support team for action. All suggestions to be forwarded will first be reviewed by the team to determine their impact on helping us to reach our goals in a cost-effective manner.

Once submitted, the team will track the suggestions on a weekly basis by contacting the support team that has accepted responsibility for the suggestion, implementation, or rejection. Feedback will then be given to the team each time there is a change in the status of our suggestions.

V. Personal Accountability. Proper feedback will also be given to each team member as appropriate. All quality and productivity information that is recorded on a daily basis will be monitored during the six-month evaluation. The six-month evaluation will also reflect worker versatility and suggestions for continuous improvement, whether implemented or not.

The team leader will also be subject to a six-month evaluation. Each team member, including the manager, will fill out an evaluation sheet on the team leader. This evaluation will help identify any areas in which the team leader is not providing adequate support for the team.

VI. Team Building/Team Business. Support for the team will also be required from management and support groups. This support can be obtained through better communication of team needs. To improve the communication of our potential parts shortages, team members will check bins each Friday morning and will list the parts that are down to a two-week or lower supply. Team members will forward a copy of this list to the general supervisor and to the production control supervisor, so that they will have the opportunity to provide us assistance proactively.

The team will continue to have a meeting each morning. At the Monday morning meeting, the team will review performance of the previous week and establish goals for the current week. To help establish goals, the internal quality consultant, production control manager, and, if possible, the general supervisor will be present at this meeting. They will be able to provide necessary information on quality, part status, and the needs of customers.

In addition, any time the team is not getting a satisfactory answer or an answer in a timely fashion on any problems or suggestions, the team leader will request the help of the general supervisor. The team would also like to meet with the general supervisor each Friday to review the progress and needs of the team.

VII. Cost-Effective Scheduling. Management can also help achieve and maintain team goals by providing the team with more control of resources. Currently, other departments rely too heavily on the services of some team members. This disrupts smooth work flow in the department and makes it more difficult to maintain a cost-effective schedule.

To maintain a cost-effective schedule for the remainder of 19X7, Department 1732 must produce an average of 374 hours per week. To meet the team performance level goal of 85 percent, we will have to produce these products with 440 hours expended. In addition to the 440 hours of planned work, 120 hours will be carried by the department to allow for vacation time, absenteeism, work on rework orders, and repairs. To maintain this cost plan, it will be necessary to limit the size of the team to 15 members, including a team leader.

As stated earlier, the scheduled needs of customers will be given priority when deciding which work will be completed during a given week. The schedule, however, does not truly reflect their needs and driving to schedule does not make this department cost-effective. The average weekly amount of work scheduled to be completed by the department this year is 346 hours. Planning for 374 hours per week will allow correction of the current "behind schedule" condition.

VIII. Administration Cost Reduction. To reduce the administrative cost of the company, the team is willing to broaden its span of control to include another department. From past experience, team members think it is possible to operate as part of a business unit with around 25 people. The team would gain by expanding the base of experience, and the company would gain through increased versatility. This would also provide for greater versatility between the two departments because of the larger base of resources with which to work. One of the two departments could also be used as a training area for new team leaders as necessary.

IX. Implementation. In closing, this department has made a great deal of improvement in the areas of quality and productivity over the past year and a half. In July and August of 19X6, the average cost was 79 hours over budget. Since then, the team managed to bring the average cost to within 15 hours of budget. The average cost has been reduced through combined efforts, support for each other, and constant feedback on our progress toward achieving our goals. Within one month, the team will provide first-time quality ailerons, shrouds, and leading edge flaps to the wing shop and final assembly at a cost that is at or below budget, and at a rate that allows the customers to meet their schedules.

[*Note:* Action plans were a part of the plan, but are not included in this example.]

BUSINESS PLANNING: CRITICAL ELEMENTS

✓ Mission or purpose statement

✓ Vision statement

✓ Specific goals

  Quality

  Schedule

  Cost

  Performance

  Attendance

  Safety

  Customer Satisfaction

✓ Action plans to achieve goals

✓ Responsibilities assigned for actions

✓ Time frames identified

✓ Budgets to support the plan

PREPARING TO DEVELOP A BUSINESS PLAN

HANDOUT 22-3

A. What does the team have working in its favor as you approach the development of a business plan?

1. ______________________________

2. ______________________________

3. ______________________________

B. What are barriers to the development of a business plan?

1. ______________________________

2. ______________________________

3. ______________________________

C. What does the team need to do in preparation for developing a business plan (for example, collect baseline data)?

1. ______________________________

2. ______________________________

3. ______________________________

D. What is your schedule for completing the plan?

1. Goals: ______________________________

2. Action plans: ______________________________

3. Budget: ______________________________

Module 23

Business Planning: Part II

(3 hours)

Objective To develop a business plan for the business team.

Materials Needed

✓ *Flipcharts:* Objectives, Key Learning Points, and Topics (copy from this page)
Business Plan Model (page 301)

✓ *Handouts:* Goals (page 302)
Objectives (page 303)
Criteria for Effective Goals (page 304)
Team Business Goals: Instructions (page 305)
Team Business Goals: Chart (page 306)
Criteria for Effective Objectives (page 307)
Criteria for Effective Action Plans (page 308)
Business Plan Objectives: Instructions (page 309)
Business Plan Objectives: Chart (page 310)
Action Plan Chart (page 311)
Evaluation (Appendix)

Key Learning Points

✓ Understanding the elements of the business plan.
✓ Writing business goals.
✓ Writing business action plans.

Topics

✓ Elements of a Business Plan
✓ Business Goals
✓ Action Plans
✓ Evaluation

Procedural Outline

Time	Activity
15 minutes	*Introduction:* Open this session by posting and explaining the objectives, key learning points, and topics to be covered. Remind the team members that this is not only the second part of the business planning process, but also the final session. Once the team has created the business plan, it is well on its way toward self-management. In the first section on business planning (Module 22), the goal was to familiarize the team members with business planning, its critical elements, and different business planning formats. The team then took the first cut at creating their customized team plan. In this module, the idea is to refine that initial plan and to finalize a business plan that all team members own and to which they are committed.

Review what a business plan is and what it stands for. Help the team understand that basically a business plan is a road map—"If you don't know where you're going, any road will get you there." We believe that you must know where you are going, the road you will take, the mode of transportation, and the budget for making the trip.

This module provides a framework for developing a business plan. It is not a complicated process, nor does it take special education to do it. Fundamentally, business planning is a logical process using a combination of building blocks (vision, goals, information, etc.) and the team's experience and creativity. As you move through the steps of developing the plan, you begin to see the links between components.

The business plan provides several guideposts for the team. As such, it includes:

- ✓ A clear picture of what you want to achieve during the period of the plan.
- ✓ A definition of the kind and extent of resources required to achieve the goals.
- ✓ Action steps and commitments the team is taking and making during the course of the business plan period.
- ✓ An evaluative process to monitor and manage progress toward goals.

The plan is essential. It is the most important tool you have for identifying the target, charting the course, and steering the business toward it.

The Place for Creativity. The planning process is also a creative process. If you just copy someone else's plan with adaptations for your business or simply pull last year's plan off the shelf and update it, you not only set the stage for a decline of the team's performance somewhere in the future, but also lose an opportunity to tap the team's major resource—talent, experience, and creativity.

In constructing a vision, developing action plans, and defining resources, you will have ample opportunity to use what you know from your time in the business. This is a big leap forward from traditional work structures. Use it—or perhaps you will lose it!

20 minutes *The Business Plan Model:* Post Business Plan Model and review with the team each of the vital components. These were developed and/or reviewed in prior modules.* Please review and, if necessary, revise these statements and information prior to proceeding with the planning process. Then proceed with the development of the action components of the plan for your business team (goals, objectives, and action plans).

The business planning model has several components:

- ✓ Mission statement
- ✓ Vision statement
- ✓ Baseline data
- ✓ Setting goals and objectives
- ✓ Action planning
- ✓ Monitoring and evaluation

10 minutes *Business Goals Versus Objectives:* Before the team can set good business goals and objectives, it must clearly understand the difference. Distribute the Goals

*The team's purpose statement was developed in Module 8, the vision statement in Module 9, and the baseline data in Modules 4 and 5.

and the Objectives handouts, and have the team discuss the distinction between the two. Summarize the discussion by suggesting that goals are much broader than objectives and tell the team that each has several specific criteria.

15 minutes *Criteria for Effective Goals:* Distribute the Criteria for Effective Goals handout. Help the team understand that the team's business goals should meet certain criteria. The goals should be:

- ✓ *Realistic:* They are not "pie-in-the-sky" statements that no one really expects to achieve, but rather realistic estimates of what can be accomplished.
- ✓ *Challenging:* Goals should "stretch" the team. Just saying that "we will improve our quality by 5 percent over last year" is not enough if you are certain you can do it. Why not try for a real challenge? Say 20 percent. Of course, the level of goal depends on how much you have improved to date, the resources available, and so forth.
- ✓ *Aligned with company mission, vision, goals, and policies:* To get the resources and support needed, the goals should be logically and empirically tied to the foundations and directions of the overall business.
- ✓ *Name the target:* Rather than say that the goal is simply to "get better this year," say something like, "We will improve productivity significantly over prior years' performance."
- ✓ *Measurable:* The goal should translate (via the objectives) into something that is measurable. If you cannot track progress toward the goal, it serves little value.

40 minutes *Team Business Goals:* After the team members have a solid grasp of the goal criteria, the next step is to actually set the goals for the team. Distribute the Team Business Goals: Instructions and the Team Business Goals: Chart handouts. Work with the team as a whole to follow each step of the instructions and to complete the goal chart.

40 minutes *Business Objectives:* After the team has clarified and set its goals, distribute the Criteria for Effective Objectives handout. Explain to the team that the criteria for effective objectives:

- ✓ *Are explicit:* Objectives are not the place for vague, flowery statements. Be clear and concise.
- ✓ *State measurable outcome or condition:* This is the key to the objective. It tells how the team will measure progress toward the goal.
- ✓ *Includes a time frame:* The objective says not only what will happen ("recordable incidents will be less than one per 100,000 hours worked"), but also when it will happen ("within a six month period").
- ✓ *Are consistent and compatible with goal(s):* Because the objective helps define the goal, it should be compatible. That is, the objective should not predict anything from the team that is irrelevant to, or incompatible with, the goals of the business.

Distribute the Business Plan Objectives: Instructions and the Business Plan Objectives: Chart handouts. Work with the team to follow each step in the instructions and to complete the chart.

30 minutes *Action Planning:* The final step in business plan development is the action plan. Distribute the Criteria for Effective Action Plans handout and help the team understand each criterion.

The criteria for effective action plans:

- ✓ *Translates goals to action plans:* The action plans provide a direct link for "how to get from here (where you are today) to there (the achievement of the stated objectives)."
- ✓ *Is specific to the problem, opportunity, or goal:* The action plans are directed at a specific objective in your business plan.
- ✓ *Specifies actions to be taken:* The action plan identifies the specific actions and/or steps to be taken to achieve the stated goal.
- ✓ *Identifies the resources needed:* The action plan identifies the resources needed to achieve the objective. These include staffing, materials, new equipment, and budget.
- ✓ *Assigns specific responsibility for implementing actions in the plan:* The action plan indicates who is responsible for what in the plan.
- ✓ *Contains specific, realistic time frames:* The plan identifies the schedule for implementing various steps.
- ✓ *Outlines the monitoring and evaluation process:* The plan specifies how and by whom the activity will be evaluated

After all the criteria have been discussed, distribute the Action Plan Chart handout and have the team as a whole complete the chart. When this is done, all the critical elements of the team's business plan should be in place. If the plan is not in a single document, encourage the team to create a single, neat, document (teams often take it to a local copy place, make several copies, and have it spiral bound) so that they may refer to it (and change it) over the year.

10 minutes *Summary/Close:* Summarize this module by congratulating the team members on a difficult job well done. They should now be considered a business team. Completing all the training and creating a business plan are no easy tasks. Remind them that their plan will probably change as they move forward and that, the more planning they do, the better they will get.

Also congratulate the team on completing the entire series of business team trainings. This learning process—never easy—is always a challenge and something about which all members should be proud.

Finally, ask the members' indulgence one last time and distribute the evaluation.

The business plan model has several components:

✓ Mission statement

✓ Vision statement

✓ Baseline data

✓ Setting goals and objectives

✓ Action planning

✓ Monitoring and evaluation

Goals: A description of the ends you want to achieve or the condition you want to create.

Examples:

✓ *We want to achieve best-in-class quality with our product.*

✓ *We want total customer satisfaction from our clients.*

✓ *We want to create a satisfying work environment.*

Objectives: The operational definition of the goal. Objectives define the what, when, and where of the goals.

Examples:

- ✓ *Our product quality will result in a .01 percent rejection/return rate by the customer during the next 12 months.*

- ✓ *Customer complaints will be less than 5 per 100,000 units sold during each quarter of the fiscal year.*

- ✓ *Employee complaints and grievances related to work conditions and work environment will be 0 during the coming year.*

CRITERIA FOR EFFECTIVE GOALS

The team's business goals should meet the following criteria:

✓ **Realistic**

They are not "pie-in-the-sky" statements that no one really expects to achieve, but rather realistic estimates of what can be accomplished.

✓ **Challenging**

Goals should "stretch" the team. Just saying that "we will improve our quality by 5 percent over last year" is not enough if you are certain you can do it. Why not try for a real challenge? Say 20 percent. Of course, the level of goal will depend on how much you have improved to date, the resources available, and so forth.

✓ **Aligned with company mission, vision, goals, and policies**

To get the resources and support needed, the goals should be logically and empirically tied to the foundations and directions of the overall business.

✓ **Name the target**

Rather than say that the goal is simply to "get better this year," say something like, "We will improve productivity significantly over prior years' performance."

✓ **Measurable**

The goal should translate (via the objectives) into something that is measurable. If you cannot track progress toward the goal, it serves little value.

TEAM BUSINESS GOALS: INSTRUCTIONS

The following handout contains a chart on which to record your team's goals. The following steps provide instructions for completing the chart.

Steps

1. Decide what business categories (column 1) you will address. Write them in the boxes.

   The categories include the outcomes of your business:

   Productivity levels

   Quality levels

   Cost levels

   Customer satisfaction

   And means to achieve those outcomes:

   Safety

   Equipment run time

   Maintenance costs

   New products developed

   Number of suggestions for improvement

   Effectiveness of internal communication

2. Enter the goal or goals for the division/company/agency in column 2. If the larger business entity has a goal, it should provide the umbrella or background for the team's goal.
3. Enter the goal for your business for the present or previous year.
4. Enter your team's goal or goals for the coming year.

TEAM BUSINESS GOALS: CHART

(1) Category	(2) Company Goal(s)	(3) Current Goal	(4) Business Team Goal
Example: Quality	To be number one in the industry in quality by the end of the year.	The team's average product rejection rate, which is significantly better than the previous year.	The product rate will be equal to or better than the best-in-class by the end of the year.

CRITERIA FOR EFFECTIVE OBJECTIVES

✓ Be explicit.

✓ State a measurable outcome or condition.

✓ Include a time frame.

✓ Be consistent and compatible with goal(s).

CRITERIA FOR EFFECTIVE ACTION PLANS

✓ Translates goals to action plans.

✓ Is specific to the problem, opportunity, or goal.

✓ Specifies actions to be taken.

✓ Identifies the resources needed.

✓ Assigns specific responsibility for implementing actions in the plan.

✓ Contains specific, realistic time frames.

✓ Outlines the monitoring and evaluation process.

BUSINESS PLAN OBJECTIVES: INSTRUCTIONS

Steps:

1. Enter the goal (from the previous goal chart) in column 1.
2. Write the objective or objectives for this goal. Use the criteria to guide the development of objectives.
3. Identify the member of the team who is responsible for:
   a. The oversight of the development of the action plan for achieving the objectives and the goal.
   b. The coordination of the action plan when implemented.

Sample Objectives Chart

(1) Goal	(2) Objective(s)	(3) Responsibility
The product rejection rate will be equal to or better than best-in-class by the end of the year.	The team will complete training in and install a statistical process control system by March 1.	Dunn
	The team will reduce scrap to the following levels: 1st quarter 2.8% 2nd quarter 2.0% 3rd quarter 1.7% 4th quarter 1.0%	Pierce
	The team's budget for product rework will be .5% of total by the end of the first six months of the fiscal year.	Coronetz

BUSINESS PLAN OBJECTIVES: CHART

(1) Goal	(2) Objective(s)	(3) Responsibility

ACTION PLAN CHART

Goal/Objective	Action Step/Description	Responsibility?	Target Date

REFERENCES

Argyris, C. and Schon, D. A. *Organizational Learning: A Theory of Action Perspective.* Reading, MA: Addison-Wesley Publishing Company, 1978.

Belasco, J. A. *Teaching the Elephant to Dance: Empowering Change in Your Organization.* New York: Crown Publishers, Inc., 1990.

Brocka, B. and Brocka, M. S. *Quality Management: Implementing the Best Ideas of the Masters.* Homewood, IL: Richard D. Irwin, Inc., 1992.

Davis, K. *Human Relations in Business.* New York: McGraw-Hill Book Company, 1957.

Deming, W. E. "Out of the Crisis," *Journal of Organizational Behavior Management, 2 (10)* (1986), pp. 205-13.

Harshman, C. L. and Phillips, S. L. *Teaming Up: Achieving Organizational Transformation.* San Diego, CA: Pfeiffer & Company, 1994.

Johnson, D. W. and Johnson, F. P. *Joining Together.* Needham Heights, MA: Allyn & Bacon, 1987.

Kuhn, Thomas. *The Structure of Scientific Revolutions.* Chicago, IL: University of Chicago, 1984.

Lee, Clyde E. *The Handbook of Structured Experiences for Human Resource Training,* Vol. 6. San Diego: Pfeiffer and Company, 1992.

Parker, G. M. *Team Players and Teamwork: The New Competitive Business Strategy.* San Francisco, CA: Jossey-Bass, Inc., 1990.

Peters, Tom. *Thriving on Chaos: Handbook for a Management Revolution.* New York: Harper & Row, 1988.

Rosow, J. M., Zager, R., and Casner-Lotto, J. *New Roles for Managers Series: The Manager as Trainer, Coach, and Leader.* Scarsdale, NY: Work in America Institute, Inc., 1991.

Schrage, M. "Managers journal," *The Wall Street Journal, 3 (19),* 1990.

Senge, P. M. *The Fifth Discipline: The Art and Practice of the Learning Organization.* New York: Doubleday/Currency, division of Bantam Doubleday Dell Publishing Group, Inc., 1990.

Webster's New World Dictionary. New York: Simon & Schuster, Inc., 1989.

Appendix

TEAM TRAINING MODULE EVALUATION FORM

TEAM TRAINING MODULE EVALUATION FORM

HANDOUT

Module:	
Department/Work Team:	**Date:**
Read the statement below.	**Circle your response on the scale below.**

Evaluation Statement	Excellent	Good	Fair	Poor
1. The printed materials were ...	E	G	F	P
2. The instructor was ...	E	G	F	P
3. The exercise(s) was/were ...	E	G	F	P

Now, read the following statements.	**Circle your response on the scale below.**			
Statement	Great Deal	Somewhat	Very Little	Not at All
4. I benefited from this module ...	G	S	V	N
5. The team will benefit from the module ...	G	S	V	N

Please answer the following questions:	**Write your answer here.**
6. What did you like best in the module?	
7. What did you like least?	
8. How would you improve the module?	

About the Authors

Carl Harshman, Ph.D., and **Steve Phillips**, Ph.D., have been on the cutting edge of the self-directed work team movement since its inception. Each author heads his own consulting company specializing in organizational change through team work; in this capacity, they have provided guidance to such clients as Ford Motor Company, General Dynamics, Taco Bell, and McDonnell Douglas. Previously they coauthored a professional handbook called *Teaming Up: Achieving Organizational Transformation*, and Phillips is also the coauthor of *The Team Building Sourcebook* and *Teambuilding for the Future*. Carl Harshman is based in St. Louis, Missouri; Steve Phillips is based in Malibu, California.